Identity and Resistance in Further Education

"Who is it that can tell me who I am?" This is the question Shakespeare's King Lear asks at the beginning of his descent into madness. It is a desperate attempt to reassert his 'position' and the Fool's reply: "Lear's shadow!" provides him with a stark and uncomfortable insight. Why is this relevant to the content of this book? There is a sense in which the storm of policy and curriculum intervention that has gripped post compulsory education over the last decade and more has caused teachers to question their selfhood, their values and principles. In recent years, stability in post compulsory education in England has been notable by its absence. While this has been a challenge for many, the creativity of teachers' responses and their often dogged insistence on sticking to their values while adapting to changing circumstances has taken on simultaneously noble and tragic dimensions.

Further education has reached a crossroads signposted with a set of questions, which include whether or not this increasingly abstract term has become merely an invitation to increasingly problematic 'sector-wide' policy interventions. Is it about a distinctive learning experience for people who may have had a negative experience at school? Is it simply about training for employment? Is its primary focus 16–19-year-olds re-taking qualifications? Or is it there to offer a second or third chance to adults who are seeking to transform their lives? Related to this set of questions is another more pressing set related to teaching: what is the role of the FE teacher? What are the key aspects of curriculum? What values should inform FE pedagogy? These questions give a sense of some of the 'unruly forces' that FE is currently subject to. They are of central concern to anyone considering becoming a teacher in FE as well as current teacher educators in FE and, increasingly, HE settings.

Pete Bennett is Senior Lecturer in Post Compulsory Education at the University of Wolverhampton, UK.

Rob Smith is a Reader in Education at Birmingham City University and Director of the Centre for the Study of Practice and Culture in Education (CSPACE).

Identity and Resistance in Further Education

Edited by Pete Bennett
and Rob Smith

LONDON AND NEW YORK

First published 2018
by Routledge
2 Park Square, Milton Park, Abingdon, Oxon OX14 4RN

and by Routledge
711 Third Avenue, New York, NY 10017

Routledge is an imprint of the Taylor & Francis Group, an informa business

© 2018 selection and editorial matter, Pete Bennett and Rob Smith; individual chapters, the contributors

The right of the editor to be identified as the author of the editorial material, and of the authors for their individual chapters, has been asserted in accordance with sections 77 and 78 of the Copyright, Designs and Patents Act 1988.

All rights reserved. No part of this book may be reprinted or reproduced or utilised in any form or by any electronic, mechanical, or other means, now known or hereafter invented, including photocopying and recording, or in any information storage or retrieval system, without permission in writing from the publishers.

Trademark notice: Product or corporate names may be trademarks or registered trademarks, and are used only for identification and explanation without intent to infringe.

British Library Cataloguing-in-Publication Data
A catalogue record for this book is available from the British Library

Library of Congress Cataloging-in-Publication Data
A catalog record for this book has been requested

ISBN: 978-0-8153-7825-9 (hbk)
ISBN: 978-1-351-23295-1 (ebk)

Typeset in Bembo
by Apex CoVantage, LLC

"It's not too late to return; this is no land
to stake out, but a state forgotten; clasp
me gently, in old ways; we'll understand
full well what we are; it's in our grasp.
I vow we will not leave until we're lost."
					(Nick Burbridge, *Arcadian*)

Contents

List of figures x
Acknowledgements xi
Preface xii

1 "Who is it that can tell me who I am?" – identity
   and resistance in further education 1
   PETE BENNETT AND ROB SMITH

SECTION I
Setting the scene 19

2 'Hello . . . who am I?' – the change agent or the game
   player of performativity? 21
   JENNIFER ADDO

3 The teacher educator experience: 'guardians of the pedagogy'? 28
   ANNE GROLL, SANDI BATES, CLAIRE SAUNDERS AND ROB SMITH

4 Through the looking glass: reflection and teacher identity 38
   DAVID WISE

5 Enquiry-based learning and adult learners: a discussion 51
   ELIZABETH A. STEVENSON

6 Something out of nothing: reflecting on the emerging
   self as teacher 61
   ANISA ALI, JOE HARRISON AND JULIE A. WILDE

SECTION II
Policy and pain 69

7 Understanding the business of failure: the educational
  disconnect between systems and so-called learners 71
  MATTHEW PARSONS

8 FE teacher identity: marketisation and metaphor 81
  CHRIS DAVIES

9 Character building: how accommodating is
  the FE Newbuild™? 96
  PETE BENNETT

10 "Feeding the monster": vocational pedagogy and
   the further education policy present 105
   DONNA DREW, EMMA LOVE, ALAN DAVIS AND ROB SMITH

11 Faith, apostasy and professionalism in FE 116
   JOEL PETRIE

SECTION III
Creativity and resistance 127

12 The experience of Ofsted: fear, judgement and
   symbolic violence 129
   CATHERINE GALLAGHER AND ROB SMITH

13 Identity and autonomy in lifelong education 139
   VICTORIA WRIGHT AND THERESA LOUGHLIN

14 Subverting the pseudo-science of inspection with
   research-informed practice and pedagogic principles:
   an ungraded approach to the evaluation of teachers 151
   MATT O'LEARY

15 Teaching an old dog new tricks: developing instructor and
   teacher identities in a military context: a conversation 161
   STEVE COLEBY AND STUART SMITH

16 Constellations of practice 170
LOU MYCROFT AND KAY SIDEBOTTOM

17 'The Marriage of Heaven and Hell': discourses
   of autonomy and reason in further education 179
   KIRSTIE HARRINGTON

18 Conclusion: identity and the collective purpose
   of further education 189
   PETE BENNETT AND ROB SMITH

List of contributors 197
Index 203

Figures

4.1	Reflection-on-practice	43
4.2	Flexion-of-practice	47
4.3	'Going through the looking glass'	48
8.1	Dave's spinning wheel	85
8.2	Sandra's 'keystone'	87
8.3	Doug's actual teaching situation	88
8.4	Liz's management clock	91
11.1	FTM model	122
13.1	An inversion model of the requirements on a PCE teacher	146
13.2	Emerging model of both quality and teacher training observations	149

Acknowledgements

Thanks to members of the PCE team, past and present at Walsall Campus, University of Wolverhampton and to the open-minded and open-hearted leadership provided by Alex Kendall and Julie Hughes.

This collection is dedicated to David Wise: teacher, colleague and friend.

Preface

This collection is forged in a time of considerable challenge. In a range of passionate, analytical and reflective pieces it explores how practitioners in post-compulsory education can continue to meet learners' needs and aspirations in a constantly changing environment. When dramatically diminishing budgets combine with increasing central control of what is taught and to whom, the space for professional autonomy is ever more constrained. It considers how best practitioners balance the needs of learners with the performance required by the State through its funding and inspection mechanisms, and reasserts the case for a vocational education that is expansive, creative and developmental.

Whilst the issues addressed in it are each grounded in the specific circumstances of post-compulsory education in England their implications are wider – both within public services in Britain, and for education systems increasingly shaped by short-term utilitarian goals elsewhere. Make no mistake – these are tough times for further education in England; tough too for the learners who rely on it. Despite Britain's spectacularly weak productivity, and its need for skilled technicians, public funding of the sector has shrunk by a quarter since 2010, whilst higher education has seen its substantially larger budgets grow by a quarter. Constant changes in regulation have been accompanied by an increasingly intrusive inspection regime, all backed by policies derived from a political nostalgia for the Britain of the fifties, and a narrow privileging of academic curricula for young people. Despite four in five of its colleges being recognised as good by the State inspection system, further education is consistently described as a problem sector. Students meanwhile enjoy few of the fiscal support measures offered to their contemporaries in higher education.

All this is happening as the onset of a fourth industrial revolution built on advances in robotics and artificial intelligence risks decimating swathes of white collar jobs in the same way that blue collar jobs went east with globalisation. You would think that that prospect alone would lead policy planners to value creativity, flexibility and innovation in teaching and learning. Yet by contrast, policymakers pursue a narrower and narrower utilitarian focus, shaping courses to the quickest routes to the labour market. Staff working in the sector, where they have established posts, experience year on year reductions in real salary as wage settlements fail to match inflation, whilst more and more workers in the sector are employed on zero hours or flexible contracts – offering little or no security.

To an extent this situation is shared in a range of other public services, but the multi-faceted denial of autonomy of action and denial of freedom for practitioners to exercise professional judgment, has been dramatic in further education. What Ruth Silver, chair of the Further Education Trust for Leadership called 'the adaptive layer' – the ready responsiveness of colleges to change, has been, perhaps, part of the problem. Like frogs in increasingly hot water, the further education sector has until now been slow to say enough is enough. This collection is by contrast strongly resistant to the tide of the times.

It was very different when I first worked in colleges and adult education centres in the 1970s. There was a clear cross-party convention then that politicians steered clear of interfering in the curriculum. On the ground, inspection visits were welcomed – as opportunities for dialogue and reflection on how best to develop teaching and learning, and a culture of inter-institutional collaboration backed by subject advisers employed by local authorities led to benchmarking best practice. Jim Callaghan's (1976) Ruskin speech marked a break with the convention, making clear that what happened in education was a proper matter for public and political discussion. Whilst he argued that 'it is not my intention to become enmeshed in such problems as whether there should be a basic curriculum with universal standards – although I am inclined to think there should be'(para. 15), the effect of the speech was the launch of a Great Debate that culminated in 1988 with the adoption of a national curriculum for schools and national targets for Education and Training.

The nationalisation of colleges in 1992 marked a second step in the reduction of autonomy. First there was a nationally approved and funded curriculum. Other studies whilst tolerated were seen as local concerns. This resulted in the development of a powerful audit culture, needed since college funding was for units of approved courses undertaken. Second, Her Majesty's Inspectorate was abolished, and FE inspectors were subsumed into the new Further Education Funding Council. Until then, no official would meet an education minister without the interests of the profession being represented through the Chief Inspector or her/his nominee. Subsequently, unlike health where it remains inconceivable that key policy meetings would exclude the Chief Medical Officer of Health, professional advice was subsumed in the Departmental brief, and the freedom to speak truth to power reduced with it.

The third step on the slope to our current difficulties followed when in 1996 OECD Finance Ministers decided that since human capital was increasingly key to prosperity, lifelong learning should be a priority. At first this led to a flowering of creative initiatives – in England coinciding with New Labour's first government. All too quickly, however, the Treasury's grip on post-compulsory education policy tightened, as education was seen primarily through the prism of economic policy, offering a supply mechanism for the labour market. The narrowing of curriculum to an increasingly gradgrindian utilitarianism followed as night follows day.

This sorry state calls for a powerful re-assertion of the case for creativity and imaginative enquiry in post-compulsory education, and for the recognition of the key role of professional teachers, and those that train them, in securing the spaces for that creativity to flourish. These essays are an important contribution to that task.

I am grateful to Richard Pring for the observation about the changing role of inspectors

Sir Alan Tuckett,
Professor of Education,
University of Wolverhampton

Reference

Callaghan, J. 'A rational debate based on the facts', speech given at Ruskin College, 18 October 1976. Accessed on 29/09/2017 at www.educationengland.org.uk/documents/speeches/1976ruskin.html

Chapter 1

"Who is it that can tell me who I am?" – identity and resistance in further education

Pete Bennett and Rob Smith

In his seminal text, *The Sociological Imagination*, C. Wright Mills declared that "'Man's chief danger' today lies in the unruly forces of contemporary society itself, with its alienating methods of production, its enveloping techniques of political domination" (C. Wright Mills 1959: 13). More than fifty years on the "unruly forces" show little sign of abating and education remains particularly susceptible to all manner of 'methods' and 'techniques'.

This introductory chapter will set out the argument of this collection by creating a brief history of its conception and development, by making explicit its central propositions and intentions and, then, by providing an overview of the ways in which each chapter contributes to the critical whole.

A brief history

In this book, we use 'further education' as an umbrella term to signify educational courses and experiences that take place in a variety of settings involving young people who have finished attending school, as well as adult returners. Further education includes vocational education and work-based learning but this book focuses mainly on the further education that takes place in colleges across England and the UK.

This project originated from a collective commitment within a community of practice/partnership of teacher educators to exploring reflective practice and teacher-scholarliness in a university in the West Midlands of England. This community of practice, spanning higher and further education settings was formed during a period in which neoliberal values and New Public Management and managerialist approaches to organising public sector education had become hegemonic cultural practice in public educational institutions across large parts of the Western world (see for example Clarke and Newman 1997; Considine and Painter 1997; Smith and O'Leary 2013). By 'neoliberal', we mean the policy paradigm traceable to Hayekian economic doctrine that seeks "to replace political judgement with economic evaluation" (Davies 2014: 4). Peck (2010) suggests that thinking about neoliberalism in "regime-like" terms renders it too "static" a concept and that a "processual definition", i.e. *neoliberalisation* is preferable (ibid. 19).

In England, this process involved the promotion of competition and international comparison by the Organisation for Economic Co-operation and Development (OECD) and specifically the Programme for International Student Assessment (PISA) in the measurement of educational and 'skills' attainment as an index of national economic potential.

In the spring of 1993 through incorporation, further education colleges had a business-orientated institutional model imposed on them. Following that, policy – driven increasingly by an instrumentalist agenda – cast further education in the role of "hand maiden to British industry" (Ainley and Bailey 1997: 14). Colleges had always been positioned as local service providers offering courses to their surrounding communities including businesses. The marketisation of the environment that followed promoted them as entrepreneurial outfits with an eye on ensuring profit came first (Smith 2015). The funding mechanism was a key aspect of this. Funding for colleges in England asserted a brutalist equivalence between different qualifications for the purpose of measuring 'productivity'. The introduction of managerialist cultures and practices were a response to this. The roll-out of managerialism resulted in dramatic changes to the constitution of the teaching workforce. The number of part-time staff in colleges in 2015 was 60%, compared to the proportion in the general UK workforce of 37% (ETF 2016: 9).[1] A third of these part-time jobs were on 'precarious contracts' (UCU 2016: 3) – suggesting that teaching in further education belongs to the emerging neoliberal phenomenon of the precarious professions. At a fundamental level, this shift constitutes an attack on teachers whose work was often socially situated in settings with strong links to community and locality.

The embedding of managerialism as orthodoxy in college cultures was exacerbated by the Global Economic Crisis of 2008 which ushered in 'austerity'. Ironically, rather than challenge the 'neoliberal restructuring' ("Epistemology, economic strategy, and moral code rolled into one" [Tuck 2013: 326]), which has so changed social attitudes to education and almost every other public sphere, this 'catastrophe of capital' seems rather to have given what Fisher has labelled 'capitalist realism' a second wind. This, for Fisher is "the widespread sense that not only is capitalism the only viable political and economic system, but also that it is now impossible even to imagine a coherent alternative to it" (Fisher 2009: 2). Neoliberalisation, to use Davies's term, is pre-eminently capable of self-reinvention and adaptation.

This book explores some of the pressures militating against any consolidation of a unifying or stable sense of identity amongst further education teachers that intensified in the period after the financial crisis. The title of the book uses a quotation from Act I, Scene IV of Shakespeare's *King Lear*. Having given away his title to his daughters, Lear begins a painful journey of understanding into how who we are is as much about how others see us as it is about who we feel ourselves to be. The current neoliberal backdrop with its "pervasive atmosphere, conditioning not only the production of culture but also the regulation of work and education, and acting as a kind of invisible barrier constraining thought and action" (Fisher 2009: 16) provides a frame for the contributions in this collection. In the so-called 'age of austerity', further education in England has been targeted for budgetary cuts more than any other sector of education. In addition, the professional identity of teachers in further education was undermined by the Lingfield Report (BIS 2012) whose key finding threw out the 2007 regulation that teachers in colleges had to acquire a teaching qualification, suggesting instead this could be left to 'the market'. More recently, colleges have been subjected to further 'rationalisation' as more efficiencies are sought through a national programme of Area Reviews. This has involved mergers, takeovers and the closing of some colleges (see Smith 2017).

This is the context that, for us, resonates so strongly with Shakespeare's Lear at the beginning of his journey onto the heath and into madness and that makes his question so startlingly pertinent for many further education teachers: "Who is it that can tell me who I am?"

The contributors to this volume straddle the divide between further and higher education. They have stark and uncomfortable insights but countering these, maintain a commitment to creativity, to practical solutions, to producing resources of hope. Like Carol Taylor in her recent work on HE teacherliness who seeks "to find or, rather, hold onto and cherish, an educative space from which to contest perceptions that the intensification of market conditions in higher education inevitably brings a deformation and derogation of teaching and learning relationships" (Taylor 2016: 1), this volume's contributors are determined to offer resistance to these phenomena as they manifest in further education while acknowledging their destructive power. This resistance necessarily seeks to deconstruct the mythic qualities of the neoliberal *faux* consensus since as Fisher points out, "emancipatory politics must always destroy the appearance of a 'natural order', must reveal what is presented as necessary and inevitable to be a mere contingency" (Fisher 2009: 17).

Propositions and contexts

The mythic 'Age of Austerity' is in truth a consciously precipitated 'age of anxiety' which has caused teachers in further education to question their selfhood, their values and principles. All this needs to be contextualised within notions of post- and hyper-modernity in order to restore its historical character in the face of claims about its inevitability and necessity. Take Baudrillard: "Today, the whole system is swamped by indeterminacy, and every reality is absorbed by the hyperreality of the code and simulation" (Baudrillard 1994: 2). Baudrillard's notion of 'simulations' displacing the real will be meaningful for any reader who, as an aspect of their job, contributes to an institutional corpus of performance data. This, often 'crafted', data is a necessary feature of accountability in marketised settings and consequently takes priority in teachers' work. These simulations are what will be judged, and on them depends market position and, for colleges, funding. This explains why fear has become such a feature of teachers' working conditions. According to Lipovetsky:

> It is fear which triumphs and bestrides the stage in the face of an uncertain future, a logic of globalisation which acts independently of individuals, an exacerbated free market competitiveness, a headlong development in the technologies of information, an increasingly precarious hold on one's job and a worrying stagnation in employment figures.
>
> (Lipovetsky 2005: 5)

The contributors to this volume speak from a position that acknowledges that, for teachers in further education a certain precariousness has become the order of the day: "a sense of insecurity has invaded all of our minds" (Lipovetsky 2005: 13). Writing and thinking about further education is in short supply. It's interesting that while educational research in the academy operates under the (market-led) restriction of the need to publish 'new knowledge', knowledge production under neoliberalisation is prolific and involves the repetition *ad nauseum* of self-interested and specious knowledge often with a spurious evidence base. How should educational research cope with the requirement to continually find new things to say when so much of what is wrong has roots in policy decisions made a quarter of a century ago and whose effects are still being experienced today? The challenges faced by teachers in further education colleges haven't stopped just because educational researchers have identified them. They haven't stopped because educational researchers have generated positive and radical versions of professional identity from outside, either. Just because they have been researched doesn't mean that people are not continuing to endure their effects.

One attritional consequence of these seemingly inevitable (and 'natural') conditions can be an inability to think through a future. These contributions are all in their own ways attempts to lay the groundwork to make thinking through a future possible. The creativity that drives this thinking constitutes a collaborative praxis "as informed, committed action which embodies certain ethical qualities oriented to improving the relations of those involved" (Taylor 2016: 2). Crucially, in this case, it also involves individuals reaching out beyond the confines of the institution to find hope and solidarity in trans-sectoral relationships. It addresses identity as it is and for what it is while understanding that an instability of identity, a sense of enveloping chaos and a testing of values and beliefs are all topographical aspects of the further education sector.

A matter of time (scales)

A central issue in contemporary education is time as a relative concept and particularly of 'timescales' which lurk unacknowledged beneath any discussions about education making them superficial or under-informed. Much education policy in the last fifty years has not only been reactive in character but also misguided in its reliance on initiatives 'transplanted' inappropriately from one context to another, such that it is alarmingly common for policy interventions to be discarded long before they have been properly evaluated. The conundrum is simple: in the UK and the US, where successive governments have taken an active interest in intervening in formal education, the appetites of a political system predicated on a five-year cycle are largely incompatible with 'learning careers' which last longer, perhaps a lifetime. At the same time the broader debate is also around temporal issues, principally whether we should look progressively to the future or, increasingly, back to 'basics' with further education regularly tipped from one side to the other in response to the latest release of longer-term data, as a feather for every wind that blows. Currently that 'fix' is the effective extension of the school leaving age for college students who are unable to prove proficiency in English and maths in a somewhat ironic reworking of the spirit of the American 'No Child Left Behind' (NCLB) riff, though many of these 'learners' know only that they have been effectively left behind, detained at her majesty's pleasure. This gives a new take also on the proud tradition within further education in particular of being the 'home of the second chance' which in a bizarre almost imperceptible shift of emphasis which has suddenly become a second chance chiefly for the governmental imperative to see all so-called 'learners' included/processed/managed. And 'included' here is more likely to be 'accounted for' than 'educated'.

While the time-space compression enacted in what in England used to be (prior to Daley, Orr and Petrie 2015) dubbed the 'Cinderella sector' (and she was a character bound to a tight schedule) is not exactly Virilio's 'speed space' with its hyper-modernist conception of an accelerated reality, there is much there that resonates with contemporary further education experience. Virilio developed the term 'dromology', the "science (or logic) of speed", which derives from the notion of a race or racetrack, to emphasise the central role of speed/relative time in contemporary life (Virilio 2006). In education, notions of 'the race' (Obama's educational initiative was entitled Race to the Top!) and accelerated/decelerated 'progress' are commonplace and not without implication. For a decade, time has been an increasingly negative element in the provision of a feasible second chance and college is currently that place where eleven years of 'difficulty' with 'the basics' might be remedied in one. This is decisively a law of diminishing returns, predicated on the vanishing point that occurs somewhere between 'being educated' and 'passing the test'. Making the tests apparently more difficult adds more friction, but the more important decision is to make the tests essential because as 'turnstiles' they control the circulation of human resources. With echoes of Tuck's notions of settler colonialism, even 'manifest destiny', Virilio describes the dromological bottom line:

> Whoever controls the territory possesses it. Possession of territory is not primarily about laws and contracts, but first and foremost a matter of movement and circulation.
>
> (Virilio 2000)

This movement in Virilio's work "from topology to dromology", from the features of the contemporary landscape to movement around and through it works for further education also. His general theoretical warning, applies disturbingly to the world addressed by this collection of interpretations: "Dromology (from Gr. dromos: race course) is this government of differential motility, of harnessing and mobilizing, incarcerating and accelerating things and people" (Bratton in Virilio 2006: 7). And all this is conducted within a paradigm of surveillance and an assumption of accountability. Nick Peim, whose *Education as Mythology* does much to advance our own arguments, characterises this as "the gift of education ... an offer that you cannot refuse" but adds sardonically that "for certain segments of the population it is also, at the same time, an offer you can't accept". And here the great refusal identifies you as a 'suitable case for treatment', "being in need of reorientation, salvation and realignment" (Peim in Bennett and McDougall 2013: 38).

One aspect of the neoliberal age is its deployment of (pseudo) onto-theological principles, heady concoctions of 'Reason' and Faith offering the consumer the opportunity to commit to notions it would be difficult to object to: Freedom, Democracy, Education, Feed the World, Every Child Matters. In the US in the zero-zero decade it went by the title No Child Left Behind, a bi-partisan commitment to recover America's competitive edge by addressing the inequalities of educational outcomes as a rather more comfortable option than addressing the social and economic inequalities that largely produced them. This for Nick Peim is where this "particular dimension of the education myth presents its most sinister motif": "the glaringly obvious fact that, as the sociologists have been telling us for years now, the apparatuses of education are clearly designed to reproduce inequality" (Peim 2013: 33). To argue this though is to lack both 'responsibility' and 'belief', to fail to embrace the project with the catchy title which hits below the intellect and which coincides suspiciously with the 2002 release of Disney's *Lilo and Stich*, a feel-good feature whose central message concerns the importance of 'ohana' (family) and a commitment that no-one gets left behind (Sanders and DeBlois 2002). Little wonder that some have suggested that we live in a cultural Disneyland, where everything is parody and nothing is better or worse.

There is a simplicity both semantic and emotional here that skilfully distracts attention from the simplest of truths that NCLB is a policy that presumes that some child has been left behind in the same way that Every Child Matters as a policy assertion is founded on an acknowledgement that some children apparently don't. Always these 'get less thick' schemes which convince us that aspiration is the midwife of achievement have a convenient bail-out point (complete with people to blame for selling short the 'message') so like unscrupulous bankrupts they can set up anew without debts being paid to those promised so much and achieving so little. This point is reached shortly after the promise (No Child Left Behind) becomes a threat. There is a parallel here with the myth of market forces surviving the Global Economic Crisis and informing that other contemporary myth 'austerity'. In each case we know what was done and who did it but find it difficult to find access to the appropriate discourse. This brings to mind Žižek's description of a "society of pure meaningless historical experience", "(o)f a society without history" (Žižek 2006).

Reason's not the need: nothing will come of nothing

There is a rich seam of critique on the impact of neoliberalisation on education. International perspectives coming from a critical race theory position are important in this regard as they can help us identify the cultural specifics of the neoliberal *weltbild*. Contributing to this in the US context, Eve Tuck identifies a binarist injunction to limit the options "to either increasing the role of the state . . . or to increasing the freedom of the market" (Tuck 2013: 328). This renders other kinds of solutions unrealistic and irrational, ultimately impossible. No wonder Maria Bargh, a Maori scholar, considers that "The usage of the term 'rational' by neoliberals can be seen as 'a propaganda coup of the highest order'" (Bargh in Tuck 2013: 328). In fact a philosophy is very much at work which is both colonising and marketising education at an enormous cost, namely the principles of a humanistic, liberal education. The totality of this leads Peim to comment that "It is ironic that today the philosophy of education has aligned itself with the nihilism of the improvement agenda and that 'leading' philosophers today actively promote a rationalist, universalist logic of well-being within unashamedly humanist discourses of 'human flourishing'" (Peim 2013: 34).

It is this nihilism that Eve Tuck identifies as an essential component of the neoliberal agendas that have dominated education policy in the United States and with which we have, like so much else this century chosen to align ourselves with in England. Teacher educator Eve Tuck's work, for example, documents how "the relentless pursuit of accountability" has created "an unworkable framework for school reform and teacher education" (Tuck 2014: 324). Tuck sees neoliberalism "as nihilistic, as death-seeking" (ibid. 324) and powerfully and controversially, finds analogy in the operation of settler colonisation, which means, of course, a process of dispossession and also, later, of an absorption and appropriation of discourses of protest (Tuck and Yang 2012).

Despite its apparent focus on individual self-responsibility and social efficiency, Tuck believes that 'neoliberalisation':

> has worked to defund the public sphere . . . at the same time diminishing the public sphere in ways that make everyday people more politically and economically vulnerable, more fully exposed to the dips and turns of the speculative market, and ultimately, more poor.
>
> (Tuck 2013: 324)

She also makes uncomfortably clear that "settler colonialism is the context of the dispossession and erasure of poor youth and youth of colour in urban public schools"

(Tuck 2013:326). Those 'poor youth' caught in the apparent 'need' for maths and English in England may seem and feel similarly dispossessed, and ultimately erased since it is a neoliberal discourse which is "shaping what is valued, replicated, exported, and vilified in public education" (ibid. 328). These processes, for Tuck and Bargh, are always paradoxical, a "conflict between not wanting to be or appear paternalistic, wanting to be seen to allow people the 'freedom' and 'empowerment to govern themselves, but at the same time distrusting the abilities of some peoples . . . to do so'" (Bargh 2007 quoted in Tuck 2014: 327). A return to high stakes and culturally biased and traditional forms of assessment in England, predicated on an apparent but unconvincing crisis in educational standards fits Tuck's model of the "logics of settler colonialism and manifest destiny" alarmingly well.

This creation of the pseudo-crisis is central to Tuck's critique as a teacher educator: "In my work as a teacher educator, I encourage current and future teachers to understand neoliberalism as a set of responses to real and perceived crises in the public sphere" (Tuck 2013: 327). It is this certainly that since 2010 has typified policies in further education in England and which Toni Fazaeli (CEO of the Institute for Learning) addressed in her inaugural professorial lecture in April 2016 entitled *Value in Our Further Education: Pride or Prejudice?* Fazaeli argued that despite there apparently being a crisis in the post compulsory sector, 82% of colleges were deemed by government to be 'good' or 'outstanding'. Once the crisis had been declared then the mechanisms of the state can be brought in to resource a recovery based on certain conditions of compliance. On both sides of the Atlantic,

> What that amounts to is a school reform movement in which, the surveillance of students, and now the surveillance of teachers (and ultimately of all citizens of a corporate state), is not covert, but in plain view in the form of tests, that allow that surveillance to be disembodied from those students and teachers – and thus appearing to be impersonal – and examined as if objective and a reflection of merit.
>
> (Thomas in Tuck 2013: 329)

Also there is a radical reimagining of the self "to encourage everyone to think of themselves as individuals who always act in ways that maximize their own interests" (Apple in Tuck 2013: 330). Tuck argues that "Pedagogies such as Self-Regulated Learning can be seen to emerge from the same ideological context as self-service tills in supermarkets", including the implicit irony about who is being served and/or is regulating in each case (Tuck 2013: 331).

The contributors to this collection would be fully conversant with Tuck's overview of literature that provides a summary of the way we (apparently) learn and teach now:

- "[T]he rising prominence of fast-track teacher certification alternatives (even as traditional teacher education programs are ever more heavily regulated)".

- "[A]n ideologically driven agenda that is fundamentally redefining what it means to be a teacher in the U.S.".
- Neoliberal reforms which "proffer a zero-sum game, where, in one way or another, half of the participants will end up with below average results".
- "[T]he fetishizing of choice, competition, and accountability within globalized and neoliberal frames has resulted in an almost grotesque pooling of wealth, power, and control".
- "[T]he invention and perception of educational crises (requiring 'triage') and their roles in ushering in policy reforms that restrict the public sphere and deregulate the private sector".
- Misrepresenting "the experiential and empirical knowledge of education scholars and teachers as 'anti-reform,' or 'using poverty as an excuse'".

(Tuck 2013: 331–335)

Resistance and creativity: austerity strikes at the home of the second chance

In his *Education as Mythology* Nick Peim identifies the kernel of our problem and the cause of much of the 'collocation' in contemporary further education of 'Policy' and 'Pain'. "Education", he claims "dominates politics", though some would reverse these, but either way, "Social policy is predicated on the myth of the necessary progression between spheres of operation" (Peim 2013: 37). Peim's analysis takes in the whole national educational 'project' ("correlated with the great economic national project" (Peim 2013: 33) but is particularly pertinent when applied to further education. For Peim, education is principally a form of "population management", producing (and here he echoes Bowles and Gintis 1976; Reay 2006; Bourdieu and Passeron 2013) "the distribution of identities within and for the social division of labour" (Peim 2013: 33). Peim is at pains to reveal (de-mythify) the ways seemingly progressive and aspirational policy initiatives, like the "ethic of lifelong learning" play their part in this.

Further education is central to this, occupying as it does the areas of liminality which exist between the compulsory and post compulsory and between 'first go' and 'last chance'. These are ever fluid concepts at a time where no 'goalpost' is static, where the school leaving age has outstripped the age of consent and where our formal responsibility to educate ourselves careers ever gravewards. Further education is always going to be particularly susceptible to this uncertainty as it exists closest to the formal designated exit and closest to the apparently real world of work, though real 'gratification' might be further, even endlessly, deferred and getting people educated seems these days a frivolous target. This is why Peim is keen to pinpoint how (and when) "lifelong 'learning' exposes its darker, governmental side" in promoting "the myth of perpetual enhancement, a life sentence" (Peim 2013: 33). The neoliberal *weltbild* positions learning as an aspect of the population's ongoing and necessary adaptation to (national) economic circumstances. This has led Biesta to urge us to stop learning and to rethink the significance of teaching (Biesta 2017).

Peim is sceptical to say the least of attempts to use education to ameliorate 'social exclusion', which he identifies as "a contemporary, fashionable euphemism for poverty" (Peim 2013: 38). He is rightly sceptical because although many (including many teachers) have a belief in this redemptive power the research evidence is thin on the ground. A major study in 2005 by two geographers, Webber and Butler, applied a robust neighbourhood classification system to the records of the Pupil Level Annual School Census (Webber and Butler 2006). Somewhat disturbingly this project found that "other than the performance of the pupil at an earlier key stage test the type of neighbourhood in which a pupil lives is a more reliable predictor of a pupil's GCSE performance than any other information held about that pupil" (Webber and Butler 2006: 4) and cast significant doubts over narratives of school improvement predicated on league tables. The influence of neighbourhood was strong enough to suggest that "a school's league position bears only an indirect relationship to the quality of school management and teaching" (Webber and Butler 2006: 4). It would seem to be fitting then that in recent years longitudinal studies have clearly suggested that the products of progressive education now in their fifties are performing much better in international comparisons for maths and literacy than contemporary teenagers brought up on a diet of high stakes assessments.

Lear, identity and the measurable subject

To use the word *identity* in the title of any book dealing with issues as they impact on different individuals in the world today is to invite critical scrutiny not least in literature that seeks to explore educational issues. So the use of this word in the title of our collection of essays needs some framing. Post-modernist thought has questioned the use of identity as a unitary concept including when linked to professionalism (Stronach et al. 2002). Among other things this has served to illuminate the particular experience of individuals and groups that until recently had remained largely obscured by a normative liberal-humanist world-view (e.g. Hall 1992). Intersectionality provides a way forward here and the idea that as subjects we are all subjected in different ways to the web of roles, meanings, expectations and limitations that connect but also shape us in the social world (Bhopal and Preston 2011; Crenshaw 1991).

So what does it mean to talk about identity when talking to and with further education teachers? Further education colleges more than any other sector of education have been subjected to attempts by central government to eliminate as far as possible the gap between policy intention and "the wild profusion" (Ball 1994: 10) of local implementation. The repeated imposition of an instrumentalist purpose on further education over almost a quarter century has led to a tightly prescribed role for college teachers and this has coincided and collided with the fragmentation of unified notions of identity. The way the chapter contributors use identity connects it to an inherited, rooted set of practices and values that, while under threat, have still not been killed off by the ravages of neoliberalism.

As can be seen in contributors' commentaries on graded observations, managerialism seeks to measure and manage individual identities through number. Presaging this current context, in Act II, Scene IV of *King Lear*, the audience witnesses Lear's power as a monarch being stripped away through a parodic inverted auction as first Goneril then Regan stipulates a reduction to his retinue of a hundred knights:

GONERIL: Hear me, my lord.
    What need you five and twenty, ten, or five
    To follow in a house where twice so many
    Have a command to tend you?
REGAN: What need one?
LEAR: O! Reason not the need.
(Muir 1982: 92–3)

Lear's despairing retort, signals his sense that his daughters' 'reasoning', a precursor of the technical rationality that underpins managerialist practices, threatens in a literal way to shrink his sense of self and to dismantle his physical and social significance. Like Lear, the contributors speak of a beleaguered experience, about struggling to maintain an identity they own and connect it to a role they recognise, while external forces attempt to wrestle agency away from them.

In the sense that Foucault talks about the subject as an "effect of power" (Foucault 1982), the corporate performative subject is a hollowed-out individual, an FE effigy. For teachers in further education who often bring their biographies and values to their role, the sense of themselves as subjects experienced in and through the corporation is simply not enough to sustain them. Not only that, but the subjectness on offer is a jealous one that seeks to shut down any rival identities. This is why Ball has written about teachers' 'souls' being put at risk (Ball 2002).

The demise of the managerialist project in educational workspace is its inability to connect with teachers' biographies and values other than through a perception that their individuality is somehow extraneous to corporate aims and culture. The individual is famously only valued inasmuch as her interests can be aligned with those of the corporation. To that extent, in the corporate performative environment, human idiosyncrasies, failings and any tendency to voice dissatisfaction or dissent fall outside what is legitimate. The cultural trajectory of performative organisations is towards the appearance of compliant homogeneity. The key quality of the FE subject-as-teacher is not to get noticed. This isn't necessarily the same thing as being compliant. Rather, the FE subject seeks to avoid the attention of centralised institutional audit. To have performance measured is inevitable, what must be avoided is additional scrutiny.

Unlike Lear, however, the contributors have learnt to look elsewhere for the affirmation of self that gives meaning to the subject. They have come to recognise that the performative institution is only capable of reflecting back a performative shadow of themselves. The resilience of this book's contributors resides not in an introverted essentialist professional identity but in identities that are connected to others: to their students, to their colleagues inside and outside of their work settings. This is a critical version of the 'fraternity' that Badiou writes about (Badiou 2007: 101–2): an affirmation of themselves through their relations with others: their students but also other staff – possibly at departmental level, or with individual allies in the workplace; or even, as in the case of this book, with others of like mind outside the institution. It is in these relationships that further education teachers ultimately locate their identities and autonomies and it is that which has ensured an ongoing resistance to the regimes of simulation that now dominate the culture of many colleges.

The current English model of a marketised, managerialist further education 'sector' has developed over almost a quarter of a century. That stretch of time enables us to identify the features that distinguish such a model. Alongside the imperative to produce simulations through performance data, and as a consequence of this imperative, we have witnessed the emergence of a debased form of education that typically infantilises and objectifies students through a reductive curriculum of spoon-feeding and teaching to the test (Edwards and Smith 2005). While giving voice to their experiences of this, the contributors to this volume insist on the primacy of the teacher/learner relationship in which the learner is seen as a whole person, rather than as a means to gain funding, a 'unit' of achievement or a 'test-ready' subject.

This collection echoes the experience of educators in different countries as teachers attempt to come to terms with the colonisation of their practice by technocratic management practices and to wrestle with the gravitational forces of centralisation amongst whose effects appear to be the obliteration of local identities. Despite the onslaught of managerialism, despite Lingfield, further funding cuts and Area Reviews, the reflexive critical identities of college teachers are still there – as evidenced by this collection. This collection constitutes material resistance to the version of identity offered by performative institutions. In place of the atomised, precarious professionalism of the part-time employee whose voice is confined to institutionalised contributions to a performative quality discourse, these contributors offer their engagement in a critical and reflective commentary. The collection bears witness to 'the way we live now' with a wish that in doing this, things might change.

Chapter overview

The first section of the book sets the scene for the collection. In Chapter 2: Jen Addo charts a steady trajectory away from the practices and values she began with as informed by her teacher training experience, to reveal the attrition contingent on working in a 'quality' role. The tone is that of a lament as the inspirational experience of learning in further education contrasts with her role as a teacher in the same setting.

Chapter 3 adopts an autoethnographic approach, as Anne Groll, Sandi Bates, Claire Saunders and Rob Smith focus on teacher educators' practice on Initial Teacher Education (ITE) courses across a partnership based in the West Midlands of England. It explores some of the issues faced by these 'HE in FE' teacher educators through the lens of Lefebvre's triadic conceptualisation of space as they mediate student teachers' journeys into the 'dominated space' of college workplaces.

In Chapter 4, in the context of initial teacher education, David Wise provides an overview of the mainstream versions of reflection, carefully outlining the provenance of the concept. From there, he proceeds to assimilate and then methodically elaborate on a modified conception: flexion, which builds substantially on a term identified (but not pursued) by Gillie Bolton. The emphasis throughout is on helping student teachers to understand what learning and teaching should be about.

Chapter 5 also explores learning approaches, this time through an investigation of the use of enquiry-based learning with adults. Using Foucauldian concepts Elizabeth Stevenson sets out to examine the subject/object relationship between the learner, learning society and the world of enquiry-based learning (EBL) in a higher education setting. The purpose of the chapter is to consider these concepts in relation to power, knowledge and subjectivity. In so doing complex considerations emerge for learners using EBL and for teachers who favour it as a contemporary strategy of learning and teaching.

Chapter 6 takes an original theoretical approach to the issue of identity construction for student teachers in further education. Anisa Ali, Joe Harrison and Julie Wilde draw on the work of Hannah Arendt and through the key concept of 'natality' – the potential to act and start something new – try to make sense of how new teachers can secure their sense of agency as they start their careers.

The second section moves away from the perspectives of student and new teachers to explore the views of established teachers. In Chapter 7, Matt Parsons challenges and deconstructs some of the key pillars of instrumentalist thought that connect education and economy. The free-floating nature of capital in our society he concludes destabilises these popular discourses and demands a re-integration of critical thinking into further education curricula.

In Chapter 8, Chris Davies draws on his doctoral study to explore the impact of the marketisation of further education on the identities of individual teachers and managers as they seek to formulate and re-formulate their roles against an ever-changing policy backdrop. The chapter uses visual images produced by research participants to explore their teacher identities. The metaphors within each image allow the writer to consider some of the key debates surrounding the agency of teachers to enact their own identities and notion of professionalism.

Chapter 9 sees Pete Bennett using Heidegger and Hölderlin to examine the essential relationship exists between spaces of learning and notions of 'health and well-being'. It may be that 'inhabiting' is inextricably bound up with those developments of human potential sometimes called 'learning'. In fact a tentative hypothesis might suggest that we will 'work'/'learn' best when best accommodated and 'most at home'. Taking these observations as a starting point, this chapter develops a critique of recently built further education colleges in Birmingham and the Black Country.

Chapter 10 centres on a discussion about vocational pedagogy. Drawing on a research project involving teachers of vocational subjects from a number of different colleges in the West Midlands region of England, Donna Drew, Emma Love, Alan Davis and Rob Smith explore the reality as experienced by practitioners behind recent policy interventions in this area. Using theory drawn from Lefebvre, it reveals how despite political rhetoric, policy initiatives to raise standards in vocational teaching and learning may not be yielding the results intended.

In Chapter 11 Joel Petrie provides a critical commentary on whether professionalism in further education derives from values or from some form of faith. The chapter considers how further education's current alienating methods of local production, and enveloping techniques of national political domination, tends to render college teachers as unwilling and apostates in their own places of work.

The third section highlights a range of perspectives that use theory and ideas not just as tools for resistance but as aids in imagining possible futures and resources of hope. In Chapter 12 concerns about the impact of Ofsted, the market regulator of education in England, surface again and Catherine Gallagher and Rob Smith theorise the inspection of an Initial Teacher Education programme, using Bourdieu to illustrate how pedagogic authority and judgement are modelled by inspectors in a ritual of symbolic violence.

Chapter 13 and 14 focus on lesson observation as prime site of struggle for identity in further education. Victoria Wright and Theresa Loughlin present a 'mosaic' of different writing approaches as they reflect on their experience as teacher educators and tease apart the distinctions between carrying out observations for quality and observations for development. The tension between the developmental and quality observer roles epitomise the way quality and management approaches are not congruent with the safe spaces to share learning that student teachers need when they first enter employment. In Chapter 14, Matt O'Leary critiques the reductive nature of inspection judgements based on the numerical grading of lesson observations. In sharing this story, the chapter raises fundamental doubts about the validity and reliability of such assessments. It also offers hope to teacher education programmes that seek to prioritise sustainable teacher growth over the pseudo-scientific practice of performative measurement.

Chapter 15 presents a conversation between two committed teachers and teacher educators, Steve Coleby and Stu Smith, who represent different ranks and experience within the RAF. Together they attempt to negotiate issues of teacher identity in this specific military context. This 'creative conversation' is not without difficulties as the contextual default culture remains a 'command' model of education where 'teaching' often seems synonymous with 'telling'. The authors each offer both a critique of the prevailing situation and an appreciation of the value of developing more effective instructor identities.

Chapter 16 sees Lou Mycroft and Kay Sidebottom examining the potential for rhizomatic working practices to produce approaches to education free from political domination. The chapter develops a case study of a teacher education programme which foregrounded a 'the work is the institution', rather than 'the institution is the work' orientation in an attempt to cultivate a pedagogy unrestricted by the further education system.

The final contributor, Kirstie Harrington, uses the backdrop of William Blake's epic poem 'The Marriage of Heaven and Hell' to highlight the congruence between modern and 18th century arguments. Blake's protestations against structures seeking to control and remove the autonomy of human beings (his railings against 'Reason') are revealed as having a striking relevance for the discourses that suffuse further education in England at the beginning of the 21st. Kirstie ends on an appropriately apocalyptic note (drawing here on the literal meaning of 'uncovering' or 'revelation') positioning the tensions that currently sit at the heart of further education as problems that sit at the heart of our existing social order. We have no option but to listen to the world and to respond with a mixture of resistance and hope.

Note

1 This contrasts with figures from 1995 of 42% (Select Committee on Education and Employment 1999).

References

Ainley, P. and Bailey, B. 1997. *The Business of Learning*. London: Cassell.
Badiou, A. 2007. *The Century*. London: Polity Press.
Ball, S. 1994. *Education Reform: A Critical and Post-Structural Approach*. Buckingham: Oxford University Press.
Ball, S. 2002. The teacher's soul and the terrors of performativity. *Journal of Education Policy*, 18 (2): 215–228.
Bargh, M. (Ed.) 2007. *Resistance: An Indigenous Response to Neoliberalism*. Wellington: Huai.
Baudrillard, J. 1994. *Simulacra and Simulation*. Ann Arbor: University of Michigan Press.
Bennett, P. and McDougall, J. (Ed.) 2013. *Barthes' Mythologies Today*. London: Routledge.
Bhopal, K. and Preston, J. (Eds.) 2011. *Intersectionality and 'Race' Education*. London: Routledge.
Biesta, G. J. J. 2017. *The Rediscovery of Teaching*. London: Routledge.
Bourdieu, P. and Passeron, J.-C. 2013. *Reproduction in Education, Society and Culture*. London: Sage.
Bowles, S. and Gintis, H. 1976. *Schooling in Capitalist America: Education Reform and the Contradictions of Economic Life*. New York: Basic Books.
Clarke, J. and Newman, J. 1997. *The Managerial State*. London: Sage.

Considine, M. and Painter, M. (Eds.) 1997. *Managerialism: The Great Debate*. Melbourne: Melbourne University Press.

Crenshaw, K. 1991. Mapping the margins: Intersectionality, identity politics and violence against women of colour. *Stanford Law Review*, 43: 1241–1299.

Daley, M., Orr, K. and Petrie, J. 2015. *Further Education and the Twelve Dancing Princesses*. London. Trentham Books.

Davies, W. 2014. *The Limits of Neoliberalism*. London: Sage.

Department of Business, Innovation and Skills (BIS) 2012. *Professionalism in Further Education: Final Report* (The Lingfield Report). London: BIS.

Education Training Foundation 2016. *Further Education Workforce Data for England*. www.etfoundation.co.uk/wp-content/uploads/2016/06/RPT-FE-Colleges_SIR_for-publication-PC.pdf. 19 January 2017.

Edwards, R. and Smith, J. 2005. Swamping and spoon-feeding: Literacies for learning in further education. *Journal of Vocational Education & Training*, 57 (1): 47–60.

Fisher, M. 2009. *Capitalist Realism: Is There No Alternative?* London: Zero Books.

Foucault, M. 1982. The subject and power. *Critical Inquiry*, 8 (4): 777–795. www.jstor.org/stable/1343197. 28 August 2017.

Hall, S. 1992. The question of cultural identity. In Hall, S., Held, D. and McGrew, T. *Modernity and Its Futures*. Cambridge: Polity Press.

Lipovetsky, G. 2005. *Hypermodern Times*. London: Polity Press.

Muir, K. (Ed.) 1982. *King Lear by William Shakespeare*. London: Methuen.

Peck, J. 2010. *Constructions of Neoliberal Reason*. Oxford: Oxford University Press.

Peim, N 2013. The Myths of Education in Bennett, P & McDougall, J (Ed.) *Barthes' "Mythologies" Today: Readings of Contemporary Culture*. Abingdon, Routledge.

Reay, D. 2006. The zombie stalking English schools: Social class and educational inequality. *British Journal of Educational Studies*, 54 (3): 288–307.

Sanders, C. and DeBlois, D. 2002. *Lilo and Stich*. Orlando, Walt Disney Pictures.

Select Committee on Education and Employment 1999. *Appendix 33: Memorandum from the University and College Lecturers' Union (NATFHE)*. www.publications.parliament.uk/pa/cm199899/cmselect/cmeduemp/346/346ap41.htm. 19 January 2017.

Smith, R. 2015. College re-culturing, marketisation and knowledge: The meaning of incorporation. *Journal of Educational Administration and History*, 47 (1): 18–39.

Smith, R. 2017. Area reviews and the end of incorporation: A Machiavellian moment. In Daley, M., Orr, K. and Petrie, J. (Eds.). *The Principal: Power and Professionalism in FE*. London: IOE Press. Pp. 6–17.

Smith, R. and O'Leary, M. 2013. New public management in an age of austerity: Knowledge and experience in further education. *Journal of Educational Administration and History*, 45 (3): 244–266.

Stronach, I., Corbin, B., McNamara, O., Stark, S. and Warne, T. 2002. Towards an uncertain politics of professionalism: Teacher and nurse identities in flux. *Journal of Education Policy*, 17 (1): 109–138.

Taylor, C. 2016. Ethically important moments in the higher education space of appearance: Renewing educative praxis with Arendt. *Educational Philosophy and Theory*, 49 (3): 231–241.

Thomas, P. L. 2013. Corporate education reform and the rise of state schools. *Journal for Critical Education Policy Studies*, 11 (2).

Tuck, E. 2014. Neoliberalism as nihilism? A commentary on educational accountability, teacher education, and school reform. *Journal for Critical Education Policy Studies*, 11 (2). www.jceps.com/archives/434. 14 September 2017.

Tuck, E. and Yang, K. W. 2012. Decolonization is not a metaphor. *Decolonization: Indigeneity, Education & Society*, 1 (1): 1–40.

UCU. 2016. *Precarious Work in Further Education: Insecure Employment and Institutional Attitudes within the English FE Sector*. www.ucu.org.uk/media/7999/Precarious-work-in-fe/pdf/ucu_precariouscontract_fereport_apr16.pdf. 19 January 2017.

Virilio, P. 2000. *The Kosovo War Took Place In Orbital Space: Ctheory Interview with Paul Virilio*. www.ctheory.net/articles.aspx?id=132. 2 October 2017.

Virilio, P. 2006. *Speed and Politics: An Essay on Dromology with an Introduction by Benjamin H. Bratton*. New York: Semiotext(e).

Webber, R. and Butler, T. 2006. *Classifying Pupils by Where They Live: How Well Does This Predict Variations in Their GCSE Results?* CASA Working Paper Number 99. UCL.

Wright Mills, C. 1959. *The Sociological Imagination*. Oxford: Oxford University Press.

Žižek, S. 2006. *Commentary on Children of Men*. Dir. Alfonso Cuarón. DVD. Universal Pictures, 2007.

Section I

Setting the scene

Chapter 2

'Hello ... who am I?' – the change agent or the game player of performativity?

Jennifer Addo

The change agent

'Why do people choose to become further education teachers?' This question is a complex and multi-dimensional one that has been researched by a number of academics over the years. An abundance of attempts to provide insight and reason into this topic comes from Australian and American research with a growing body emerging from the rest of the world. I am not going to synthesise a literature review of the many pieces of research conducted in this field, nor shall I endeavour to answer the initial posed question objectively. Instead, I will lay out my own reasons for becoming a further education teacher through reflecting upon my inspirations, motivations and experiences regarding learning and teaching in further education since the beginning of my professional career.

"*Ipsa scientia potestas est*" translated from Latin means "for knowledge itself is power" (Sir Francis Bacon, 1597). Bacon's original use of the phrase carried a religious meaning, but since then it has been used profusely across the centuries as an empowering and liberating meme in many different contexts and many different societies, to the extent that today it seems almost clichéd. Even so, the reason that I draw upon it here is that it is central to my own personal reasons for pursuing a career in teaching and learning in further education. My father had always told me that in order to be successful in society (a society that seemed to me, to be somewhat obsessed with 'order' and 'status'), I had to become knowledgeable, academic and educated to a high level. He said that this would ensure that I had the "best career opportunities".

As a young Black-British African female I always felt compelled to use education as a vehicle to realise my aim of becoming an educated and inspirational individual, like my father, who had overcome many socio-cultural barriers to become an academic and a respected professional. Despite my father's achievements, I always envisaged the academically able as white and middle class, yet the multi-cultural landscape of further education showed me something different. It allowed me to see that academic success was not determined by a person's race or social status, but rather by a person's aspirations, dedication and support from the educational environment, which positioned its students' achievements at the heart of everything it did.

I knew that I wanted to become an academic and have a close relationship with education . . . but I realised early on that the traditional route was not available to me, due to personal, unpredictable and disadvantaging circumstances – namely my becoming a mother at a young age and having to exit my VIth Form education early. My experience of VIth Form education caused me to question my position there. I was different; I had responsibilities that school could simply not accommodate. Upon reflection, the traditional route of education seemed linear, rigid and one dimensional; and for me it was like *putting on a shoe that did not fit*. I could not meet the demands of the traditional route – or rather the traditional route did not understand my needs: being a mother and a worker trying to complete education simply did not fit; and it was at that time in my life (a time when I had decided I wanted to re-engage and continue my education) that further education proved to be a saviour.

As a working-class teenager, I knew, after exiting my A-levels, that I still wanted to study, that I still wanted to be academically successful and that I would have greater capacity to do so if I re-entered education. The perfect place for me to pursue this was in a further education college. Why? . . . you might ask. Well, because this was a place that would help me to grow and develop intellectually and socially and most importantly – regain my lost confidence – confidence that was lost through leaving VIth Form early and feeling that I wasn't 'good enough' or 'able' to learn any longer. Yet little did I know that further education would be a place where I could feel equal, valued and not be judged. Interestingly, at this time in my education I felt like a 'forgotten-middle child' in a family, one that had been left behind or neglected almost; coincidentally, a nickname applied in 2005 to further education itself by Sir Andrew Foster (Foster, 2005).

You see I had seen the power of further education at play before. My older brother and sister had both completed BTEC qualifications and continued on to university whilst working and managing multiple responsibilities, and are now extremely successful individuals. Based upon their accounts of their experiences at college, I expected further education to be an educational environment that held out its hand, extended feelings of warmth and welcome to those who felt unwelcome or as though they were coming back into education with *baggage*. I expected further education to be a place that understood the difficulties faced by those who may not have had the same advantages as 'the privileged'; a place that creates a neutral platform for self-discovery, achievement and fulfilment for each individual entering it, *baggage* and all. Upon entry to college I remember feeling nervous, worried, and anxious, like I was transitioning from the "known to the unknown" (Perry and Allard, 2003: 75). However, my feelings of anxiety were soon overcome, as I became a member of the college community. Further education was caring, understanding, non-judgemental and compassionate; always seeking to understand one's position in life, including the multiple life events that cause hindrances and limitations for those who sought to improve, enhance and upgrade themselves. So what is further education to me? Further education is the teachers, the students, the colleges and the communities.

During the period of time before I entered further education I had feelings of being forgotten, as though education had carried on without me since I became a mother and I had no choice but to refocus and move on. Looking back I can comfortably say that there was a force that kept me going, a great power that kept me swimming against the tide; that was my ongoing belief that just as it had proved successful for my brother and sister – further education could do something for me too. It could help me to learn and permit me access to study my chosen vocation, whilst understanding the complexity of my needs and my responsibilities that came to college with me each day. Something had happened to me, and I now felt and saw the true potential of further education from the student's perspective. I was experiencing the purest form of encouragement, acceptance, empowerment, belonging and respect on a daily basis at college. Further education supported me in building and establishing a heightened internal locus of control (Rotter, 1954; Rotter, 1966), enthusing me and giving me belief that I had control over my future and the events that were to come. It raised my self-esteem and deepened my sense that I was in control of my education and had the power to set and achieve my own goals.

I had been empowered by my new environment and the educational and social activities that I had become a part of; I was empowered to break free from one *habitus* (Bourdieu, 1977a in Sullivan, 2002) and look to the future in a more positive way, an experience that I wanted to reciprocate for prospective further education students (particularly the 'non-traditional' kind who may well have become alienated from education due to an ingrained *habitus*). This Bourdieusian philosophy, upon reflection, played a key part in the transformation of my identity as a student in further education, and motivation to become an FE teacher. My time as a further education student awakened me to the habitus that I had previously become locked into and the impact this had upon how I perceived the world, and my own capabilities and opportunities within it. Further education increased my level of self-belief bringing about greater opportunity for me, irrespective of my working-class background, multiple responsibilities or BME status; and I recognised that the metamorphosis I had gone through could be an absolute 'game-changer' for future further education students with similar characteristics. As a student at college I was encouraged, I was praised, I was given choice, I was made accountable, I was given autonomy but most important of all . . . I was given *hope*.

Further education itself can be seen as positioned in the lower ranks of the "educational strata" inasmuch as research suggests that some further education teachers themselves view the sector as a "dumping ground" for young people (Hyland and Merrill, 2003: 60). However, from the inside looking out, my experience was very much to the contrary. Sullivan (2002: 145) in reference to Bourdieu (1977a: 494) explains Bourdieu's view that social inequalities are legitimated by credentials and this means that in today's society students who are in the stronger position to attain better, more highly valued qualifications (those coming from more affluent backgrounds where cultural capital is stronger) will generally be more successful, and potentially have more opportunities in life than students coming from lower social classes. However, it is my belief based upon my experience as a further education student, that further education itself can break this presupposition, and therefore can be the embodiment of hope and a 'second chance' or an alternative for those from less affluent backgrounds, lower social status and for 'non-traditional' students. Further education teachers, including myself, have created a shift in their identities and their roles. They are now addressing the 'elephant in the room', recognising that further education students (particularly mature students and returning students falling outside of the 16–19 age bracket) bring with them an array of complex issues and needs, as manifested in my own case.

There is the acknowledgement by commentators and college teachers themselves that the sector is in a constant state of flux with respect to policy change, the aftershocks of incorporation in 1993 and the new competitive arena of further education and skills, and of how work intensification impacts on the ability and willingness for teachers to pursue improving the pedagogic aspects (see Clow, 2001). However, that being said, my own fundamental aim was to help in the collective creation of what Lareau and Weininger call "the transmission of advantage" (2003: 568). For me this meant the same advantage that further education had offered me as a returning student.

My commitment to enabling students who enter the sector with a smaller amount of cultural capital (Bourdieu, 1977b), namely those from lower social status or disadvantaged backgrounds, contributed to the impetus that led me to choose a career as a further education teacher. I decided that my aim would be to teach students but also to support them in developing their personal *potential*, go against the status quo and be academically successful; in turn reducing the life-limiting effects on a student who begins in education with a lower cultural capital. My desire to become a 'change agent' in re-aligning social equality through the means of re-education in further education resonates with the work of the great educator and philosopher Paulo Freire.

The work of Paulo Freire introduced me to the idea that, for me, my passion to become a teacher originated in my passion to achieve social equality through the means of a 'teaching revolution'. Freire's work awakened me to the underlying purpose of education: "*society producing what society wants*" through the use of "banking" (Freire, 1972) to meet the needs of ever-changing political agendas; and the need to combat this with a different approach. With limited knowledge (at that time) of the true potential of education – outside of the world of occupational preparedness, credentials and academic prowess – I rejected John Locke's (1690) 'Tabula Rasa' concept and became more committed to Freire's 'race for humanization' (Freire, 1972). Placha (2007: 123–4) writes in *The Journal of Thought* of the moral challenges faced by teachers who choose to teach for a revolutionary purpose. She talks of how "teaching as revolutionary" is "essential in building the foundations of democratic citizenry". My goal was to become an active part of this movement, not only to become educated but also to teach others to educate and share this two-way, equal and reciprocal process with the students that I encountered. My goal was to be a part of this constant renewal of society for the greater good. Türkkahraman asserts "One of the mechanisms which provides and maintains this renewal is education" (2012: 40).

Such a notion has been strongly supported by the likes of Dewey and Alfred North Whitehead who stated in his famous essay "The Aims of Education" (1929), "Education with inert ideas is not only useless: it is, above all things, harmful – *Corruptio optimi, pessima (the corruption of the best is the worst)*". Education with "inert ideas", here, refers to 'an education' that is non-moving and non-changing. So if we consider an education trapped in a web of ideas that are inert and non-growing, one could argue that it is detrimental to our society, naturally because society moves and society grows. Dewey (1916: 3) goes deeper than this and proposes that "Society exists through a process of transmission, quite as much as biological life", suggesting that the groups in society enter and exit through birth and death and that this is a natural happening. The essence of what Dewey is saying is that if we did not allow attitudes, values, ideals, hopes, expectations and standards (not solely taught facts) to be transmitted through the renewal of social groups then the constant "reweaving of the social fabric" (Dewey, 1916: 3) would not take place, therefore preventing society from growing and bringing about an inevitable 'death of a *developing* society'.

So from my perspective, what is important is that society's renewal through education includes the idea that society itself should become more equal or at any rate less unequal. Therefore if we consider the power of further education in developing and growing an individual's potential (as it did for me), where better a place to continue the renewal of society, but in further education?

However

Moving on from being 'the change agent' and marching forward in unison with the army of revolutionary teachers, where am I half a decade on? The truth is I am 'disillusioned' and 'institutionally schizophrenic', as though my soul has become entrenched in the policy epidemic that has overrun education (Ball, 2003; Levin, 1988). When I wrote about further education at the beginning of this chapter, my meaning centred on the value of further education and the heart of the further education teacher being aligned to: supporting the disadvantaged, supporting those who wish to pursue a vocation, growing an individual's sense of cultural capital and potential, developing a sense of belonging and self-fulfilment in students. My view of further education was that it was a system that was non-judgemental, fair and accessible.

Now, after being immersed in the marketisation (Lucas and Crowther, 2016) of the sector (since incorporation) – and taking on a new role in Quality Improvement, I have been exposed to cultures of *performativity* and the incessant need for college managers to measure and monitor what they do to prove their efficiency (see O'Leary, 2013). I have had to comply with an institutional "focus on growth and increased efficiency" (Lucas and Crowther ibid.: 588) as policy, money-pots and the demand from bureaucratic systems fluctuate erratically. From the inside looking out, I question what has happened to the professional autonomy that I once enjoyed? Being judged on my performance in one teaching and learning session in time, and being given a number or a subjective ranking to represent the value of my teaching does not wholly reflect me as a teacher, or my purpose in further education. Surely this valorisation of my worth is not the culmination of my experience of the true value and purpose of further education: the life-changing impact that aroused my initial passion to teach in the sector?

References

Bacon, F. (1597) *Sacred Meditations* accessed on 18/12/2017 at https://en.wikisource.org/wiki/Meditationes_sacrae.

Ball, S. (2003) The teachers' soul and the terrors of performativity. *Journal of Education Policy.* 18(2): 215–228.

Bourdieu, P. (1977a) 'Cultural Reproduction and Social Reproduction'. In Karabel, J. and Halsey, A. H. (eds.). *Power and Ideology in Education.* Oxford: Open University Press.

Bourdieu, P. (1977b) *Outline of a Theory of Practice.* Cambridge: Cambridge University Press.

Clow, R. (2001) Further education teachers' constructions of professionalism. *Journal of Vocational Education and Training.* 53(3): 407–419.

Dewey, J. (1916) *Democracy and Education.* New York: Macmillan.

Foster, A. (2005) Oral Evidence Taken before the Education and Skills Committee on Wednesday 16 November 2005 accessed on 17/12/2017 at https://publications.parliament.uk/pa/cm200506/cmselect/cmeduski/uc649-ii/uc64902.htm.

Freire, P. (1972) *Pedagogy of the Oppressed.* Harmondsworth: Penguin.

Hyland, T. and Merrill, B. (2003) *The Changing Face of Further Education.* London: RoutledgeFalmer.

Lareau, A. and Weininger, E. (2003) Cultural capital in educational research: A critical assessment. *Theory and Society.* 32: 567–606.

Levin, H. M. (1988) Cost-Effectiveness and Educational Policy. *Educational Evaluation and Policy Analysis.* 10(1): 51–69.

Locke, J. (1690) *An Essay Concerning Human Understanding.* (Ed. Winkler, P. K.). Indianapolis, IN: Hackett Publishing Company.

Lucas, N. and Crowther, N. (2016) The logic of the incorporation of further education colleges in England 1993–2015: Towards an understanding of marketisation, change and instability. *Journal of Education Policy.* 31(5): 583–597.

O'Leary, M. (2013) Surveillance, performativity and normalised practice: The use and impact of graded lesson observations in further education colleges. *Journal of Further and Higher Education.* 37(5): 694–714.

Perry, C and Allard, A (2003) Making the connections: Transition experiences for first-year education students. *Journal of Educational Enquiry.* 4(2): 74–89.

Placha, T. C. (2007) Teaching for democracy: The risks and benefits of teaching in the danger zone. *Journal of Thought.* 42: 123–138.

Rotter, J. B. (1954) *Social Learning and Clinical Psychology.* New York: Prentice-Hall.

Rotter, J. B. (1966) Generalized expectancies for internal versus external control of reinforcement. *Psychological Monographs. 80*(1): 1–28.

Sullivan, A. (2002) Bourdieu and education: How useful is Bourdieu's theory for researchers? *Netherlands Journal of Social Sciences. 38*(2): 144–166.

Türkkahraman, M. (2012) The role of education in the societal development. *Journal of Educational and Instructional Studies in the World. 2*(4): 38–41.

Whitehead, A. N. (1929) *The Aims of Education.* New York: Williams and Norgate.

Chapter 3

The teacher educator experience

'Guardians of the pedagogy'?

Anne Groll, Sandi Bates, Claire Saunders and Rob Smith

Context

In the last decade in England, routes into teaching school leavers who are 16+ has undergone a major upheaval. From a situation in which all such teachers were expected to gain a teaching qualification, in 2012 Lord Lingfield's report into professionalism in further education removed all compulsion (BIS 2012). The routes into the sector are now deregulated and largely shaped by market demand, which often translates as the growth and contraction of subject areas according to shifts in funding. That said, most further education teachers still undertake Initial Teacher Education (ITE), either once employed (in-service) or in a one year postgraduate course (like that explored by David Wise in Chapter 4). Since 2014, in-service teachers have been divided loosely into three groups: unqualified staff, those who study a set of government-endorsed qualifications as organised by their employer and those whose college belongs to a partnership with a local Higher Education Institution (HEI). The courses they study range from those that are very focused on achieving learning outcomes to those that are founded on critical reflective practice.

The shifting sands of the market landscape in England provide an interesting contrast with the situation in other countries. For example, in the US, a teaching certificate for community college and postsecondary teachers is not mandatory, although a bachelor's or master's degree in a relevant subject specialism is required. Interestingly, community colleges in the US are seen as embedded in local communities and as important providers of teacher education programmes with their ability to address teacher shortages and to supply teachers from under-represented groups (Coulter and Vandal 2007). In contrast, the Australian context sees VET teachers being required to hold a Certificate IV in training and education (Guthrie et al. 2011). In England, post Lingfield, the situation in further education colleges hovers somewhere between the two. In some vocational subjects, unqualified teachers may be appointed; in others, they may be qualified below degree level. But in the US and now English contexts, despite this movement away from mandatory teacher certification, there is evidence of a push for greater accountability of teacher education programmes (Cochran-Smith et al. 2016 and see Gallagher and Smith: Chapter 12).

The neoliberal instrumentalisation of further education in England is highly visible in a policy discourse that utilises the notion of the 'FE sector'. The use of this abstract term contributes to conditions that make it acceptable to impose generalised, decontextualised meanings on very heterogeneous provision. Lefebvre's triadic conceptualisation of space as 'conceived space', 'perceived space' and 'lived space' (Lefebvre 1991) can provide some theoretical insights into this kind of abstraction. Lefebvre argues for a blurring between physical and mental space – seeing the duality as a false one and the categories as interpenetrating. For Lefebvre, conceived space links to abstract space as:

> an apparent subject, an impersonal pseudo-subject . . . and – hidden within it, concealed by its illusory transparency – the real subject, namely state (political) power. . . . (Here), lived experience is crushed, vanquished by what is 'conceived of'.
>
> (Lefebvre 1991: 49–51)

In this sense, further education – conceived of as 'the FE sector' – can be viewed as an 'abstract space': generalised and instrumentalised by policymakers. This abstract space is reified through the production and use of performance data: colleges are required to quantify teaching and learning in order to draw down funding, transforming social processes into numerical form so this simulation can be fed back into the policymaking cycle (O'Leary and Smith 2012; Smith and O'Leary 2013). This is the abstract space in which teaching and learning is conceptually reduced to the 'delivery' of a curriculum that produces students with the skills needed by industry and who are therefore 'employable'. Through abstraction, the significance of context is dismissed as performative relations require interaction at the level of the symbolic and through the co-construction of simulations. In this way, the abstract space of 'the FE sector' articulates with the spoon-feeding/transmission approach to education inasmuch as 'surface' data is taken to signify the complex diversity of teaching and learning experiences.

Against the idea of abstract space (or rather nestled within it), Lefebvre counterposes 'differential space':

> abstract space carries within itself the seeds of a new kind of space. I shall call that new space 'differential space', because, inasmuch as abstract space tends towards homogeneity, towards the elimination of existing differences or peculiarities, a new space cannot be born (produced) unless it accentuates differences.
>
> (1991: 52)

Lefebvre theorises how even totalising discourses are unable to exclude the potential re-appropriation by ordinary people of abstract space. If the abstract space of the 'FE sector' is founded on a conceptualisation of teaching and learning that corresponds to the delivery of a curriculum and the transmission of knowledge, then the differential space that is recuperable within it is space in which teaching and learning is something more and different. In this chapter we will propose that the differential space of further education can be a space in which critical pedagogy is espoused. This approach to teaching and learning originating in Freirean pedagogy (Freire 1995) connects to transformative approaches (Duckworth and Smith 2017) and views students in a holistic way, as reflexive and dialogical co-constructors of meaning; it views teaching successfully in further education as depending on a critical understanding of the policy context in which it takes place. In turn, this means that ITE courses for college teachers necessarily involve a 'conscientisation' of student teachers. This theorisation enables us to understand how the version of further education envisaged in the neoliberal imaginary of policy-makers contains within it transformative learning opportunities and environments.

This chapter will focus on the experiences of teacher educators belonging to one ITE partnership in the West Midlands. It will explore the tensions experienced by them in upholding a set of pedagogical values that do not always harmonise with the culture of their workplaces. We are not claiming that all college ITE programmes are founded on the principles of critical pedagogy but rather that the relative status of teacher education teams can be taken as a cultural barometer in any given college because teacher educators often find themselves positioned at the interface between data-driven college processes and the attitudes and values associated with critical pedagogy and transformative learning (Duckworth and Ade-Ojo 2014; Duckworth and Smith 2017). In 'expansive' (Fuller and Unwin 2004) college environments, teacher educators are ideally positioned to act as disseminators of good practice and even to facilitate spaces for discussion around what effective pedagogy is. However, in more 'restrictive', managerialist college environments, they are likely to find themselves either marginalised as 'outliers' or assimilated into quality assurance (qa) mechanisms and deployed in order to enforce staff compliance with performance data production procedures (the tension between these roles is explored by Victoria Wright and Theresa Loughlin in Chapter 13).

This chapter will foreground the voices of teacher educators from a college and university partnership and will attempt to represent their experience of functioning at the meeting point of these distinctly different value systems.

Values: countering symbolic violence

The partnership teacher educators identified values as lying at the heart of their ITE practice. These values had a significant impact on their work and their approach to it. These teacher educators' values transcended neoliberal prescriptions for college education. They believed that further education has a broader impact on society than just through raising skills levels. The role of colleges as contributing to social cohesion and community well-being as well as goals connected to social justice also featured strongly in the values set.

One way of viewing this value set is to see it as a response to the symbolic violence that the 'FE sector' visits upon learners in objectifying them in human capital terms, i.e. as repositories of skills required for the nation's economic needs. Learners often arrive in further education colleges with negative prior educational experiences. Young people's experiences of schools often leave them believing they are 'not academic' or 'thick' and can attach stigma to their home culture and backgrounds. Bourdieu and Passeron see education as asserting the legitimacy of the dominant culture on members of dominated groups, classes and individuals, and as imposing on them by the inculcation of exclusion, a recognition of the illegitimacy of their own culture. Labelling is one aspect of this where symbolic violence takes the form of an ongoing assessment of 'ability' that shapes social (and institutional) interactions between teachers and students. Symbolic violence then can be viewed as an outcome of the way teachers relate to and interact with students. The teacher educators in this partnership saw it as their role to counteract this symbolic violence. To gain a clearer picture of how this could be undertaken, we need to revisit Bourdieu's original conceptualisation of symbolic violence.

Bourdieu and Passeron (2013: 3–68) see education as imposing a standard culture whose values reflect the social structure and the power relations that underpin it. In other words, education is instrumental in perpetuating a stratification of individuals in a way that helps to replicate social inequality. Teachers play a role in this through 'pedagogic action'. Pedagogic action for Bourdieu and Passeron constitutes symbolic violence because it entails the imposition of arbitrary meanings and cultural values on learners. Pedagogic authority is necessary for pedagogic action to take place. They see pedagogic authority as:

> a power to exert symbolic violence which manifests itself in the form of a right to impose legitimately (which) reinforces the arbitrary power which establishes it and which it conceals.
>
> (Bourdieu and Passeron 2013: 13)

Bourdieu and Passeron argue this means there is a 'twofold arbitrariness' in pedagogic action (ibid. 5–6). The first arbitrary is the power underpinning pedagogic authority; the second is the 'cultural arbitrary' that the pedagogy seeks to impose. In other words, for Bourdieu and Passeron, pedagogic action involves a set of power relations in which authority is established and then, using that as a basis, curriculum content can be imposed. They appear to dismiss the possibility of any pedagogy which foregoes symbolic violence, as they see no pedagogic action as 'culturally free' (ibid. 17). That said, their model is very transmission-orientated. It adopts a view of educational experiences as those in which learners are passive recipients rather than being dialogically engaged in meaning-making.

So how is it possible to theorise teaching and learning and step outside this notion of symbolic violence and the 'twofold arbitrariness of pedagogic action'? The critical pedagogy espoused as the preferred approach by the college teacher educators in this partnership addressed the twofold arbitrariness of pedagogic action through critical reflective practice. The first arbitrary: the power underpinning the pedagogic authority is something that is addressed through the egalitarian relations that the teacher strives to establish. The classroom where ITE courses convene is a space for sharing experiences and for joining with others to reflect in a community of practice. The egalitarian ethic within this between teacher and students is a cornerstone of this approach. The second aspect, the 'cultural arbitrary' that pedagogic action seeks to impose according to Bourdieu and Passeron, is addressed through critical reflective practice itself and through the biographical elements of ITE programmes that centre curricula on student identity and the construction of a teacher identity. Holistic approaches, that view students' experiences as a learning resource and see narratives and (written) critical reflection as a primary tools in development, exemplify a pedagogy that eschews the symbolic violence as theorised by Bourdieu and Passeron. But while teacher educators may have the ability to shape spaces in which teaching and learning take place, this doesn't make these 'differential' spaces immune to the pressures of pervasive neoliberal cultures. The next section looks more closely at some of these pressures.

From differential to dominated space

The partnership teacher educators had extensive experience of inspections and a consciousness that student teachers needed to be equipped to deal with the performative environments that many colleges have become. Two key areas were viewed as important in this regard: Ofsted and placement college observation schemes.

The use (or not) of lesson plans provides a point of intersection for the different issues. The use of lesson plans is another example of where practice in ITE provided a sharp contrast to practices in performative college environments. In ITE, the lesson planner can be used to make visible the student's thinking as regards teaching and learning strategies – in other words as a reflective tool designed to illuminate the choices student teachers make in the way they organise teaching. To date, the impact of Ofsted has been mainly around teachers producing formulaic lesson plans that ticked the appropriate boxes and name-checked the latest policy fad (e.g. equality and diversity or 'safeguarding'). In the last two years however, Ofsted has retreated from erstwhile prescription and signalled a move away from favouring lesson plans. The change has caused consternation. One teacher educator explained:

> When Ofsted said they wanted to see 'evidence of planning' and not necessarily a lesson plan, there was discomfort and incredulity in college. How could it possibly be true/safe to teach during an Ofsted inspection without a lesson plan? But a lot of the documents we produced were just for them,

e.g. folders and folders of material, for example, on enrichment activities undertaken, community involvement and 'green' projects.

This is an example of self-consuming performativity which functions to produce the abstract space of the 'FE sector'. In the same way that 'teaching to the test' subverts and makes meaningless assessment as a measurement of learning, teachers spending inordinate amounts of time preparing paperwork specifically for Ofsted can be seen as actually detracting from the improvement of teaching and learning. Ofsted's influence as an integral part of the machinery of market accountability has led to colleges recording and evaluating absolutely everything, a habit which takes time away from teaching and learning and certainly increases the pressures on teachers. But this reaction also points to the dominated space that further education has become. Ofsted's unquestioned legitimacy as an assessor of further education means that when it comes to the judgements made during inspections, less prescription provides greater room for the arbitrariness that is the hallmark of Bourdieusian symbolic violence.

Observations and in particular graded observations have become an aspect of unintelligent accountability that has signally failed to contribute meaningfully to positive change in further education for the last two decades (see Chapter 14). Rather, there is a case for viewing graded observations as playing a pivotal role in the production of further education space in deficit terms in order to provide the pre-conditions for the operation of a marketised system.

The Ofsted report *Teaching, Learning and Assessment in Further Education and Skills – What Works and Why* (Ofsted 2014) provides good illustration of the abstraction of 'the sector' and was a source of much grim amusement in colleges. For example, the report states that some colleges had "a culture driven by policies, strategies and documentation and not by practice in the classroom" (ibid: 4). This was acknowledged as a 'statement of the bleeding obvious' as these cultures were perceived to have arisen *in direct response to* Ofsted inspections and their requirements for 'policies, strategies and documentation'. The statement suggests an inability on the part of Ofsted to understand that Ofsted itself is the author of the entrenched practices it now wishes to see abandoned. This epistemological blindness and the paradoxes it gives rise to surface elsewhere in the report, for example, when a need is identified to:

> ensure that the results of rigorous observation of teaching and learning are used to manage teachers' performance and provide relevant staff development.
> (Ofsted 2014: 5)

This passage betrays a failure to understand that the 'management of teacher performance' may not be compatible with the 'expansive' cultures of teaching and learning and 'managed risk-taking' previously mentioned. In other words, it speaks to the spoon-feeding delivery system, cloaked in a technical pseudo-scientific discourse centred on 'how the brain works' or 'how learning works'. In this context, the judgement that there is "a lack of rigour in evaluating the quality of provision" (Ofsted 2014: 4) once again positions Ofsted as an educational regulator aligned with the cultures and metrics-mindedness of managerialist positivism that have become pervasive amongst senior management teams in further education settings.

Partnership teacher educators were keenly aware of the pressure exerted on teachers by some colleges' in-house observation schemes. Teachers were perceived to be under pressure to perform and graded observations added considerably to this. The impact of these observations was all the more apparent because it contrasted so sharply with the developmental focus of their ITE observations. One teacher educator reported:

> Recently, one of my very able PGCE students, who has sailed through the course observations, lapping up the feedback and happy to engage in reflective dissemination of the lesson, was in tears because she was so worried about her college observation. She knew that a poor grade could be the end of her teaching career. As her course mentor, her teacher, and a decent human being, I spent an hour with her building her confidence and bringing her to a level where she was able to feel able to cope. To see a strong and capable teacher in this state and seriously considering leaving teaching is disheartening to say the least.

This passage suggests the fragility of the inchoate teacher identities that student teachers find tested in some college settings. It also suggests that potentially strong teachers may be lost to colleges because of the trauma of the transition experience from studentship to employee. Furthermore, it underlines how critical pedagogies in ITE that counteract the symbolic violence that appears to be a widespread feature of teaching and learning in further education settings are boundaried by classroom walls. For partnership teacher educators, how these pedagogies were sustained by student and newly qualified teachers in their first years of employment was an abiding concern. Before we address this concern, the next section will look at the teacher educators' perceptions on the other pressures facing college teachers. Overall, the partnership teacher educators felt that good ITE provision was facilitated when a supportive culture and common expectations were shared between the student teacher, the ITE team and the student teacher's own organisation. But this was undermined by a number of key pressures.

The devolution by management of extensive, time-consuming bureaucratic tasks onto teachers could be interpreted as a sign that management is not 'taking care of business'. But such a perspective hinges on a particular view of management as having a functional role, a role in managing and coordinating data and data collection without allowing these activities to colonise cultures of teaching and learning. Sadly, in most colleges, and due to the saturation of the sector with discourses of efficiency and productivity, devolution of this kind of activity is common. A key counter-metric in an 'expansive' teaching and learning environment might be the extent to which college managers free teachers up to teach rather than embroiling them in the production of often meaningless accountability data.

The pressure placed on newly recruited (and qualified) staff in terms of teaching load and performance expectations in their first year of teaching was viewed as a significant problem by the teacher educators. One consequence of the performance management approach newly qualified teachers were subjected to was that teacher educators spent a lot of time helping them to 'fire-fight' in order to 'keep their heads above water'. The teacher educators saw themselves as role models for the student teachers and as such, felt it was important to act in a way that showed a confidence in their values and professional identities. This was easier in contexts in which pockets of critical pedagogical culture had been established but was more difficult in contexts in which their roles had been colonised by quality discourses.

The critical reflective practice that is the primary vehicle for developing a teacher's identity on ITE courses provided a potential means of support. In some settings, students' critical reflection was online and involved the use of an interactive blog which the students and teacher educators used as a discursive and dialogical tool. Blogging helped students to move their thoughts and ideas forward, as well as providing a 'differential space' for dialogue which helped the teacher educator to understand the individuals they were working with more deeply. This space is described by Lefebvre as:

> The space of a different (social) life and of a different mode of production . . . that straddles the breach between science and utopia, reality and ideality, conceived and lived. It aspires to surmount these oppositions by exploring the dialectical relationships between 'possible' and 'impossible'.
> (Lefebvre 1991: 60)

It is this space that offers a resource of hope (Williams 1989) for teacher educators and newly qualified college teachers alike. In the final section, we will elaborate on how this hope is sustained.

Looking ahead

With the drop-out rate of teachers at a ten-year high in England (Weale 2016), this suggests that colleges should see it as their responsibility to nurture their new and qualifying staff. While in some colleges, teacher education teams are positioned as overseers of 'quality' processes, an alternative and more constructive approach sees them as providing a focal point for ongoing critical reflection for all (but particularly new) staff on what it means to teach in further education settings. The work of Ernst Bloch positions hope centrally as a key motive force in history through which we as people can act on reality. In the current, grim context of further education in England, rekindling teachers' hope seems vital. For Bloch, hope is:

> indestructibly grounded in the human drive for happiness and . . . has always been too clearly the motor of history.
>
> (Bloch 1986: 443)

The joy, passion and achievement that student teachers experience in their teacher education courses are emotional rewards that motivate and inspire. These are the experiences that sustain teachers in their working lives and which lead them to enthuse and inspire the learners in their classrooms. The hollowed-out teaching role of spoon-feeding and metrics contrived by the neoliberal *weltbild* can offer only an etiolated and ersatz alternative. In the current economic and political conditions, it may be that hope has to be re-learned:

> Hope has to be learned. . . . It does not just come about automatically but is the produce of experience, failure and resistance to an everyday acceptance of reality. . . . Hope therefore learns but it also teaches as well as constitutes its own conditions.
>
> (Thompson 2013: 7)

Teacher educators can play a crucial role in the (re)kindling of hope. The critical reflective practice that is the primary vehicle for developing a teacher's identity on ITE courses can extend beyond that. Online communities are disruptive of the kind of institutionally boundaried cultures that the market relies on but that pose such a threat to sustaining cultures of critical pedagogy. The teacher educators whose views feature in this chapter find sustenance in the extended critical community of the partnership. Online networks make this a possibility not just for new but for all college teachers. Partnerships for critical pedagogy offer a technology to escape from and coordinate resistance to 'dominated space'.

To return to the national and international context, it is significant that despite the removal of mandatory certification, there is still an appetite for teacher qualifications in further education colleges in England. This may be down to more highly developed systems of accountability, but it might also speak to the notion that however economised colleges have become, there is still a strong cultural memory of the distinctness and value of pedagogical knowledge. Our claim is not that all college ITE educators provide the kind of educational experience that we have written about here, but that this space is a key battleground for challenging and subverting the processes of symbolic violence that the current neoliberal policy context presents as normal and legitimate. In that sense, teacher educators can and should be allowed to act as Guardians of the (Critical) Pedagogy in a broader historical movement to reclaim further education as 'differential space'.

References

Bloch, E. 1986. *The Principle of Hope.* Volume 1. Cambridge, MA: MIT Press.

Bourdieu, P. and Passeron, J.-C. 2013. *Reproduction in Education, Society and Culture.* London: Sage.

Cochran-Smith, M., Stern, R., Sánchez, J. G., Miller, A., Keefe, E. S., Fernández, M. B., Chang, W., Carney, M. C., Burton, S. and Baker, M. 2016. *Holding Teacher Preparation Accountable: A Review of Claims and Evidence.* Boulder, CO: National Education Policy Center. http://nepc.colorado.edu/publication/teacher-prep. 17.08.17.

Coulter, T. and Vandal, B. 2007. *Community Colleges and Teacher Preparation: Roles, Issues and Opportunities.* Education Commission of the States. www.ecs.org/clearinghouse/74/01/7401.pdf. 15.07.17.

Department of Business, Innovation and Skills (BIS). 2012. *Professionalism in Further Education: Final Report* (The Lingfield Report). London: BIS.

Duckworth, V. and Smith, R. 2017. *Interim Report: Further Education in England – Transforming Lives and Communities.* London: UCU.

Duckworth, V. and Ade-Ojo, G. (eds.) 2014. *Landscapes of Specific Literacies in Contemporary Society: Exploring a social model of literacy.* Monograph: Routledge Research in Education: London.

Freire, P. 1995. *The Pedagogy of the Oppressed.* New York: Continuum.

Fuller, A. and Unwin, L. 2004. Expansive learning environments: Integrating organisational and personal development. In: Fuller, A., Munro, A. and Rainbird, H. (eds.), *Workplace Learning in Context*, pp. 126–144. London: Routledge.

Guthrie, H., McNaughton, A. and Gamlin, T. 2011. *Initial Training for VET Teachers: A Portrait within a Larger Canvas.* Adelaide: National Centre for Vocational Education Research (NCVER).

Lefebvre, H. 1991. *The Production of Space.* Oxford: Blackwell.

Ofsted. 2014. *Teaching, learning and assessment in further education and skills – what works and why.* www.thegrid.org.uk/learning/1419/curriculum/documents/ofsted_report.pdf. 25.03.16.

O'Leary, M. and Smith, R. 2012. Earthquakes, cancer and cultures of fear: Qualifying as a skills for life teacher in an uncertain economic climate. *Oxford Review of Education*, 38:4, 437–454.

Smith, R. and O'Leary, M. 2013. New public management in an age of austerity: Knowledge and experience in further education. *Journal of Educational Administration and History*, 45:3, 244–266.

Thompson, P. 2013. Introduction: The privatisation of hope and the crisis of negation. In Thompson, P. and Žižek, S. *The Privatisation of Hope*, pp. 1–20. Durham, NC: Duke University Press.

Weale, S. 2016. Almost a third of teachers quit state sector within five years of qualifying. *The Guardian.* Monday 24 October 2016. www.theguardian.com/education/2016/oct/24/almost-third-of-teachers-quit-within-five-years-of-qualifying-figures. 10.08.17.

Williams, R. 1989. *Resources of Hope.* London: Verso.

Chapter 4

Through the looking glass
Reflection and teacher identity

David Wise

Drawing on my experience supporting groups of pre-service student teachers on a Postgraduate Certificate in Education (PGCE) course for further education teachers at the University of Wolverhampton, this chapter provides an overview of different models of reflective practice before developing a hybrid approach to reflective practice that I think offers

Exploring the literature – an overview

The literature on reflective practice offers a range of different perspectives. I will begin this chapter by providing a critical overview of this through the use of six themes: (i) reflective thinking and learning, (ii) experiential learning, (iii) critical reflection, (iv) reflection-on-action, (v) reflection-on-practice and (vi) reflection as professional knowledge – before moving onto a newer hybrid model.

(i) Reflective thinking and learning

The work of John Dewey is a good starting place for any discussion on reflection as it influenced a number of key later writers such as Schön and Kolb; Moon (1999: 11) refers to his ideas as providing the "backbone philosophies of reflection". Dewey (1910) believed that reflective thinking originates in tackling troubling situations and saw reflection as the use of a set of skills to manipulate knowledge and apply it with intent.

> Reflective thinking is always more or less troublesome because it involves overcoming the inertia that inclines one to accept suggestions at their face value; it involves willingness to endure a condition of mental unrest and disturbance.
>
> (Dewey, 1910: 13)

For Dewey, the process of reflective thinking, leading to learning, is best captured in a five-stage model of problem-solving, as follows:

1 Suggestions. Considering possible solutions to the problem.
2 Intellectualisation. Defining the problem more systematically and devising a series of questions that may lead to a solution.
3 Hypothesising. Formulating a number of possible solutions or explanations.
4 Reasoning. Assimilating other information into deliberation over the solution.
5 Testing. Trying the solution out.

Dewey's five-stage model of reflective thinking can be viewed as extending outside classroom walls to address wider social and political concerns. There are echoes of this approach in Habermas's work which came much later in the twentieth century. Habermas's theory of 'communicative action' (1987) as an everyday feature of human being has much in common with reflective practice. The work of these writers suggests that reflective thought and practice has strong roots in political philosophy. For the purposes of this chapter however, the focus is on reflective practice as a tool for teachers to interact with and develop their classroom practice.

(ii) Experiential learning

Dewey's philosophy is social and goal-directed and this latter feature is also evident in the works of experiential theorists such as Kolb (1976), Boud et al. (1985) and Mezirow (1990). Kolb (1976) famously created a model or cycle of experiential learning with four stages: concrete experience, observation and reflection, forming abstract concepts and testing in new situations. This model, which was further developed by Gibbs (1988) who introduced two new stages – 'analysis' and 'conclusion' has become a touchstone on teacher education courses throughout England.

In earlier work, Kolb and Fry (1975: 35–6) claimed that for effective learning to take place an individual required four associated abilities. Kolb thus created a learning styles inventory (Kolb, 1976) which positioned learners within a framework of four related learning 'styles'. This notion, coming long before the now largely discredited Honey and Mumford formulation (1986) and the specific concept of a learning cycle through which all learners must move for learning to take place have attracted criticism. For example, whilst Boud et al. (1985) acknowledge that the concept:

> has been useful in assisting us in planning learning activities and in helping us to check simply that learners can be effectively engaged . . . it does not help . . . to uncover the elements of reflection itself.
>
> (Boud et al., 1985: 13)

In other words, reflection as action is identified as an important and necessary component of learning but encouraging and supporting reflection is not examined. Furthermore, the learning style inventory and the cycle ignore the impact of cultural, social and situated learning.

The work of experiential theorists asserts that reflecting on experience is an inherently human capability. In an educational context, this is a vital skill for learning that involves a practical element. However, experiential theorists do not explain the relationship between reflection and learning (Moon, 1999) and certainly not in the very specific circumstances of supporting beginning teachers.

(iii) Critical reflection

A voice that has influenced other thinkers and teacher educators on reflection is that of Brookfield (1995), who argued that *critical* reflection must involve the identification and close scrutiny of the assumptions that underpin how we operate and that these assumptions need to be discovered through careful examination of our practice. The assumptions that Brookfield is interested in are the ideas that we never consciously question. In other words, critical reflection involves developing an awareness of ideology. This approach encourages learners to take responsibility for their own learning, promotes peer learning and therefore models democracy in the classroom. To this end, Brookfield (1995) advocates the use of four critical lenses and these are (1) the point of view of the teacher, (2) the point of view of our learners, (3) the point of view of our colleagues and (4) the perspectives offered by theories and literature.

This approach is readily adaptable to provide a writing framework for those required to write reflective journal entries on teacher training programmes. However, whilst one can see the appeal in viewing things from the perspective of others, the lens metaphor becomes strained in the classroom. Are we simply asking learners to gather other people's opinions on their practice? Is that the same thing as seeing things from their perspective? In my experience, the model does not always lead to effective reflection-on-practice.

Furthermore, Brookfield distinguishes his approach from earlier conceptions of reflective practice by making much of its critical nature. In part, this is about positioning his work within the tradition of Critical Theory – suggesting as it does his emphasis on the importance of tearing the ideological veil that clouds all our perceptions. Ultimately however, each learner's interpretation and mobilisation of the model will stand or fall on the ability and desire to be critical of those involved in the reflective exchange. As with all the models discussed in this chapter, the framing is everything!

Brookfield (1995) usefully makes reference to peer support and views the reflective process as inherently social:

> The importance for critical reflection of belonging to an emotionally sustaining peer learning community cannot be overstated. *Community* might seem rather a grandiose word to describe the clusters of four or five good friends that teachers say they value so highly. But the emphasis the members

of these groups place on the emotional warmth and psychological security they provide makes the term *community* more appropriate than, say, *network*.

(Brookfield, 1995: 244)

Drawing on this, on the pre-service PGCE course this chapter comes out of, all students engage in dialogical blogging with their tutor, but also with their peers. Indeed the course as a whole both promotes and supports the sharing of reflection and sees the social aspect of this as essential.

Writing with Gupta and Greaves (2001: 141), Ecclestone also foregrounds the social aspect of reflection: "if individual portfolios are shared within a community of practice, and if a debate is generated about individual experiences, then this can lead to developing a body of practical knowledge." Whilst most students are already familiar with microblogging tools such as Twitter, which provides a mechanism for quick and short messaging, "blogs invite longer responses and can support deeper reflection, discussion . . . analysis, and application of critical thinking" (Bozarth, 2010: 87).

In response to a widespread use of reflective practice, Ecclestone (1996) argues that reflective discourses have tended to focus upon reflection only as technical enquiry. Like Brookfield, Ecclestone warns of the danger of viewing reflection as an end, rather than a means or learning process. Brookfield's assertion that reflection is an ongoing process rather than an isolated event strikes a chord here. He writes of the lost innocence beginning teachers associate with the realisation that the complexity and inherent dilemmas in the teaching function have no ultimate solution.

> It dawns on us that becoming a skilful teacher will always be an unformed, unfinished project – a true example of lifelong learning.
>
> (Brookfield, 1995: 239)

(iv) Reflection-on-action

Along with Dewey, the other most commonly referenced author of key texts on reflective practice is Schön. Schön (1983) identified a number of key concepts which are useful for this discussion. The first of these, *knowledge-in-action* has two components. The first is that teaching and learning starts with a reflection on what we, as teachers do. This builds a bank of knowledge rooted firmly in practice. Our personal and collective teacher knowledge is then drawn upon to transform and reconstruct what we do (Valli, 1993). The second element of *knowledge-in-action* is that this store of practical knowledge is then drawn on to inform our teaching, thus becoming *knowing-in-action*. This knowing is often described as intuitive, unconscious and experience-informed.

Reflection-in-action, another of Schön's key concepts, builds on our *knowing-in-action*. A surprise event or critical incident in our classroom is a common trigger for the process and, as the term suggests, our response occurs on the hoof. This is distinct from Schön's concept of *reflection-on-action* – which is the type of reflection that occurs after the event. According to Ghaye and Ghaye, *reflection-on-action*:

> is a deliberate, conscious and public activity principally designed to improve future action.
>
> (Ghaye and Ghaye, 1998: 5)

It is this key concept and its near relation *reflection-on-practice* that underpin this chapter and connect most closely with reflective practice as experienced by my tutor group. Their student webfolios and integrated blogs are tools which capture those public reflections-on-action and, at the same time, aid the formation of peer learning communities and teacher identities.

(v) Reflection-on-practice

Following on from the last point made above, Ghaye and Ghaye (1998) suggest:

> Reflective practice is a research process in which the fruits of reflection are used to challenge and reconstruct individual and collective teacher action.
>
> (Ghaye and Ghaye, 1998: 5)

This is a helpful notion, linking as it does research with reflection as well as taking us another step closer towards research-informed practice and community action. These ideals helped guide Ghaye and Ghaye (1998) towards a new term – *reflection-on-practice*. From this, I have developed a model that draws on theirs and adapts it. The key difference is that this new model does away with the idea that reflection is necessarily a cyclical process. This reworking is illustrated below.

This adaptation of the original model devised by Ghaye and Ghaye (1998) provides flexibility in its non-cyclical design. Learners and teachers can start anywhere within it as the next section will illustrate. This is appropriate because reflection-on-practice can actually be quite a messy process. It may involve one, two, three or all four of the elements of reflection-on-practice in single or multiple visits.

An example

Reflecting on a successful classroom experience, one student wrote:

> So, it was my first lesson with the 16–19 year olds since that heated lesson and . . . they were really good! And not only good but the girl who gives me trouble was as good as gold! I could not believe! All the way through the lesson I thought they were going to go crazy on me or do something but nope!
>
> (Tanvee, PGCE PCE student)

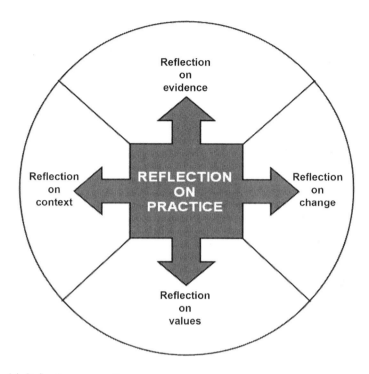

Figure 4.1 Reflection-on-practice

Source: Adapted from Ghaye and Ghaye (1998: 7)

Prompting Tanvee to reflect further on why she felt the improvement had occurred revealed the following:

> I changed the way I taught the lesson. With these guys I have realised to simplify things as much as possible is the best way and I think I have a habit of using language that they may not understand so I simplified everything! A few of them said they really enjoyed the lesson too. I was well chuffed! It's the little things!! Hopefully, onwards and upwards with this group from now!!
>
> (Tanvee, PGCE PCE student)

To which I responded:

> Excellent. How much of this is down to what happened last week do you think? How much is down to the approach you're now taking in simplifying things?

The reason I responded in this way was to prompt Tanvee to think even more deeply about the event – a strategy often used to promote further reflection. It had the desired effect. Tanvee wrote:

> I think it was all to do with last week. The conversation I had with her was really frank and it really cleared the air. Simplifying my language and the way I explained things was key in today's lesson. I was thinking a lot over the weekend about why the adults I teach are really receptive to me and the 16–19 year olds . . . don't seem as co-operative in class. I realised that I tend to use jargon that may a bit too complex for them so today when I actually got into the class, I deviated from the lesson plan slightly by breaking down my PowerPoint into the most simplified way I could and they really got it. They all wrote extra notes, asked me questions about the topic and didn't even take their break. The girl who has been trouble nominated herself for tasks that I had set and was polite and courteous all the way through. . . . It felt really good actually. I can see how this experience could impact on the way I teach other groups too.
>
> (Tanvee, PGCE PCE student)

This example illustrates how the models so far offered do not extend enough into an understanding of the interactive and dialogical aspect of reflective practice. The way in which I interacted with Tanvee was particular to her and needed to reflect the stage of her development. As such, it needed to be flexible in order to reflect (1) the fact that teachers reflect-on-practice in different ways and from different starting points, and (2) improving teaching and learning rarely happens in a neatly linear or cyclical fashion and needs to be responsive to the way individuals learn. This means effective reflective dialogue needs to be holistic, linking values with practice as developments in teaching and learning do not occur in a vacuum, but are affected by the wider landscape of further education settings, which are in an almost permanent state of flux at the current time.

In the next section, I will explore the four core foci of reflection-on-practice, namely reflection-on-change, reflection-on-evidence, reflection-on-context and reflection-on-values.

- **Reflection-on-change**

    If one of the principal objectives of reflection-on-practice is to improve the quality of teaching and learning, it is important to explain why reflection-on-change rather than reflection-on-improvement is a feature of the emerging model. Put simply, this is because all reflection-on-practice does not, necessarily, improve practice. Sometimes we may try something innovative in our classroom that adversely affects teaching and learning. That in itself can be a learning experience, which may well impact on future reflection-on-practice, but it does not in itself improve our craft in the classroom.

- **Reflection-on-evidence**

    The second focus, reflection-on-evidence, is an appreciation of the way that information gained from primary or secondary means can impact on practice. Reflective teaching and learning should strive to be evidence-based, be that evidence obtained from one's own practice, the practice of others, or as a result of educational research.

- **Reflection-on-context**

    Reflection-on-context links back to Brookfield's interest in criticality: events, organisations and externally imposed frameworks all shape the way we construct our working lives. In further education, this is exemplified by the recurrent impact of changes to government policy, the deregulation that has removed the necessity of being a qualified teacher and the recent introduction of new Professional Standards.

- **Reflection-on-values**

    The final core focus is reflection-on-values. Values are often strongly held beliefs that make us as individuals the people we are and, in the same way, make teachers the teachers they are. Consequently, individuals' values affect their practice, even at a time when the current context within which teachers are operating may seem to militate against this.

(vi) Reflection as professional knowledge

Moving away from process, the idea of reflection as 'professional knowledge' generated within a community can offer exciting contestations of accepted 'norms' (Hughes, 2007). This brings together the social aspect of reflection with some of Brookfield's criticality. Multiple layers of dialogue challenge hierarchies, blurring the roles of mentor/tutor/peer and student, particularly in a forum such as the tutor group blog. Professional knowledge can be seen as actively under construction and review.

> It is this very strange-seemingness or extraordinariness which will enable students to formulate their own questions about the situations in which they find themselves (reflective), and the self they find there (reflexive).
> (Bolton, 2010: 58)

Bolton's (2005: 32) foundations for a 'through the looking glass model' of reflection are: "certain uncertainty, serious playfulness and unquestioning questioning". This model stresses the contingent and dynamic nature of professional reflection. She emphasises that this should become a state of mind for the practitioner.

Hughes (2007) sees serious playfulness as a powerful tool in the teacher educator's toolkit to promote critically engaged reflection-on-practice. Adopting and supporting a culture of serious playfulness allows for diversion and risk. Community plays a vital role here: while new practitioners are often looking for a straightforward scaffold (Loving et al., 2007), a simple linear or cyclical model, anything that takes them outside of their comfort zones towards risk-taking may be regarded as too risky. However, a reflective horizontal community (such as that promoted by the tutor group blog) may allow for the playing out of stories of risk and experimentation in ways which allow empathetic reflection-on-practice especially when carefully promoted by an experienced tutor. Risk connects with another of Bolton's principles of reflective practice: a "willingness to risk abandoning previous 'truths' and sit with not knowing" (Bolton, 2005: 34). Bolton suggests that creative letting go is an aspect of the formation of a new teacher identity leading:

> to the discovery of other possible selves – the myselves of whom I am not habitually aware, the myself I might be and the selves I am becoming.
>
> (Bolton, 2005: 34)

Developing an adapted model of 'flexion'

In this section I will build further on Bolton's work and incorporate aspects of the other approaches considered so far to develop a new, integrated model. Bolton (2005) sees the terms *reflection* and *reflective practice* as related to metaphors associated with mirrors that simply reflect back exactly what is in front of them. Instead, she suggests we should be aspiring to go "right through the glass to the other side of the silvering" (Bolton, 2005: 4). This requires changes in relation to the evidence we consider, our working context and our underpinning values.

In Bolton's thinking, by (re)telling the past, we become more enabled to shape the future.

> Perhaps this approach should be called *flexive*. Flexion means 'alteration, change, modification', and 'bend, curve, and a joint', whereas reflection means 'the action of turning back or fixing the thoughts on some subject' (*Shorter Oxford English Dictionary*), with the associated definition of the reversed reproduction of an image.
>
> (Bolton, 2005: 4)

If the mirror image model of reflection is located in modernist duality (Bolton, 2005), suggesting that there is a me teaching *out there* while reflection goes on *in here*, in my head, then the through-the-looking-glass model "opens up more developmental reflexive and reflective space than is possible with a Cartesian-based one" (Bolton, 2005: 5).

Reflection-on-practice may lead to real change or flexion-of-practice as revealed by that change. As such, if Figure 4.1 represents one side of the looking glass, then the elusive 'other side of the silvering' would look like this:

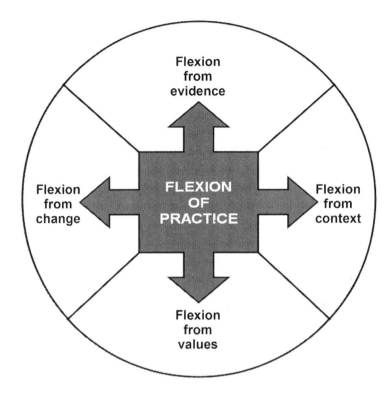

Figure 4.2 Flexion-of-practice
Source: Adapted from Ghaye and Ghaye (1998: 7)

I will now develop a discussion on the difference in emphasis between these four foci.

- **Flexion-from-change**

    Practitioners whose approach to professional reflection involves risk-taking in their practice can develop the 'state of mind' Bolton sees as accepting of uncertainty and not-knowing (2005), which helps them continually to review and develop their classroom craft. Flexion-from-change, therefore, can be the outcome of effective reflection-on-change. A commitment to uncertainty and not-knowing might underpin the process of flexion. This would involve practitioners living out change in a constant cycle of reflective renewal.

- **Flexion-from-evidence**

    The second focus, flexion-from-evidence, is an indication of the practitioner's altered approach to using evidence, be it evidence from their own practice, the practice of others or as a result of educational reading and/or research. It is also active: given that truth and knowledge are contested, it is also about the interpretation of that evidence.

- **Flexion-from-context**

  Flexion-from-context refers to a new approach to external influences on our practice. As events, organisations and externally imposed frameworks impinge on the context of our practice, we may choose to adapt minimally. Alternatively, we may uncritically allow ourselves to be directed by the change. A flexive practitioner, however, might choose to work positively in an attempt to embrace and help shape the new context itself and the way in which paper policies become practical reality.

- **Flexion-from-values**

  The final core focus is flexion-of-values. If going through the looking glass is experienced as challenging but enriching and beneficial then practitioners will become eager to do so again. This might allow for the practitioner to embrace flexion as a core component of their value system. Not only will values shape interpretations, they can and do affect practice. The interaction of students' values with the values they encounter in their placements can feed into a creative cycle. Valuing this interactive dynamic, seeing flexion itself as a fundamental aspect of practice opens the door to change and development in teaching and learning.

Between Figure 4.1 and Figure 4.2 lies the looking glass. So, how is it possible for an individual to go 'through the looking glass' into the brave new world on the other side of it? Flexion is the key: an open mind and a preparedness to change. This is illustrated below:

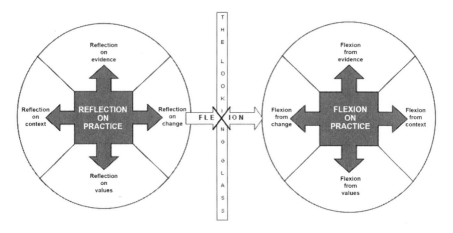

Figure 4.3 'Going through the looking glass'

Source: Adapted from Bolton (2005)

From this perspective, the more flexive a practitioner is (is prepared to be?) – the more naturally they commit to the transformative process of change that is flexion and the more readily they will be able to go through the looking glass. It may be that we need to view this 'state of mind', this openness as an important (even requisite) quality in the successful reflective practitioner.

While the adapted model illustrated in Figure 4.3 has proved helpful for students when reflecting-on-practice with their peers and with me, their tutor, others will continue to fix on the approaches advocated by others (Brookfield for example), as the ones that work best for them. This is entirely appropriate as to fix on flexion of practice as an orthodoxy would be contradictory. In any case, as Bolton (2005: 76) states it is "a mistake to privilege one kind of reflection over another". She goes on to suggest:

> Essentially, reflective practice can always be seen as a process of careful evaluation and questioning: of classroom practice; of approaches to teaching and learning; of one's own beliefs and understanding what learning and teaching should be about.
>
> (Bolton, 2005: 76)

References

Bolton, G. (2005) *Reflective Practice: Writing and Professional Development*, 2nd ed. London: Sage.
Bolton, G. (2010) *Reflective Practice: Writing and Professional Development*, 3rd ed. London: Sage.
Boud, D., Keogh, R. and Walker, D. (1985) *Reflection: Turning Experience into Learning*. London: Kogan Page.
Bozarth, J. (2010) *Social Media for Trainers*. San Francisco: John Wiley and Sons Inc.
Brookfield, S. (1995) *Becoming a Critically Reflective Teacher*. San Francisco: Jossey Bass.
Dewey, J. (1910) *How We Think*. Amherst, NY: Prometheus Books (1991 edition).
Ecclestone, K. (1996) The reflective practitioner: Mantra or a model for emancipation. *Studies in the Education of Adults*, 28(2), pp. 146–61.
Ghaye, A. and Ghaye, K. (1998) *Teaching and Learning through Critical Reflective Practice*. Abingdon: David Fulton Publishers.
Gibbs, G. (1988) *Learning by Doing: A Guide to Teaching and Learning Methods*. Oxford: Further Education Unit.
Gupta, S., Ecclestone, K. and Greaves, D. (2001) *Portfolio based learning as a tool for insider practitioner research: Developing professional knowledge*. Paper given at the Third International, Interdisciplinary Evidence-Based Policies and Indicator Systems Conference, July 2001. (accessed 28th April 2009). Available from: www.cemcentre.org/Documents/CEM%20 Extra/EBE/EBE2001/P135-144%20Shashi%20Kant%20Gupta%20et%20al.pdf
Habermas, J. (1987) *The Theory of Communicative Action: Lifeworld and Systems, a Critique of Functionalist Reason, Volume 2*. Oxford: Polity Press in association with Blackwell Publishers Limited.
Honey, P. and Mumford, A. (1986) *The Manual of Learning Styles*. Oxford: Peter Honey Associates.
Hughes, J. (2007) Possibilities for patchwork eportfolios? Critical dialogues and reflexivity as strategic acts of interruption. Wolverhampton University: Julie Hughes. Unpublished dissertation for Module ED4112 of MA (Education).

Kolb, D. A. (1976) *The Learning Style Inventory: Technical Manual.* Boston, MA: McBeer.

Kolb, D. A. and Fry, R. (1975) Toward an applied theory of experiential learning, in Cooper, C. (ed.) *Theories of Group Process.* London: John Wiley.

Loving, C., Shroeder, C., Kang, R., Shimek, C. and Herbert, B. (2007) Blogs: Enhancing links in a professional learning community of science and mathematics teachers. *Contemporary Issues in Technology and Teacher Education,* 7(3).

Mezirow, J. (1990) *Fostering Critical Reflection in Adulthood: A Guide to Transformative and Emancipatory Learning.* San Francisco: Jossey Bass.

Moon, J. (1999) *Reflection in Learning and Professional Development.* London: Kogan Page.

Schön, D. (1983) *The Reflective Practitioner: How Professionals Think in Action.* New York: Basic Books.

Valli, L. (1993) Reflective teacher education programs: An analysis of case studies, in Calderhead, J. and Gates, P. (eds.) (1993) *Conceptualising Reflection in Teacher Development.* London: Falmer Press.

Chapter 5

Enquiry-based learning and adult learners
A discussion

Elizabeth A. Stevenson

Introduction

I discovered Christopher Logue's poem 'Come to the Edge', originally written for a poster advertising an Apollinaire exhibition, during my formative years as a nurse lecturer in higher education. It is a poem of thresholds, transitions, of a fear both of flying and falling. What struck me was its congruence with my own philosophy of teaching. 'Come to the Edge' speaks of risk but also of nurturing, of instilling confidence, encouraging resourcefulness and fostering independence and self-sufficiency.

One might assume as I did in those formative years that adult learners not only have the potential to become independent and self-sufficient in their learning but they actually *aspire* to do so. As Duckworth (2014) reminds us, these assumptions can lead to unrealistic expectations about adult behaviour. My own experience of working with adult learners has revealed them to be far more complex and variable than theories of adult learning suggest. Despite their enthusiasm for learning they often lack the skills or confidence to be self-sufficient and need a bit of 'hand holding'. And so it was with some degree of scepticism several years later that I was introduced to the concept of enquiry-based learning (EBL) in my role as an external examiner; an approach with which I was previously unfamiliar. EBL attracts no commonly agreed definition but it has been described as a broad umbrella term where learning is driven by a process of enquiry that is owned by the learner in which the teacher acts as facilitator (Kahn and O'Rourke, 2005). And as I have come to learn, it is a pedagogy whose underlying philosophy reflects many of the aspirations embodied within 'Come to the Edge'.

Using Foucauldian concepts this chapter sets out to examine the relationship between the learner and the world of EBL within the higher education setting. Despite its increasing popularity within higher education EBL is not without its critics and contested landscapes. The chapter therefore aims to do what Michel Foucault encouraged scholars to do – to think EBL afresh. In order to provide structure to the chapter a framework adapted from Rose (1999) based on the Foucauldian concepts of problematisations, explanations, technologies, authorities, subjectivities and strategies is employed. The framework enables the examination of how presuppositions about learning are built into the pedagogic practice of EBL whilst enabling an analysis of the structural processes within the world of EBL and how these might influence learner development. The framework also enables the analysis of the systems of power and subjectification about which Foucault problematised (Walshaw, 2007) that are inherent within EBL; systems that Foucault might say produce and sustain the meanings that learners might make of themselves within the EBL process. Taken together these dimensions do not, as Rose (1999: xii) cautions, "amount to a formal analytical grid", rather they have helped as Rose suggests, to generate the kind of questions about EBL that creates sensitivity to the connections and relations in informing contemporary ways of thinking about EBL. In particular the analysis generates questions about the concepts of power, knowledge and subjectivity about which Foucault problematised and in so doing generates important considerations for learners who are asked to utilise EBL and for teachers who favour it as a contemporary strategy of learning and teaching in higher education.

EBL originated from McMaster University Canada in the 1980s under the label of 'PBL' (problem-based learning) from research suggesting that problem-solving situations worked more effectively than memory-based learning in educating medical students (Barrows and Tamblyn, 1980). EBL differs from the more traditional didactic model of teaching and learning that is premised on cognitive transmission where the teacher is considered a sovereign thinking individual. Rather, EBL empowers learners to research, individually and collaboratively in groups, their response to a real world scenario (Deignan, 2009). The teacher in adopting the role of facilitator places the learner in a position of discovery where they construct their own reality through experience and interaction with the environment (Spronken-Smith, 2008). Price (2003) identifies five stages to the enquiry process:

- Developing an enquiry focus or 'trigger'
- Shaping the enquiry and creating a framework for investigation
- Gathering and evaluating information
- Refining understanding
- Reaching closure.

(adapted from Price, 2003)

EBL has adopted many hybrid forms depending on the context in which it is employed but it usually involves the use of a 'trigger' to provide a focus for investigation. Ground rules are established to promote a safe and democratic environment and in addition to the role of facilitator, who acts as enabler and guide; other roles are assigned to facilitate the enquiry process such as chairperson, scribe and timekeeper. Typically the process begins with a broad discussion to determine what is known and to identify a plan of action. The group undertakes division of labour in which various tasks are allocated to smaller groups whose findings are collated through a series of whole group meetings. The focus of these meetings is to sift and refine knowledge whilst identifying gaps, problems and new lines of enquiry. The process continues until the group reaches natural closure and prepares to present their findings. Unlike PBL, EBL does not seek a solution; rather it is driven by an ethos of discovery in relation to a real-world scenario to which there is often no solution or answer.

Problematising EBL

Foucault (1984) described problematisation as a technique of posing questions, of highlighting paradoxes and difficulties in relation to the world in which we live. Problematising EBL therefore enables us to critique it. And this is important given the mixed philosophical and socio-cognitive views about its merits as a newer 'Aristotelian' social model of learning in which the learner has the freedom to develop 'know how' or 'learning by developing', as opposed to 'know this' associated with the more traditional Cartesian style of instructionism (Jones, 2011).

Much of EBL's discourse suggests it has many educational virtues. EBL can help the learner to find his or her voice and develop the self-confidence to take control of their learning. Jones (2011) observes how learners are more likely to gain from approaches like EBL than if purely exposed to instructionism. Jones uses the 'catch and toss' model to illustrate; the teacher pitches knowledge, the learner catches and in return throws knowledge back in the form of an assignment or an exam. As Jones points out, learning may not even arise from teaching. So why is it, as Deignan (2009) observes, that despite its perceived merits, EBL has been described as 'difficult' for both learners and teachers? In my own experience of using EBL one of the biggest challenges for learners is in making the transition from the traditional instructionist model of being 'taught' to the more student-led approach that EBL demands. Similarly, it has been noted that working in a more facilitative capacity can be challenging for teachers as they move away from what Jones (2011: 1004) calls the "serried and ordered didactic model". And this is significant since the facilitator's role is fundamental to EBL in ensuring that learners progress towards their goal through mediation and coordination. Moreover, in calling for a level of freedom way beyond the instructionist model some argue that EBL induces cognitive overload. The inductive style of EBL does not suit all learners (Spronken-Smith, 2008). It is therefore important to strike a balance in learning and teaching given the technologies of EBL require a different approach by the learner and the teacher. To that end if EBL is embedded within the curriculum at whatever level we should be asking questions about fairness and parity and what can reasonably be expected from the learner given the structural processes involved in EBL have the potential to contribute significantly to the learner's development and the kind of learner they become.

These differing perspectives are important to acknowledge since within higher education learners are expected to engage in learning that is meaningful; learning that promotes self-direction, critical thinking, autonomy, creativity and problem-solving (Quality Assurance Agency [QAA], 2008). And whilst EBL promotes these skills it does so by shifting the power relationships between learner and teacher to create an environment that is learner-led rather than teacher-led. In this sense although EBL can be liberatory when compared to traditional instructionism which can stifle opportunities for autonomy and creativity, it could also disenfranchise. And this is because although the philosophical basis of EBL supports the freedom to develop, its technologies also reveal the omnipresence of power and in different modalities; power that seriously questions its liberatory identity. While the discourses and practices associated with EBL aim to liberate learning by "setting collective minds loose to learn" (Jones, 2011: 997) it seems the 'rules' of EBL also have the potential to be repressive and constraining. For the adult learner who lacks the confidence to work autonomously EBL can pose a serious threat. Equally inadequate preparation can throw the success of EBL in the balance (Deignan, 2009). This raises questions about how the learner is supposed to confront their existence within the world of EBL. We should therefore be asking questions about the identity of EBL; what it is and how it is that we have come to think about it as an emerging pedagogy.

Explanations of EBL

Fairclough (1992, cited in Motion and Leitch, 2007: 5) describes ideational, relational and identity functions, which have been applied here in order to explore the relationships between the subject, object and the world of EBL.

Ideational functions

The ideational functions of EBL shape how we consider ideas about learning and pose questions about the differences between EBL and other types of learning. It is possible to conceive that all learning involves 'enquiry' to some extent but the outcome of which is arguably dependent on the level of learner curiosity. However, as Jones (2011) observes it is EBL's architecture that situates it differently from the dominant classical legacy of representation (know-this). EBL is predicated on phronesis or know-how. To illustrate this we must turn to EBL's archaeology. Implicit within is what Rose (1999) describes as an epistemological assemblage based on a number of theoretical foundations. EBL hinges heavily on pragmatism where 'truth' is relative and dynamic as opposed to essentialism where the common core basics of knowledge are learned. EBL assumes there are no straightforward answers, that knowledge is constantly evolving and moreover, continually contested. For the adult learner developing a professional identity such as the health care professional, this is particularly significant; they must learn to recognise and respond appropriately to the ever-changing knowledge base that supports patient care. In this context it is clear to see how EBL's ideational function is to generate knowledge whose focus is practical rather than 'knowledge-in-the-world-about-the-world' (Jones, 2011). Learners are involved in a logical process of determining the outcomes of their learning by engaging with a complex real world scenario as opposed to one that is detached from reality (Spronken-Smith, 2008). Acknowledging this relative and dynamic basis of truth reflects EBL's constructivist archaeology; the learner is encouraged to interact with new knowledge within the context of their environment whilst reflecting upon prior learning in order to create their own understanding of reality as Dewey (1933) suggested. The responsibility for learning rests with the learner who is perceived to own his or her own work. Learning therefore shifts from simply accepting knowledge to acquiring knowledge through a more natural method of 'active learning' that would not be possible within the constraints of the instructionist model (Hutchings, 2007). The ideational functions of EBL should therefore be considered within the context and cultures of different learning environments since as Deignan (2009) and Jones (2011) observe; there are things that learners simply have to learn – 'know-this' whilst other learning calls for 'know-how'.

Relational functions

Relational function refers to the construction of power relationships between discourse actors or 'stakeholders' (Motion and Leitch, 2007). Here examination of the relational functions of EBL enables us to reveal potential power relationships not only between learner and teacher but also between learners themselves. According to Foucault (1977) power lies beneath all aspects of human society and although often represented in a negative light is often productive, positive and enabling. For Foucault power produces reality. The relational function of EBL clearly shifts the relationships between learner and teacher by placing the learner in a more empowered and active role. The learner becomes the performer who leads learning as opposed to assuming the role of fielder or "coconut with cerebellum" described by Jones (2011). Conversely, the teacher shifts from sovereign thinker to facilitator adopting a scaffolding role which Jones (2011: 998) considers more crucial than their subject expertise. These relational functions are central to the identity function of EBL.

Identity functions

Motion and Leitch (2007) define identity functions as subject positions available to actors within discourse. In relation to EBL identity functions reveal something about the creation and transformation of learner within the EBL process. Taking Foucault's belief that systems of power both produce and sustain the meanings that people make of themselves, EBL arguably sets out to positively transform the EBL group into what Peim (2001: 179) describes as self-disciplined citizens of modernity. EBL learners not only take on an empowered role but utilise what Peim describes as an array of spaces, techniques and occasions for the transformation of learning rather than the conventional classroom setting with which learning is often associated.

Technologies of EBL

According to Willcocks (2006) Foucault rarely sought to define his use of the word 'technology' but 'power' was always inherent within his concepts of technology whether at behavioural or architectural levels. Foucault acknowledged that various technologies govern our society and that power can exist as a means of liberation despite being associated with repression (Brookfield, 2001). As Brookfield reminds us, Foucault would argue that power relations are inherent within all modes of adult education even those that seem the most unconstrained such as EBL. Brookfield echoes Foucault in reminding us not to perceive power as wholly repressive or constraining in learning, rather to consider the notion that power can also produce effects at the level of desire. Setting collective minds loose to learn through EBL as Jones (2011) describes would seem to support this notion. However, as Fendler (2010) observes democratic systems contain different modalities of power that operate within what Foucault called rules and the rules of EBL arguably make EBL a 'machine of cultural regulation' as described by Peim (2001). EBL represents an epistemic shift in the way we think about learning; it seeks to change the ontology of learning at a time when the more traditional methods of teaching such as lectures are being replaced or supplemented by approaches that call for different roles and identities. These changes can bring about societal mechanisms of control and can become repressive if they are executed in a haphazard and accidental way rather than being deliberately organised as Brookfield (2001) observes. In relation to EBL's ethos of self-directed discovery this is significant; learners may inadvertently acquire misconceptions or incomplete or disorganised knowledge if effective scaffolding is not in place. Moreover, EBL has the potential to bring about the Janus-like phenomenon described by Brookfield (2001) in which the two contradictory faces of power come into play: repressive and liberatory. For the less confident learner the culture of EBL may pose a real threat whereas for the more loquacious learner, for whom the culture of EBL holds relatively few concerns, their experience can be truly liberating (Brookfield, 2001; Spronken-Smith, 2008; Jones, 2011). These notions of power thereby accentuate the need for solid preparation for both teacher and learner and emphasise the significance of effective scaffolding throughout the EBL process.

Foucault saw power as omnipresent, etched into everyone's daily lives. And it is clear that despite its democratic intent EBL does not promote total freedom. Rather the notion of power as a technology seriously challenges the idea that EBL equates to a level of freedom that is synchronous with converting power '*over*' learners to power '*with*' them. To this end Foucault (cited in Rabinow,

1991: 252) might argue that EBL is somewhat heterotopian since its social space can have different functions for the individual and the collective. The use of 'language' within the enquiry process as a tool for thinking, learning and sharing information illustrates this. In conveying the rich conceptual structure of language Gutting (2005) refers to Shakespearean English, a language considered fluent and accessible at the time, but which now presents a certain difficulty since it is not readily available to all of us. The point here is that during the enquiry process language may be generated through discourse that not all learners are able to understand or more importantly assimilate into their real world. This poses significant challenges for the EBL facilitator or 'architect' (Price, 2003) whose role is not simply to oversee group activities through surveillance, a role that Peim (2001: 182) would describe as 'shepherd' style; rather it is to transform the unregulated EBL group into "self-disciplined citizens of modernity" by fostering communication and understanding. However, because of EBL's heterotopian nature the facilitator may have limited control over the "territory, communication and speed" that Foucault (cited in Rabinow, 1984: 244) spoke of without taking over the EBL process completely through 'disciplinary power'; power through finer channels based on "knowing the inside of people's minds" (Foucault, 1982: 214, cited by Brookfield, 2001: 9). It is then perhaps through self-surveillance that disciplinary power ensures the EBL group 'watches itself' and monitors its own behaviour in an attempt to stay close to the culture of EBL (Brookfield, 2001; Gutting, 2005).

Authorities associated with EBL

In contemplating authorities associated with EBL, Rose (1999) would question who pronounces upon it and the rivalries between their claims. This is difficult for a number of reasons. First, EBL has contested landscapes in which no one singular definition emerges. Second, there is no apparent agreement about the scope and limitations of human cognitive architecture. Third, studies about EBL are largely interpretivist in nature and this has generated multiple realities of EBL. Deciding what constitutes 'truth' about EBL is therefore complex given that each authority as Brookfield (2001) observes, has its own regime of truth and discourse that it accepts and makes function as 'true'. This is particularly important where authorities are in positions of power and in arguably stronger positions to support their knowledge claims. For the teacher who chooses to employ EBL these intricacies have important consequences. In attempting to do what is best and in making the learning environment as open and democratic as possible, they are unwittingly servants of power (Rose, 1999).

Subjectivities within EBL

Rose (1999) describes subjectivities as ontological in that they are present in various guises such as consciousness and emotion and are related to, amongst other things, the practices or regimens by which subjects should act. Foucault referred to subjectification as a process whereby "individuals become accountable to specific discourses that claim their hold" (Walshaw, 2007: 114). EBL could be presented as a tool of subjectification since as we have already outlined, it is predicated on assumptions associated with adult learning. In this sense EBL assumes the development of a more critical analytical independent learner capable of the self-regulating citizenry that Peim (2001) describes through its architecture and apparatus. Learners are positioned as teacher-scaffolded performers (Jones, 2011) becoming 'agents of power' in which they are "perpetually channelling disciplinary power but also possessing the capacity to subvert dominant power relations" as Brookfield (2001: 144) observes. The power of the teacher is thus far less emphasised but because the power relations within EBL are diverse and contextual they might originate in unpredictable ways. As Walshaw (2007) points out, most of us like order, consistency and predictability and EBL is unlikely to afford this. In many senses this is what gives it an appealing identity. It is after all a culture within which freedom of exploration and discussion should play a central role if learners are to demonstrate a suitably intellectual level of discourse in an informed, thoughtful and insightful way (Brookfield, 2001). Essentially discussion must address the fundamental epistemological question "what is knowledge?" which is precisely what EBL demands. As McCormick (2008: 51) points out there may be a "cognitive conflict between how a learner construes or conceptualises something and the evidence they are confronted with". And this further illustrates the challenges as well as the values of the inductive style of learning on which EBL is predicated.

Strategies with which EBL can be aligned

Foucault might observe that during the last decade higher education has been the object of 'biopower' a form of power to emerge in modern democracies (Fendler, 2010). Indeed higher education has been under close scrutiny in relation to the ways in which it can aid workforce skills and subsequently economic productivity. Arguments that state academic qualifications are no longer enough have generated a focus on other skills that are transferable to the workforce environment. As Malcolm (2014) reminds us, communication skills, numeracy skills, the use of information technology and learning how to learn are now critical to the success of higher education graduates. EBL demands of all these skills by shifting away from the dominant classical legacy or know-this to phronesis, know-how through empowerment and discovery. EBL can therefore be considered an instrument of person formation; a condition for contemporary social formation as described by Peim (2001: 178). As such EBL represents a subtle form of 'biopower' a concept that was arguably central to the Dearing Report (1997) that is more recently reflected in *We Think That's the Future: Curriculum Reform Initiatives in HigherEducation* (Higher Education Academy, 2013). Both call for a discourse of challenge and change in reshaping curricula to reflect new models of learning and teaching like EBL; models that are required to meet the needs of contemporary higher education learners in preparing them for future employment.

Conclusion

Like every pedagogic practice, EBL is influenced by the same complex social relations that exist between learners, teachers, knowledge and institutions that promote learning. And despite the call for a redefinition of teaching that fosters learning as a social outcome achieved by collaborative efforts, EBL is not a panacea as the preceding pages have shown. Drawing on Foucault's work has made it possible, within the limits of this chapter, to explore how the technologies, architecture and apparatus of EBL can influence adult learning particularly in relation to different modalities of power. And whilst EBL should be celebrated on the one hand for its emancipatory and democratic intent it should not be overlooked that EBL involves exercising power as a controlling influence that hovers over learners, and that seems to a large extent unavoidable. But as Foucault (cited by Gutting, 2005: 6) said "the main interest in life and work is to become someone else that you were not in the beginning". And despite its contested landscapes, complexities and difficulties, EBL at least engages with this aspiration by empowering students to 'become' while helping teachers to do what Jones (2011) advocates; hand out the cultural tools and establish the new social settings for learning.

References

Barrows, H. S. and Tamblyn, R. M. (1980) *Problem-Based Learning: An Approach to Medical Education*. New York: Springer.

Brookfield, S. (2001) Unmasking power: Foucault and adult learning. *Canadian Journal for the Study of Adult Education*. 15 (1): 1–23.

The Dearing Report. (1997) *Higher Education in the Learning Society*. London: Her Majesty's Stationary Office.

Deignan, T. (2009) Enquiry-based learning: Perspectives on practice. *Teaching in Higher Education*. 14 (1): 13–28.

Dewey, J. (1933) *How We Think: A Rethinking of the Relation of Reflective Thinking in the Educative Process*. New York: D. C. Heath.

Duckworth, V. (2014) *How to Be a Brilliant FE Teacher: A Practical Guide to Being Effective and Innovative*. London: Routledge.

Fairclough, N. (1992) in Motion, J. and Leitch, S. R. (2007) A toolbox for public relations: The oeuvre of Michel Foucault. *Public Relations Review*. 33 (3): 263–268.

Fendler, L. (2010) *Michel Foucault*. Continuum Library of Educational Thought. Volume 22. London: Continuum International Publishing Group.

Foucault, M. (1977) *Discipline and Punish: The Birth of the Prison*. New York: Vintage.

Foucault, M. (1982) in Brookfield, S. (2001) Unmasking power: Foucault and adult learning. *Canadian Journal for the Study of Adult Education*. 15 (1): 1–23.

Foucault, M. (1984) *The Use of Pleasure: The History of Sexuality*. (R. Hurley, Trans.). London: Penguin.

Gutting, G. (2005) *Foucault: A Very Short Introduction*. New York: Oxford University Press.

Higher Education Academy. (2013) *We Think That's the Future: Curriculum Reform Initiatives in Higher Education*. York: Higher Education Academy.

Hutchings, W. (2007) Enquiry-Based Learning: Definitions and Rationale. Centre for Excellence in Enquiry-Based Learning Chapters and Studies [online] Available from: www.campus.manchester.ac.uk/ceebl/resources/guides/ceeblrp001.pdf [Date accessed: 14 May 2017].

Jones, A. (2011) Philosophical and socio-cognitive foundations for teaching in higher education through collaborative approaches to student learning. *Educational Philosophy and Theory*. 43 (9): 997–1011.

Kahn, P. and O'Rourke, K. (2005) "Understanding Enquiry Based Learning". in Barrett, T., Mac Labhrainn, I., Fallon, H. (Eds.) *Handbook of Enquiry and Problem-based Learning. Galway: AISHE and CELT, NUI Galway*. Chapter 1.

Malcolm, M. (2014) Transforming lives and 'the measure of their states'. *Journal of Pedagogic Development*. 3 (3): 1–15.

McCormick, R. (2008) "Threshold Concepts and Troublesome Knowledge" in Land, R., Meyer, J. H. F. and Smith, J. (2008) *Threshold Concepts within the Disciplines*. Rotterdam: Sense Publishers, pp. 51–74.

Motion, J. and Leitch, S. R. (2007) A toolbox for public relations: The oeuvre of Michel Foucault. *Public Relations Review*. 33 (3): 263–268.

Peim, N. (2001) The history of the present: Towards a contemporary phenomenology of the school. *History of Education*. 30 (2): 177–190.

Price, B. (2003) *Studying Nursing Using Problem-Based & Enquiry-Based Learning*. Hampshire: Palgrave MacMillan.

Rabinow, P. (Ed.) (1991) *The Foucault Reader*. London: Penguin Books.

Rose, N. (1999) *Governing the Soul: The Shaping of the Private Self*. Second edition. London: Free Association Books.

Spronken-Smith, R. (2008) *Experiencing the Process of Knowledge Creation: The Nature and Use of Inquiry-Based Learning in Higher Education*. Dunedin, New Zealand: University of Otago [online] Available from: http://akoaotearoa.ac.nz/sites/default/files/u14/IBL%20-%20Report%20-%20Appendix%20A%20-%20Review.pdf [Accessed 14 May 2017].

Walshaw, M. (2007) *Working with Foucault in Education*. Rotterdam: Sense Publishers.

Willcocks, L. P. (2006) *Michel Foucault in the Social Study of ICTs: Critique and Reappraisal*. Working Paper Series 138. London: London School of Economics and Political Science.

Chapter 6

Something out of nothing
Reflecting on the emerging self as teacher

Anisa Ali, Joe Harrison and Julie A. Wilde

Knowing who we are as ourselves is significant for being a teacher in PCE; without self-knowledge and reason how can we be autonomous teachers? Reflective practice may play a part in making sense of our lived reality however it does not fully provide the political space for negotiation, collaboration or freedom. This chapter offers a critique of reflective practice using the work Hannah Arendt and her notion of 'natality', that human capacity to create new ideas, institutions and frameworks out of nothing. Natality is a condition of human existence in that we have the potential to act and start something new regardless of the persuasive and, at times, powerful discursive practices within the sector. Thus we share with Taylor's (2016) recent work on 'ethical praxis' (also derived from Arendt) the "desire to find or, rather, hold onto and cherish, an educative space from which to contest perceptions that the intensification of market conditions in higher education inevitably brings a deformation and derogation of teaching and learning relationships" (Taylor 2016: 1). This 'ethical practice' promises "action which embodies certain qualities" which include "a commitment to human well-being and the search for truth, and respect for others [and] it requires that a person makes a wise and prudent practical judgement about how to act in this situation" (Taylor 2016: 3).

The PGCE in post-compulsory education (PCE), which we three authors shared in 2013–15, has been designed to support a critically reflective (Brookfield 1995, 2005), personalised and shared experience of the emerging self as teacher. Biesta (2013) argues that there are three domains in which educational purposes can be articulated: qualification, socialisation and subjectification (referring to the self/selfness). The PGCE in PCE acknowledges that individuals will have significantly different learning autobiographical experiences as they travel through their PGCE course; each person will bring own preconceived ideas, assumptions and lived realities to the new situation. The diversity in lived experience and subjectness means that initial teacher education (ITE) is a unique and 'risky' encounter; after all it is about human interactions and lived experiences (Biesta 2013). The risk is there because students are not to be seen as objects to be moulded and disciplined, but as subjects of action and responsibility (Biesta 2013: 1). Likewise Arendt (1958) argues that the human condition of plurality, action and natality provide a context to guide education which is diverse and wide ranging

The manner in which education ought to be is framed by Arendt's (1958) *Human Condition* and theory of action. Arendt's conceptions of the human conditions of plurality, natality and action offer educators an improved grounding for their theoretical foundations and crucial points of emphasis for teacher education (Hayden 2012: 239). There are key lessons to be learned from Biesta's (2013) notion of subjectness and Arendt's (1958) human conditions in exploring teachers' natality and action. Therefore this chapter considers the complex negotiations of beginning teachers' subjectness and action in exploring how beginning teachers create something out of nothing whilst working within the political discursive practices of education.

Similarly, to Biesta's (2013) domains of education, teacher educators work within the parameters of the qualification and towards the socialisation into a professional practice; however the rewarding and challenging aspects of the PGCE course are much more risky for all participants, the shared and negotiated experience of self-emerging as teacher. This chapter has been co-written with student teachers who have shared their experience of emerging selves as teachers in PCE.

The PGCE in PCE is an endorsed qualification governed by quality assurance (QA) mechanisms and external regulatory bodies such as Ofsted and the Education Professional Standards (ETF 2014). The teaching profession and being self/subject as teacher are also influenced by politicians, policymakers as well as personal ethics. In this chapter we take look at the experience of two PGCE PCE students in making sense of their emerging selves as teachers. We consider the implications of reflective practice and discuss Hannah Arendt's notion of 'natality' where the freedom to act and create something new is significant for emerging as self as teacher.

As previously stated Biesta (2013) considers three domains for education which, for the purposes of this chapter have been interpreted below:

- Qualification – Qualifying for ITE (PGCE in PCE)
- Socialisation – Sense of professional practice endorsed by organisational expectations and ideologies, ETF professional standards and Ofsted requirements
- Subjectification – Self/ness and the emerging self as teacher.

The chapter offers a new take on reflection in an attempt to reclaim reflection as an essential critical attitude, using the work of Arendt and her notion of 'natality'. For Arendt natality is that ability, which she would see as essentially human, to create new ideas, institutions and frameworks out of nothing. Higgins (2011) claims that within Arendt's work we find the resources for developing a revised account of teaching as an activity affording contact with one's natality and spaces for self-enactment.

Arendt's work *The Human Condition* (1958) claims there is no invariable human nature, there are a number of inescapable conditions which limit, shape and inspire what humans do and become (Higgins 2011: 87). According to Higgins (2011) these conditions are analogous to the 'rules of the game' where there are endless variations and freedom of choice and movement. He continues that the freedoms are based on observing the boundaries and rules whereas natality is a condition of human existence in that we have the potential to act and start something new. The primary role of education is to preserve natality and ensure that the gap between past and future 'remains a space of freedom and possibility' (Levinson 2001: 30). Creating space for dialogue and reflection is often woven into PCE ITE programmes but is reflection itself enough? One student teacher writes:

> Many authors have said that teaching is a solitary profession and after a few months on placement I agreed with this. However, my belief now is that those authors couldn't be further from the truth and that working in collaboration with others is much better for sharing and developing my practice.
>
> (Reu PGCE PCE 2014)

Reflection is often at the heart of initial teacher education programmes in all sectors of education and is evident within subdivisions of the externally set professional standards (ETF 2014). Thus student teachers are constantly reminded to engage in reflective practice in order to critically dissect their lived experience as teachers. Kinsella (2009) points out that the practice of reflection is one of the most popular theories of professional knowledge where in the last three decades it has been widely adopted by educationalists. However, Kinsella (2009) also adds that there is little agreement as to what reflective practice is and highlights that it is not a new concept. Consequently reflective practice is in danger of being adopted without rigorous interrogation of the central notion of reflection. In this way reflection becomes both constant and problematic, the worst of both worlds, both critical and beyond reproach.

In teacher education reflective practice might be something student teachers do in order to judge the strengths and limitations of a particular teaching practice and own professional development. Hence reflection is most likely to influence a change in teaching behaviour. It is well known that Schön (1983) remains a popular reference for reflective practice and discusses notions of reflection-on-action and reflection-in-action. These concepts relate to a behavioural change in planning for a developed practice either after an event or during the very moment of an event. Schön's (1987) reflection-in-action links closely to Arendt's thinking, where we may pause in the midst of action to make what Arendt calls a 'stop-and-think' (Schön 1987: 26). Schön claims that our knowledge is ordinarily tacit, implicit in our patterns of action and intuitive perceptions of the stuff with which we are dealing. Subsequently he summarises that, it seems right to say that our knowing is in our action (Schön 1987: 49). However, do we always know why we do what we do?

Our actions, according to Arendt, are often initiatives or trying something new in a situation; thus they are likely to be 'unknown', unforeseeable, unpredictable and risky. Uncertainty is frequently experienced by beginning teachers and often by their more experienced colleagues too. We may think about what we intend to do but the interactive nature of teaching and learning means that action and response is not easily predictable. Arendt claims that 'to act' first of all means to begin something new, to bring something new into the world (Biesta 2013: 105) and whilst action has a revelatory character about the self, action cannot always foresee outcomes. Therefore Arendt sees action as changeable depending on how others take up these new initiatives (Biesta 2013). What Arendt does suggest is that with word and deed we insert ourselves into the world (Arendt 1958: 178). Thus her notion of action provides a stirring vision of interpersonal responsiveness and self-enactment that transcends our modern moral talk of duty and interest (Higgins 2011: 86). She provides a framework for thinking about how work practices are rooted in fundamental human needs and aspirations (Higgins 2011: 108). Lilly (PGCE PCE 2014) summaries her ideas 'emerging self as teacher':

> The challenge whilst on the PGCE is not having enough freedom . . . there is a set structure that every teacher needs to abide by. The structure may be different depending on the educational institution. Different educational institutions have a type of culture attached to them.

Here a teacher, her career barely begun, shares her concern of not having enough freedom. So how can teacher educators support fundamental human needs and aspirations? How might teacher educators advocate action whilst working within the parameters of both a qualification (PGCE) and a professional field? What are the risks? It is clear that the implications for teacher educators are to ensure spaces for freedom and possibility (Levinson 2001). Teacher educators must allow for the space and risks for student teachers to emerge as self as teacher. As previously stated, one consideration is through encouraging reflective practice despite the reprimands.

It is important to note that if we do not consider the problematic nature of reflective practice there might be more implicit and daunting consequences. Erlandson (2005) argues that the way in which reflection has often been adopted means that reflection has the potential to control the thinking and perceptions of teachers. He also suggests that reflection is a subtle way to control thoughts and thinking about teaching practice and eventually teachers become compliant through self-surveillance. According to Erlandson (2005) teachers are encouraged to employ reflection to gradually discipline and judge themselves and therefore normalise their teaching practices using powerful discourses within organisational culture and policy which is inferred in Lilly's earlier point.

This is where Arendt's work is useful in promoting the need for critical dialogue and action. Arendt is a campaigner for the 'active life'; she returns to philosophy to remind us about the quintessential qualities of being human where thought and action enable subjects to initiate something new in the world (Biesta 2013: 105). Arendt's work draws from social history, philosophy and phenomenology to assert what it is to be human and how thinking and action are the combination of self/ness and social interactions. This is Arendt's reading of praxis that Taylor also explores where she sees teaching praxis "as informed, committed action which embodies certain ethical qualities oriented to improving the relations of those involved" (Taylor 2016: 2).

Within Arendt's work we can identify that the experience of inner freedom (reflection) is therefore derivative in that it presupposes "a retreat from a world where freedom is denied" (Arendt 1961: 146). For Arendt we first become aware of freedom or its opposite in our interaction with others and not in the communication with ourselves. Arendt asserts that sharing with others (plurality) is essential for freedom and action; self-reflection is not enough. She suggests that freedoms in our imagination remain only partial freedoms and it is when we act with others in plurality that freedom is most likely to be experienced in full. Gordon (2002) asserts that Arendt's consideration of humans as both free and having the propensity to act is clearly significant for teachers, teaching practice and concepts of reflection. To engage in individual acts of reflection in making sense of our experiences has it uses but it is not freedom. It is possible, however, that most teachers, even at the beginning of their careers, are aware of the implications of reflection and the discursive expectations of being teacher. Reu (PGCE PCE 2014) writes that:

> during the PGCE teaching placement there is a strange compression of identity. We are constantly asked to look at who we are as teachers and how our personality reflects our practice and vice versa. The problem is that, as a training teacher, you must impress (or at least not upset) your colleagues. Is there a job at the end of it? Am I going to pass my observation etc.? As a consequence of this there is very limited scope to really express yourself and have a lasting and meaningful impact on the students. Your time is mostly taken up ensuring that pre-determined criteria set by an outside body are being met. It is a slightly robotic process which lacks depth and emotion.

Atkinson (2003) and Harrison et al. (2007) claim that the social and political processes that student teachers experience when learning to teach are closely associated with a discourse of professionalism and accountability. Professional discourses originate from government and college managers in an attempt to control teaching (Harrison et al. 2007: 60). In this way a 'professional standards' discourse becomes an idealised benchmark against which effective teaching can be measured (Atkinson 2003). Atkinson continues that a 'professional standards' discourse contains much to be valued; however we ought to also consider the social and political processes that student teachers experience when learning to teach. How can teacher educators and student teachers guard against becoming a compliant and automated workforce where emphasis is placed upon consistency and conformity and thus confirms PCE's totalitarian tendencies along with its cult of performativity?

Arendt left an impressive intellectual legacy that continues to act as a provocation to think about current human predicaments in fresh and challenging ways (Gunter 2013: 16). The work of Arendt is worthy in understanding the complex interplay of personal history, lived experience, teaching practice and personal ethics. Arendt suggests that we are capable of developing our sense of self within a socially and politically driven lifeworld. The importance of being teacher is being human, where self/ness and action are significant for emerging self as teacher. Arendt's political thinking challenges contrived and limiting conceptions of reflective practice because of her understanding of being human and the ability to act. Thus if we want to confirm Arendt championing the 'active life' over a merely contemplative, reflective life we need to explore the ways this active life is achieved by student teachers. This is expressed by Reu towards the end of his PGCE year.

> You should consider the rules as simply guidelines . . . many of those rules are there as a toy to play with. Sometimes toys break, but more often than not they are just bent or bruised. The bit that is me as a teacher is that my classroom is a fun, happy and enjoyable place to be for everyone that enters it. Relating to students is more than half of the battle, having stories and banter and giving praise and smiling and genuinely enjoying the experience creates a wonderful learning environment. I do what is needed for teaching but my way and a way my students enjoy.

Reu's response is very much as Van Manen (1995) suggests when he claims that novice teachers should not be cheated out of learning a wealth of rules of thumb, techniques, skills, knacks, models, theories, etc. that can furnish them with a rich and an effective body of knowledge (Van Manen 1995). Van Manen argues further that the ultimate success of teaching actually may rely importantly on the 'knowledge' forms that are inherent in practical actions, in an embodied thoughtfulness, and in the personal space, mood and relational atmosphere in which teachers find themselves with their students (Van Manen 1995). Arendt (1993) suggests that a teacher is someone who stands between their students and the broader world into which we were all thrown at birth, and a good teacher is someone who is able to lead them into an understanding of the world that inspires a renewed commitment to it. Teachers, in other words, seek to help students feel at home in the world by accomplishing their transition from their beginning as 'strangers and newcomers' in an already existing world to their maturity as people ready and willing to assume responsibility for the world through their freedom to act and change. The following extract from Reu (PGCE PCE 2014) shares Arendt's ideas:

> Taking the time to have a coffee with a student and finding out the core of the problem, looking at them as human beings whose future is in part your responsibility. Laying it all out on the table in real person to person terms and then making those people feel welcome and comfortable and encouraging them to identify all of the positive things about themselves. Letting them walk away knowing that you have their back and will have until they give you significant reason not to. This works and guess what? There is no paper work required!

Arendt produced texts that challenged notions of freedom and politics, and examined the lives of people, ideas and historical events in ways that are pertinent to the purposes and practices of education (Gunter 2013). As Reu (PGCE PCE 2014) suggests in his responses, without freedom, without the possibility of disrupting, shaking and creating ruptures, and without the capacity to generate breaches within the structures . . . life as such would be meaningless (Arendt 1993: 146). The teacher's undertaking consists in knowing the world and being able to instruct others about it (Arendt 1958). Thus Arendt's notion of freedom offers a powerful insight and reminder of what it is to be human. Reu (PGCE PCE 2014) shares this point well:

> If you want to follow every rule in the book, including hitting targets for retention and grades the easy option is to follow the rules and play along. It's a bit like playing pretend as a child . . . but if you want to make a difference. . . . If you want to build lots of new relationships, make people smile and open previously closed minds, then being a teacher it is. Of course there are boundaries but we create our own freedom within those and that is what being a good teacher is!

In his professorial lecture the French philosopher and great public teacher Roland Barthes clarified the problematic of all teaching, that "what can be oppressive in our teaching is not finally the knowledge or culture it conveys, but the discursive forms through which we propose them" (Sontag 1993: 476). He also clarifies the relation teacher freedom must have with the inevitability of power: "method can really bear only on the means of loosening, baffling, or at the very least, lightening this power". Twenty years earlier Barthes had proposed to "live in the contradictions of our times where sarcasm might be a condition of the truth" (Barthes 1972: 11) which is indeed resonant with Deleuze's call for 'creation' rather than 'conversation', for 'resistance to the present'([Deleuze, G and Guattari, F. (1991) Equally for Arendt to be human and to be free are one and the same (Arendt 1993: 167). She modelled, for her audience, a mode of world engagement that is responsive to the rich and contingent complexity of lived reality which accounts for power and resistance dynamics (Schutz 2001: 130). It is Arendt's notions of action and plurality that teachers can become freer to emerge as self as teacher.

References

Arendt, H. (1958) *The Human Condition*. Chicago: University of Chicago Press.

Arendt, H. (1961) cited in Coutler, D. and Wiens, J. R. (2002) Educational Judgment: Linking the Actor and the Spectator Educational Researcher, Vol 31, No 4,

Arendt, H. [Ed.] (1993) *The Crisis in Education: In between Past and Future*. New York: Penguin Books.

Atkinson, D. (2003) Theorising How Student Teachers Form Their Identities in Teacher Education. *British Educational Research Journal*. Vol 30, No 3.

Barthes, R. (1972) *Mythologies*. London: Jonathan Cape. Biesta, G. (2013) *The Beautiful Risk of Education*. London: Paradigm Publishers.

Brookfield, S. (1995) *Becoming a Critically Reflective Teacher*. San Francisco: Jossey Bass.

Brookfield, S. (2005) *The Power of Critical Theory for Adult Learning and Teaching*. Maidenhead: Open University Press.

Deleuze, G. and Guattari, F. (1991) *What Is Philosophy?* London: Verso.

The Education and Training Foundation (ETF) (2014). www.et-foundation.co.uk/supporting/support-practitioners/professional-standards

Erlandson, P. (2005) The Body Disciplined: Re-Writing Teaching Competence and the Doctrine of Reflection. *Philosophy of Education*. Vol 39, No 4, pp. 661–670.

Gordon, N. (2002) On Visibility and Power: An Arendtian Corrective of Foucault. *Department of Politics and Human Studies*. Vol 25, pp. 125–145.

Gunter, H. M. (2013) *Education Leadership and Hannah Arendt*. Oxon: Routledge.

Harrison, J. K., Lawson, T. and Wortley, A. (2007) Mentoring the Beginning Teacher: Developing Professional Autonomy through Critical Reflection on Practice. *Reflective Practice*. Vol 6, No 3, pp. 419–441.

Hayden, M. J. (2012) Arendt and Cosmopolitanism: The Human Conditions of Cosmopolitan Teacher Education. *Ethics and Global Politics*. Vol 5, No 4, 2012, pp. 239–258.

Higgins, C. (2011) *The Good Life of Teaching: An Ethics of Professional Practice*. West Sussex: Wiley-Blackwell.

Kinsella, E. (2009) Professional Knowledge and the Epistemology of Reflective Practice. *Nursing Philosophy*. Vol 11, pp. 3–14.

Levinson, N. (2001) The Paradox of Natality: Teaching in the Midst of Belatedness. In G. Mordechai (Ed.), *Hannah Arendt and Education*. Boulder, CO: Westview.

Schön, D. A. (1983) *The Reflective Practitioner: How Professionals Think in Action*. Aldershot: Arena.

Schutz, A. (2001) Theory as Performative Pedagogy: Three Masks of Hannah Arendt. *Educational Theory*. Vol 51, No 2, pp. 127–150.

Sontag, S. (Ed.) (1993) *A Roland Barthes Reader*. London: Vintage.

Taylor, C. A. (2016) Ethically Important Moments in the Higher Education Space of Appearance: Renewing Educative Praxis with Arendt. *Education Philosophy and Theory*. Vol 49, No 3, pp. 231–241.

Van Manen, M. (1995) On the Epistemology of Reflective Practice. *Teachers and Teaching: Theory and Practice*. Vol 1, No 1.

Section II

Policy and pain

Chapter 7

Understanding the business of failure

The educational disconnect between systems and so-called learners

Matthew Parsons

Education vs. economics

There is an explicit and implicit assumption that education drives economic and personal success as well as civilised progress, in general, though there is strong evidence only for the opposite: "Growth generates education, whether or not education generates growth" (Wolf, 2002: 976). The idea that education is a key driver of economic outcomes in its current configuration is only true for a certain few at certain levels, in particular areas of society since "Education in England is still far too weak an engine of social mobility, skills and citizenship" (Adonis, 2012: 78).

This work contends that, financially and technically, our current educational system is not the driver of economic or personal success. Moreover, it seems unaware that it is actively blinding its participants, by exclusion, to what is: The Money System. There is a disconnect between economic reality and education and as a result education fails to see its supportive role in keeping its citizens ignorant and conditioned to accept the status quo. In this way, it suppresses opposition and analysis. Its hubris is blinding it to the real 'education' and conditioning by mass media, advertising, debt-money and fear-mongering politics.

The response from 'education' is to pour more funding into, constantly reorganise and sporadically reinvigorate its systems (Adonis, 2012), and to exhort its participants, as individuals, to greater efforts to improve their personal prospects, all the while, increasing the debt burden of both. There is little or no mention of the crucial societal mechanisms which are dictating outcomes nor are these system disorders covered in any meaningful way. To highlight this disconnect, individuals eventually arriving at a reasonable understanding and knowledge of such issues (through their own endeavours and self-education) find themselves bereft of any effective, democratic mechanism to air concerns and work towards solutions.

There is no alternative

> There are some people who think we don't have to take all these tough decisions to deal with our debts. They say that our focus on deficit reduction is damaging growth. And, what we need to do is to spend more and borrow more. It's as if

they think there's some magic money tree. Well let me tell you the plain truth: there isn't.

(David Cameron, in Robinson, 2013)

The baseline reason for a nation's financial woes is simply put that there is not enough money/funding to go round (scarcity) and that is why difficult decisions have to be made.

This whole premise is predicated on this one simple point: there is not enough money and the current systems are the best way to allocate it. This very point requires careful examination.

Taking university fees as an example, the government is adamant that the country can no longer provide funding – except through debt. Should an individual not have sufficient funds to pay their way through higher education, they have the option to take out a student loan. This would be paid back over time from taxes on earnings over a certain amount. Should the graduate not reach this level of earnings, the government will not only underwrite the loan but 'write it off' (Lewis, 2015).

The question to be asked is: where did the money for the loan to the student come from? The answer to this question should form the basis of a complete rethink and reorganisation of not just education but of society itself, particularly following the financial crisis in 2008 and the subsequent austerity programme referred to by the former prime minister above.

Re: money and remuneration

So, can we afford education, can we alleviate social inequality (to promote easier engagement with education for students: the Finnish model), can we provide reasonable livelihoods for our graduates? To answer these questions, the nature of money needs to be understood.

Typically, money is said to have four key functions: (1) store of value, (2) medium of exchange, (3) unit of account, (4) means of payment/settlement (Ryan-Collins *et al.*, 2012). In simple terms, money should represent *something real*. What that something is differs in detail from culture to culture. Generally, it is considered to stand for goods and services manufactured, grown, bought and sold. Ultimately, it is really a set of signals – to initiate a productive activity of some sort.

> [M]oney has no reality in itself . . . it is either gold, silver, copper, paper, cowrie shells, or broken tea-cups. The thing which makes it money, no matter of what it is made, is purely psychological, and consequently there is no limit to the amount of money except a psychological limit.
>
> (Douglas, 1935: 16)

Fundamentally, money systems are about trust, faith and consistency (Pettifor, 2014). These are the only things that give any currency its *actual* value;

not its precious metal value, nor its asset price or scarcity but the philosophical and ethereal notion of abstract value to the society using it. Controlling the production and value of money should, therefore, be the highest priority of any nation's government that uses a currency. The government's main task should be to ensure, absolutely, that no private interest inserts itself, parasitically, into this process. The greater good, for the benefit of all, should be, must be, the highest priority for leaders of a nation (Still, 2012; Werner in CBFSD, 2012).

Unfortunately, this public service principle rarely gets a look in. Currently, 97% of our money is commercial credit not created by the government.

> New money is principally created by commercial banks when they extend or create credit, either through making loans, including overdrafts, or buying existing assets.
>
> (Ryan-Collins *et al.*, 2012: 276)

The answer to where does money come from for student loans is rather circuitous. Ultimately, it is created, *out of nothing*, by private, profit-making institutions such as banks. If the government does not have enough revenue (the 'national deficit'), it borrows from the international money markets, usually via a bond. If students don't pay back all of their loans in the 30-year period, the government 'writes it off' (adding it to the 'national debt'). The buyers of bonds will take out substantial loans from private banks to finance their bond purchases. And where does this bank credit come from? It is loaned into existence – as a series of entries in an accounting ledger. Banks and extenders of credit carry out a business risk assessment and allocate credit/money as suits their profit-making, self-interested business models – and, for no other reason (Pettifor, 2014). In essence, this credit becomes a 'claim' on future earnings and production with the added burden and penalty of a compounding interest rate.

> Private investors demand the highest possible private profit, which is not consistent with providing financial security, equitable service, and ready credit to the population.
>
> (Brown, 2013: 1029)

It is a vital point to absorb and understand for all citizens in a currency-based society: money/credit is a purely man-made, artificial construct. It can be created, in seconds, either with the stroke of a pen or pressing keys on a computer keyboard. *As a nation, you can never run out of money.* As long as the money represents real value, wealth, productive activity, create what you need, when you need it. Anything produced in this way should give a lasting value (real wealth) and, therefore, not create inflation (Werner in CBFSD, 2012).

The next question we should be asking in order to fund education (or any other useful work, but, debt-free) is why is the government not creating money out of nothing if private institutions are allowed to do it anyway? The answer is in a historical and legal abdication and transfer of this power to the private banking sector.

> Ever since the passage of The English Bank Act of 1844, the creation, issuance, and the regulation of the circulation of the current medium of exchange, though being duties that constitute the most conspicuous and sacred responsibilities of government, have been in large measure delegated in blind faith and absolute confidence to bankers and financiers.
> (McGeer, 1936, in Brown, 2013: 3168)

Fundamentally, there is no practical or technical reason why a government shouldn't be able to create credit to fund what it requires if a revenue shortfall exists from publicly owned business income or taxes. In this case, the credit would be underwritten by the entire wealth and credit of the whole nation for the nation (Brown, 2013). All that would be required is another Bank Act to reclaim sovereign, democratic control of money creation for the productive benefit of the nation. This is an act of democratic will – a policy decision by the people.

The production triad

On a regular basis, we hear members of the public, politicians, businessmen, economists and experts of all kinds pontificate about how "we can't afford to do . . ." well, just about anything and everything. If a nation's people think they can't afford to do something that they are *physically capable of*, then, they won't. If manpower/skills, raw materials and means of production exist (the Production Triad) and work is required, an artificial construct called money should not hinder production. Money should not dictate production; necessity should dictate production and money should facilitate it.

The principle we have lost is: if we can *do* it – we can *afford* it – simply create the money signals to represent the work and make it happen. This is the real value and power of money. With debt-free, productively representative credit/money you can *achieve* whatever you can practically *do*. This is a total sea-change in thinking and the complete opposite of what we are told by all mainstream politicians and experts.

Nations choose to organise their production and distribution via signals in the form of money. So, for a nation's economy, where several million able and qualified or *trainable* personnel were under/unemployed while raw materials and factories lay idle and work was needed, the simple act of creating credit against a robust, production triad, risk assessment would send the signals to initiate economic activity. This publicly controlled bank credit could be either loaned out at viable, *non-predatory* low rates of interest to private business (particularly small and medium enterprises at the regional level) or created to pay directly for goods and services the country required (again, to private firms where appropriate). In fact, anything the nation deemed necessary could be funded. This is the secret to funding specific projects, political aspirations, indeed, a whole civilisation.

> among the most productive investments are those in human resources, *such as university education and research*, and green, sustainable infrastructure or energy.
>
> (my italics; Werner, in CBFSD, 2012: 4)

> Children growing up in the most deprived and challenging circumstances need the very best schools and teachers and not, as too often happens, some of the shabbiest and ill-equipped buildings, or least experienced, temporary or demoralised and exhausted staff.
>
> (Adonis, 2012: 1092)

What should now become apparent is that far from there being no "magic money tree", it is currently controlled by purely private, profit-maximising institutions – and they, in effect, decide what gets done in our society and, further, create the artificial scarcity society has to contend with.

> There need never be a shortage of money to invest in and create economic activity and full employment. There need never be insufficient money to tackle energy insecurity and climate change. There need never be a shortage of money to solve the great scourges of humanity: poverty, disease and inequality; to ensure humanity's prosperity and wellbeing; and the ecosystem's stability.
>
> (Pettifor, 2014: 203)

There is, certainly, no requirement to borrow it from private sources that do not have it in the first place, would create it out of nothing as a claim on future earnings and production and then attach a hefty interest rate.

The Student Loan ~~Scam~~ ~~Shame~~ Scheme

Unfortunately, with the rise in tuition fees using the Student Loan Scheme, the education sector has hitched its wagon to the debt-money system, to the very model that causes the problems each person and the nation is trying to cope with. This is a tacit and wilful declaration of intent: the individual is to be burdened with phenomenal debt to go along with other areas of life debt (housing, transport, business, national debt). Any benefit gained from this education will need a high paying job to pay off the loan – no indication, whatsoever, of how, *en masse*, this is to be achieved. Individuals may fare relatively well, but as a system for the majority? Especially considering that democracy is *about* the majority. Instead, what has been created is an educational aristocracy.

> The stark reality is that what the few can achieve the majority cannot *regardless of how educated they are*.
>
> (my italics; Ashton *et al.*, 2011: 287)

As an 'unintended consequence' (at least for graduates, if not for employers), another disconnect between the promise of improving one's education and, therefore, one's prospects, is the saturation of the graduate pool and its effect on this educational investment's return. With an average 1:46 jobs-to-applicants ratio in the graduate job market (thus, an implicit employers' market), bargaining power and wages are also suppressed (Huffington Post, 2013; Prentis, 2013) literally devaluing qualifications (in line with supply and demand). Job insecurity and lower wages do not contribute positively to the healthy growth of an economy or an individual, nor the repayment of debt. Also, the individual still carries an extra tax burden that reduces their purchasing power and further undermines their role as a consumer, thus *harming* the economy. Reggie Middleton (2013) concludes that excess debt is chasing funding for educational assets (qualifications) which have questionable, inflated or even fictitious value. This 'education bubble' is directly analogous with the 'sub-prime' mortgage bubble – and that didn't end well at all.

Furthermore, as Brown (2013) and Robinson (2010), almost casually, remind us, a degree qualification no longer leads to degree-level jobs and pay. This fact alone should spark a massive public debate on what education is for, how it is funded and the return on that funding (Kemp-King, 2016) and why we should continue this model. The student loan system, itself, is a dead give-away, here. Many students' worries about debt repayment are being placated with the fact that they do not have to begin paying if they earn below £21,000 (Lewis, 2015) – a poor aspirational bar if ever there was one. The inference to be drawn from this repeated palliative is that many are unlikely to earn any more even across the 30-year loan term. The ideological schizophrenia of urging individuals to take up higher education to improve the individuals' and the economy's prospects can be seen in the system's lack of faith in its own economic *raison d'etre*.

Supposedly, education and an individual's efforts are able to counter a money system that colludes with, and thus favours, big finance and business, politicians, specialised education departments and special interest lobby groups. This is highly questionable. To illustrate this point, consider that the complete budget of Education was around £90 Bn for 2014 (Chantrill, 2015). It is very unlikely that even this seemingly vast sum of money can counter *unlimited, almost interest-free credit* at the push-button behest and disposal of an elite who can obtain/coerce a government guarantee underwritten as a future claim on the productive economy at large. A repeating mantra from this critique is: why credit creation for private profits and not for the public that underwrites it? Talk of 'innovating' our way out of the current crisis repeats this anomalous thinking with concerns about increasing or maintaining funding for science and research of £1.1 Bn and £4.6 Bn (Cable, 2014). These sums pale into insignificance when compared to £1 Tn "mobilised (. . . almost overnight) to bail out the British banking system" (Pettifor, 2014: 1354).

Regarding infrastructure funding, once the principle of 'productive credit' issued against a production triad is understood, it should be easy to question why PFI/PPP were even *considered* as the best way to fund our schools. It is clear, even a little alarming, that PFI will prove to be a scandalous waste of public money by further indebting the nation for decades to come and, absurdly, with no tangible benefits that couldn't have been achieved with 'ordinary' public funding (i.e. straight from the existing bond markets) – and for a *lot* less (Al Jazeera TV, 2008). Craig and Brooks (2006: 153) warn: "parents should probably start saving up now to buy books, computers and other supplies for schools, as we increasingly find education budgets are being given to PFI suppliers rather than being spent on children's educational needs". At the very least, *the whole economy* will feel the burden of the national deficit and debt. Our education leaves us blind to the mechanics of finance and totally at its mercy.

Purse and perspiration

It is interesting to note that economic models predicated on productive credit via interest-free fiat money systems have existed for centuries. History is replete with examples from Chinese emperor Kublai Khan, the medieval tally system instigated by William the Conqueror's son Henry I to American colonial scrip and Abraham Lincoln's greenbacks. Mainstream education covers history with barely any or no reference to these examples. Today, nations such as Germany and China bolster their economies with publicly created credit via non-profit or government-owned banking institutions (Brown, 2013).

Additionally, when considering the extremely poor funding options available to today's students, one should be aware of past experiences for work, earnings and study. With reference to historian Thorold Rogers, Brown (2013: 1789) recounts the economic experiences of the middle ages, at a time of, largely, manual technology and production, when, "a labourer could provide all the necessities for his family for a year by working 14 weeks." Moreover, Brown continues:

> The rest of the time, some men worked for themselves; *some studied*; some fished. Some helped to build the cathedrals that appeared all over Germany, France and England during the period – massive works of art that were built mainly with *volunteer* labour. Some used their leisure to visit these shrines. One hundred thousand pilgrims had the wealth and leisure to visit Canterbury and other shrines yearly.
>
> (my italics)

In today's culture, this would be impossible, almost laughably so, and amply illustrates the surrealism and almost irrational focus on blame towards individuals for not being able to provide and support themselves financially whether through waged labour or otherwise. This medieval experience would seem an ideal model for accessing higher education – work for a quarter of the year and attend college/university for the remainder. A medieval peasant could do it yet, a 21st century worker can't – a system disorder if ever there was one. Over the course of an indebted lifetime, not only do we produce a huge amount just to pay off an artificially imposed burden, but we are also, therefore, diverted from a broader ability to 'progress' either personally or societally. Debt mires us in economic drudgery.

Democratic disconnects: the citizen/student

> [A] broad understanding of money and credit, and of the way in which the banking system operates is essential if citizens of democratic states are to reinvigorate and empower the democratic process, and override the despotic, unaccountable power of today's financial plutocracy. Such knowledge or understanding is vital if we are to see through the academic obscurantism and economic 'quackery' of much debate around monetary systems.
>
> (Pettifor, 2014: 313)

Our education systems have left most of us with a conditioned ignorance and inability to define what the problem is, let alone come up with solutions.

If Wolf (2002) is correct and mass education emerges from increases in the economy, then sorting out the economy (really the money supply) must be the priority, not education – unless this *first* addresses money systems. Public credit creation, its principles and benefits have to be inculcated as standard if we are to make our education effective, re-align the economy and remain a democracy. If, as Wolf (2002, loc. 988) comments "illiteracy brings misery to people, erecting barriers in front of them and their children" why not so for financial illiteracy?

A more fitting education would create the "Critical Citizen" not narrow them to merely a "Consumer Citizen" (Arthur, 2012: 1) giving them the background knowledge and intellectual tools to analyse and problem-solve. The new financial education curriculum proposed in 2013 (Lewis, 2013), while a step in the right direction, exists within the same, flawed constraints: we concentrate on teaching youngsters how to calculate APR etc. instead of urging them to question why it is our economy requires us to borrow and pay APR, in the first place.

Currently, education, in all its forms and guises, is subservient to, and reliant upon, the money system for the quality of both its students (their social capital) and its graduates (their prospects), and its infrastructure, content and staff. Yet, it is blamed for its ineptitude as if *it* has set these conditions for learning (Robinson, 2010). But, it is largely or even wholly unaware of this inconsistency. We must raise this awareness. As a minimum, there must be full disclosure of all available systems of finance, taught and debated, *educated*, in an open, accountable, democratic way.

> Money is only a mechanism by means of which we deal with things – it has no properties except those we choose to give to it. A phrase such as 'There is no money in the country with which to do such and so' means simply nothing, unless we are also saying 'The goods and services required to do this thing do not exist and cannot be produced, therefore it is useless to create the money equivalent of them.' For instance, *it is simply childish to say that a country has no money for social betterment, or for any other purpose, when it has the skill, the men and the material and plant to create that betterment.* The banks or the Treasury can create the money in five minutes, and are doing it every day, and have been doing it for centuries. (my emphasis)
>
> (my emphasis; Douglas, 1922: 9)

References

Essential

Ashton, D., Brown, P., Lauder, H. (2011) *The Global Auction: The Broken Promises of Education, Jobs and Incomes*. New York: Oxford University Press.

Brown, E. (2013) *The Public Bank Solution: From Austerity to Prosperity*. Baton Rouge: Third Millennium Press.

Kemp-King, S. (2016) *The Graduate Premium: Manna, Myth or Plain Mis-Selling?* [online]. [Accessed 6 June 2017]. Available at:<www.if.org.uk/archives/8403/the-graduate-premium-manna-myth-or-plain-mis-selling>

Pettifor, A. (2014) *Just Money: How Society Can Break the Despotic Power of Finance*. Commonwealth Publishing.

Wolf, A. (2002) *Does Education Matter? Myths about Education and Economic Growth*. London: Penguin Books.

Further

Adonis, A. (2012) *Education, Education, Education: Reforming England's Schools*. London: Biteback Publishing Ltd.

Arthur, C. (2012) *Critical Education* [online]. [Accessed 29 January 2015]. Available at: <http://ices.library.ubc.ca/index.php/criticaled/article/view/182350>

Cable, V. (2014) *Innovation and the Uk's Knowledge Economy* [online]. [Accessed 29 January 2015]. Available at: <www.gov.uk/government/speeches/innovation-and-the-uks-knowledge-economy>

CBFSD (2012) *Policy News: Vol 3. Issue 1 (8th Feb 2012) Featuring: Prof Richard Werner, Caroline Lucas MP Brighton, Green New Deal Group, Green QE*. Southampton: University Management School.

Chantrill, C. (2015) [online]. [Accessed 4 July 2015]. Available at: <www.ukpublicspending.co.uk/total_spending_2014UKb>

Craig, D., Brooks, R. (2006) *Plundering the Public Sector*. London: Constable.

Douglas, C. H. (1922) *The Control and Distribution of Production* [online]. [Accessed June 2017]. Available at: <www.socred.org/index.php/pages/the-douglas-internet-archive>

Douglas, C. H. (1935) *Warning Democracy* [online]. [Accessed June 2017]. Available at: <www.socred.org/index.php/pages/the-douglas-internet-archive>

Huffington Post (2013) More Graduate Jobs But There's Still 46 Applicants Competing For Each Vacancy [online]. [Accessed 22 February 2015]. Available at: <www.huffingtonpost.co.uk/2013/07/01/graduate-job-competition_n_3527767.html>

Lewis, M. (2013) Financial-education-on-the-national-curriculum-the-work-starts-here? [online]. [Accessed 4 July 2015]. Available at:<http://blog.moneysavingexpert.com/2013/11/06/financial-education-on-the-national-curriculum-the-work-starts-here/?_ga=1.203543504.1991819803.1435988410>

Lewis, M. (2015) Student-loans-tuition-fees-changes [online]. [Accessed 4 July 2015]. Available at: <www.moneysavingexpert.com/students/student-loans-tuition-fees-changes>

Middleton, R. (2013) *The Keiser Report*. Episode 392 RT TV.

Prentis, D. (2013) There-are-too-many-people-chasing-every-job [online]. [Accessed 22 February 2015]. Available at: <http://labourlist.org/2013/03/there-are-too-many-people-chasing-every-job/>

Private Finance or Public Swindle (2008) Al Jazeera TV. Viewed 17 March 2008

Robinson, K. (2010) *Changing Education Paradigms* [online]. [Accessed May 2013]. Available at: <www.youtube.com/watch?v=mCbdS4hSa0s>

Robinson, N. (2013) [online]. *There Is No Alternative (TINA) Is Back*. [Accessed 23 September 2015]. Available at: <www.bbc.co.uk/news/uk-politics-21703018>

Ryan-Collins, J., Greenham, A., Jackson, A., Werner, R. (2012) *Where Does Money Come From?* 2nd Ed. London: New Economics Foundation.

Still, W. (2012) *No More National Debt*. Jacksonville: Reinhardt & Still Publishers.

Chapter 8

FE teacher identity
Marketisation and metaphor

Chris Davies

Introduction

This chapter draws on a doctoral research study and takes the incorporation of further education colleges in 1993 as a starting point from which to investigate the impact of the marketisation of the further education (FE) sector (Hall and O'Shea 2013) through successive government controls (Randle and Brady 1997) on the identities of individual teachers and managers within FE colleges in the West Midlands. The chapter will consider the political and ideological context that Beck concludes both Conservative and Labour governments have adopted over the last forty years in seeking to 'restructure and 'modernise' the teaching profession in England and Wales (Beck 2009: 121).

The chapter will begin by outlining the political context post-incorporation, before defining teacher identity (Ti) and outlining some of the key changes to FE and their impact on individual teacher identities and professionalism. The discussion will focus on the ability of teachers to enact their own identities against the backdrop of a neo-liberal reform agenda, which has focused on transforming public sector working practices and culture through the imposition of private sector managerial practices (Devine et al. 2009) and a focus on educational outputs (Ball 2003).

The FE sector context post-incorporation

The FE sector post-incorporation has seen huge changes in the level of government involvement and control in almost every aspect of what individual teachers and colleges do. Wolf describes these changes impacting the FE sector for well over twenty years at an ever-accelerating rate.

Further and adult education have been subjected to comprehensive and unprecedented levels of centralised planning, and to sudden and repeated changes. Detailed, expensive and overlapping bureaucratic control has been imposed on all aspects of people's work, and there has been cavalier destruction of large parts of the sector's historic and popular provision. Current arrangements undermine innovation and make it completely pointless for 'providers' – the government's favoured term – to undertake any sort of long-term thinking (Wolf 2009: 28)

This resonates with Lucas and Crowther who suggest that the logic of incorporation has taken on a life of its own and blocked innovation and educational change, 'making it impossible for FE colleges to find stability or resolve important areas including the strategic place and purpose of FE' (2016: 584). Successive governments have developed a range of policy initiatives and mechanisms to measure and quantify the quality and value for money provided by FE. These have sought to control the sector and led to a potential conflict within colleges between structures developed by organisations in response to government changes, and the agency of teachers in developing their identities (Gleeson et al. 2005). Fenwick (2006) defines teacher agency as the 'means to make occupational choices concerning one's core work and interests' and Vähäsantanen (2015) points to it being dynamic, fluid and impacted by the characteristics of the individual and the nature of the social setting. In comparison, structure can be seen as the 'recurrent patterned arrangements which influence or limit the choices and opportunities available' (Barker 2005: 448).

Following incorporation, a focus on breaking long-established conditions of service agreed with trade unions (called 'the Silver Book') through financial incentives and the development of an output-based funding methodology (Smith 2015) ensured colleges focused on results (product) potentially reducing the focus on the (process) of education. More recently, the use of a wide variety of managerial controls including performance management systems and graded lesson observations have all sought to influence the behaviour of teachers in the work place (Hamilton 2007; O'Leary 2013). New regimes of audit through the national standards regulator Ofsted to determine what is and isn't good practice, have meant that the culture of colleges has altered and a far higher degree of managerial direction has been imposed to meet the output-based measures of student success, retention and achievement. In turn, this has impacted on the capacity of teachers to enact their own-values and priorities in relation to education (Ball 2008).

Smith (2007) describes the attempt to create markets as creating a quasi-market, highlighting the fact that these markets do not operate in the same way as free markets, in that they are 'engineered competitive environments that are superimposed over existing public-sector services' (p. 54). He contends that they bring with them 'the inference that the existing, non-marketised structure requires reform' (p. 54), and this highlights the ideological assumptions that underpin this approach towards controlling education. Further to this, Coffield et al. (2005) refers to college staff no longer occupying the position of trusted public servants, and now being regarded as licensed deliverers of nationally produced materials, targets and provision.

The importance of teacher identity and professionalism

Cote and Levine (2002) define teacher identity (Ti) as being made up of different aspects of social behaviour that involve an individual's presentation of 'self' and construction of reality through social interactions. Ti can be seen as the ongoing process of change and development teachers go through as they constantly re-appraise their role within the organisation, with students and their values and beliefs in relation to education (Jeffrey and Woods 1996; Gee 2001; Keltchermans 2005; Boylan and Wolsey 2015). Sachs points to Ti providing

> a framework for teachers to construct their own ideas of 'how to be', 'how to act' and 'how to understand' their work and their place in society. Importantly, Ti is not something that is fixed nor is it imposed; rather it is negotiated through experience and the sense that is made of that experience.
>
> (2005: 15)

The governmental changes outlined have impacted the nature of professionalism within the FE sector and Jephcote and Salisbury (2008) argue that the current model of professionalism adopted in FE is focused on very specific measures of competence about the teaching role. This limits the ability of teachers to exercise their professional judgement: one of the key aspects of being professional. Robson et al. (2004) found that there was real conflict between the professional ideology of the individual teacher and the organisation, which led to a sense of bereavement as teachers found they were unable to act based on their own professional ethos (Stronach et al. 2002). It is also argued that FE teachers are not only marginal to the hierarchy of professions, but also lack a well-bounded unifying culture (Viskovic and Robson 2001).

Shain and Gleeson (1999) point to teachers in FE engaging in a variety of responses to the changes outlined, which consist of strategic or subversive compliance to redeem the relationship between the teacher and student based on educational as opposed to managerial values. This shows that there are a variety of 'creative responses' to de-professionalisation (Colley et al. 2007). The tension between managerial control and an individual's agency to act is mediated by teachers as they seek to re-construct and debate current notions of professionalism. Gleeson and Knights (2006) argue that public professionals are 'neither simply de-professionalized "victims", who feel oppressed by the structures of control, nor strategic operators seeking to contest the spaces and contradictions of market and audit cultures' (p. 279). They feel that both of these extremes may apply in some circumstances but that professional practices in the public sphere are mediated or co-produced outcomes of structure and agency. This highlights the importance of organisational culture in allowing individual teachers the freedom to develop their identities and notions of professional development which link to broader educational values and ideals (Hoyle and Wallace 2007). In my view, the ability of individuals to be able to mediate, moderate and reconstruct notions of professionalism in relation to enacting their own values and beliefs about teaching is key to developing Ti.

The research question

This background forms the basis for a central research question study I sought answers for, namely:

> How do teachers form, maintain and develop their professional identities set against the interplay and tension between government intervention and the agency of individuals to enact their own beliefs, values and attitudes towards teaching?

Methodology

A purposive sample was used within the study to capture the identity stories of teachers and managers from a variety of backgrounds as they developed their professional identities against a backdrop of an ever-changing policy environment. The stories were unique (Sfard and Prusak 2005) and provided individual accounts of the working lives of teachers within different environments.

The study design included the use of narrative and semi-structured interviews with each participant, based on the completion of two visual tasks. The first reviewed their notion of being a teacher (Johnson 2001) and the second considered their journey into teaching and the key influences and critical incidents that made them the teacher they had become (Day et al. 2006).

Findings

This section will use a selection of visual images and narrative from four teacher and manager respondents to provide an insight of into some of the key debates associated with the main research question.

Participant Dave, a science lecturer with over thirty years of experience within the FE sector teaching at all levels and abilities, developed an image which reflected the relationship between the teacher and the organisation through a period of ongoing change. The metaphors based on Dave's image serve to illuminate the complexity of the professionalism debate within the FE sector. In particular, the image communicates a sense of powerlessness created by the pace of change and increasingly complex nature of the teaching role. Dave's teaching metaphor **(Figure 8.1)** is represented by a spinning wheel, with the lecturer at the centre and the many spokes outlining the varied and different skills required to undertake the teaching role.

The participant discussed the number of spokes representing the complexity of the role increasing substantially since entering the profession, which had led to a 'whittling away' of the thickness of the main spokes he originally developed to be a successful teacher in order to develop a range of thinner spokes associated with performativity tasks (Ball 2007). He felt time spent developing new

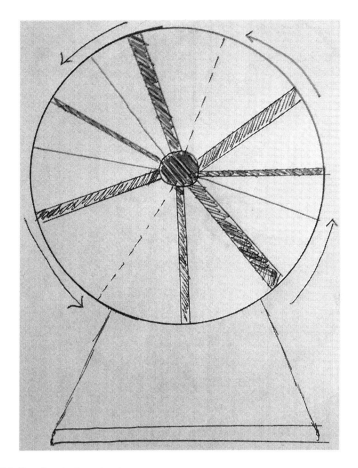

Figure 8.1 Dave's spinning wheel

skills, associated with managerial requirements for data had diminished his core strengths as a teacher.

He commented:

> My job in the centre of the wheel is to keep myself balanced and to balance the myriad of jobs that make up the role of being a teacher. This carries a huge burden keeping the wheel revolving and balanced. The wheel represents the forces that impinge on the lecturer, what is not well thought through is the emotional balancing act that the lecturer undertakes.

When asked whether depicting teachers at the centre of the wheel represented their power, Dave commented that lecturers were positioned by the organisation to be in the middle, so they absorbed organisational pressure acting as a mechanism through which to get things done.

> Yes it appears that way but the power is illusionary, students have power over the lecturer, managers have power over the lecturer, support-staff have power over the lecturer and other agencies have power over the lecturer. The lecturer has to absorb all this pressure, all these shocks, and it suits people to keep the lecturer in the middle, because otherwise the pressure would be on them.

The notion of being positioned is an important one as it is likely to impinge directly on an individual's perception of their role and relationship with the organisation. Several participants within the study discussed being positioned by the organisation and the effect of this on their development as a teacher. Gleeson and James. (2007) discuss teachers being positioned by the organisation as part of the development of a new discourse within FE, which is part of the wider public sector modernisation project. The discourse embodies a synthesis of public and private sector values, which includes a focus on markets and individual choice. This privileges recipient needs rather than providers, and this helps re-inforce the shift in power from teachers to central government (Leitch 2006).

Participant Sandra, a mid-career teacher produced a strong visual image focused on the relationship between the teacher, learner and the purpose of the organisation. The image refers to the importance of the student teacher relationship and sees teachers as the 'keystone' in a bridge **(Figure 8.2)** with the institution depicted as the bridge. The metaphor sees the role of the college as enabling learners to travel from one side of the bridge to the other. Without the bridge, students are unable to complete their educational journey, while at the same time 'the journey' is the reason and purpose for the bridge and holds up the education process. Importantly, these two elements are depicted as the purpose of a college, as opposed to the grandeur of the bridge (college) as a structure.

An essential element of the educational process is the teachers, who both support the college and also enable students to complete their educational journey. When asked 'Do you think the institution sees the relationship between the student and the teacher as the keystone in the bridge?' Sandra replied:

> No, I think the institution sees the institution, I think the institution sees the bridge, I don't think the institution is very good at seeing what it is that if you take it out, the bridge will fall apart.

The participant felt the low value given to the student/teacher relationship was at least in part because managers did not see the importance of teachers as the keystone of the organisation. Instead, value was given to the buildings and structures of the institution and the maintenance and development of these was seen as a measure of success of the college.

The strong sense of purpose and values outlined provide a clear view of Sandra's priorities and role as a teacher, which were echoed by several participants

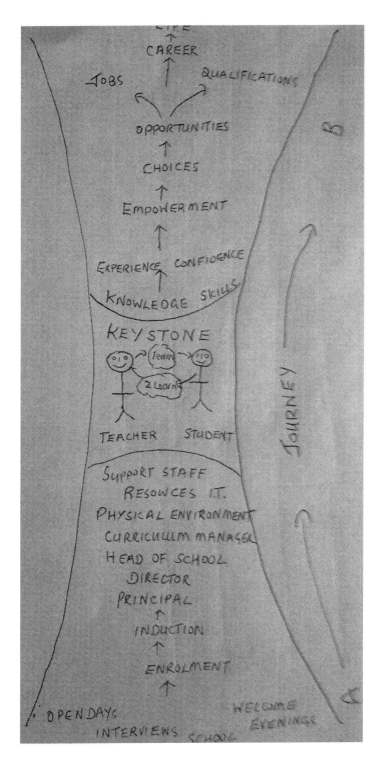

Figure 8.2 Sandra's 'keystone'

88 Chris Davies

within the study. One teacher referred to the classroom as his domain, where he was 'lord and master' and exercised his professional judgement. This positioning gave many of the teachers agency within a classroom environment, but less so in the wider college where to many competing variables allowed less control:

> We could work smarter, be more effective. I think there is a lot of fear, I think a lot of my colleagues don't feel positive in the way I do. I think for a lot of teachers teaching is a stress generating aspect of their life not a positive aspect.

The idea of teachers enacting their identities and professionalism within a classroom setting is a powerful one suggesting a separating out of the college, between the classroom associated with teaching and learning and the wider college environment influenced by managerialism (Fligstein and McAdam 2012).

In comparison to the two teacher images outlined, participant Doug, a senior manager, was clear about the potential conflict between his formal organisational position and his teaching role. In the discussion about his teaching metaphor **(Figure 8.3)**, he used the notion of an idealised teaching situation in terms of student numbers and classroom layout which would facilitate the best learning environment. He contrasted it with the actual teaching situation, where the group size was larger and there was less room to enable the best layout to facilitate learning. This actual teaching number was seen as more economic in terms of maintaining the financial prosperity of the college. As can

Figure 8.3 Doug's actual teaching situation

be seen, this image of the teacher student relationship is far more ordered and static than Sandra's journey across the bridge, which suggests movement and change. It reflects a more hierarchical relationship and different view of knowledge acquisition, learning and the role of the teacher. These differences give an insight into the identities of Sandra and Doug as teachers and how they see the student/teacher relationship and the role and function of the organisation.

When Doug was asked: 'Do you think as a teacher you are still concerned with getting the most people in the class?' he replied:

> If I'm a teacher no, but I'm a management teacher, aren't I? Here, I'm trying to get the balance between the minimum class size and learning space for me to get around.

Although Doug had a sense of an idealised teaching environment this was tempered by responsibility as a senior manager to operate as a 'corporate agent' (Briggs 2003), maintaining a secure financial base for the college. These competing responsibilities are mediated by the individual and moderated by the policies and procedures of the organisation, relationships with other colleagues and perhaps most importantly the wider post-incorporation political landscape (Gleeson and Knights 2006).

Briggs (2003) sees managers mediating the tension between managerial control and their individual agency to act. Doug's pragmatic view of the teaching situation is arguably related to his role and identity within the organisation as a (manager/teacher). As a senior manager Doug was regularly exposed to college finances and the need to maximise resources. These factors had shaped both his identity as a manager, and impacted his identity as a teacher. However, when asked about whether teaching and learning was at the centre of the business Doug replied:

> Yes and no, I think it should be, but I think often it isn't it gets side-lined, it should be as that's the business.

This further insight points to the potential for organisations within a competitive environment to promote self-interest and survival above the wider social goals of education (Davies 2017). It also reflects the development of a 'new culture' within further education colleges, which provides less space for individual teachers to enact their own values and beliefs (Jephcote et al. 1996). This cultural change not only reduces the individual agency of teachers, but also affects the agency of managers in undertaking their roles (Page 2011).

Doug also discussed some directors not being prepared to say anything in meetings or challenge the status quo; he felt you shouldn't surround yourself with people who just say yes:

> I get quite frustrated with some directors who are not prepared to say what they think, because they pay me quite a bit of money and if they don't want

to know what I think then just tell me and I'll just pick up the money. I should be there to say something; you're hopefully not paying me the salary you're paying me to just sit there and agree with everything that is being said, because otherwise I don't need to be there. There are some people who wouldn't say stuff, even when they disagreed with what was being put forward and you knew they disagreed with what was being put forward. They would either politically keep quiet, or nod or stuff like that.

This glimpse into decision-making at a senior level within a college environment shows that some managers clearly do not act on their own values and beliefs and in so doing do not act as moderators of external changes. This may have a negative effect on both the mission and values of the college, it also serves to further legitimate and enforce the neo-liberal ideology outlined.

In comparison, participant Liz, a line manager, commented on feelings of a lack of agency linked to her managerial role. As opposed to Doug who was able to distinguish between what he saw as idealised and pragmatic views concerning the purpose of the college and the teacher's role within it, Liz felt her lack of agency came in part from a lack of formal organisational authority. As a first tier manager (FTM) the participant felt there was a real tension between having a heavy teaching load and significant management responsibilities. The role involved an equal split between the teaching and managerial aspect of the job, however she felt that the management aspect occupied far more time than teaching.

> The management role is much larger than the 50% and the day to day tasks scream at you, there are dire consequences if they aren't completed. I would say that the management function makes up more than 75% of my time.
> This means you condense the teaching into this smaller portion of time, but you use your experience to help you to enable that to happen.

Liz felt unable to focus on teaching, which was the aspect of the role she got the most pleasure from (Figure 8.4).

LIZ: The image shows me stuck on the clock, this is the management clock.
RESEARCHER: It looks as though you are part of the clock's machinery. You are a hand of the clock, and you are controlled by the machine.
LIZ: Yes, and therefore other things become secondary. At my level, the management role is about compliance. It is a role of complying with other people's requests rather than the scope to develop your own ideas. It's not empowering.

Page (2011) discusses the potential of FTMs in FE experiencing trialectic as opposed to the dialectic pressures of middle and senior managers. For Page, these trialectic pressures apply more specifically to FTMs because of their position within the organisation. The pressures are outlined within a model **(See Chapter 11's**

FE teacher identity 91

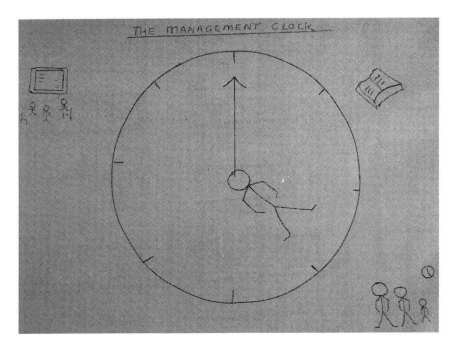

Figure 8.4 Liz's management clock

Figure 11.1), which identifies the three competing forces at the points of the triangle. These include organisational influence on the manager to conform and act as 'corporate agents' working towards college targets.

Page refers to many FTMs having very widely defined job descriptions, with in one case forty-six separate areas of responsibility. In addition, FTMs in Page's study referred to being used as 'dogsbodies' to complete almost any task required by the organisation. Responsibility for staff and students are the other two pressures faced by first tier managers. However, Page points to the conflict between three elements of the trialectic and the FTMs' time.

> Rather than operating with a unified focus, FTMs were dragged between the competing and concomitant demands of the triumvirate, which precipitated the reactive management style they were forced to adopt. From this perspective, 'firefighting was not a product of a lack of planning efficacy, but a direct outcome of the trialectic'.
>
> (2011: 111)

Page points to the data being clear that each participant prioritised one or more elements of the trialectic, and that this was 'hugely influential in how they perceived their role and how they performed their work' (p. 111). He refers to four positions within the triangle represented by religious metaphors which the individual can adopt in trying to resolve this role conflict. Each of these positions can be seen as a strategy adopted by the individual to cope with the external pressures within the role.

For 'fundamentalists', the key responsibility is for students and their militancy is educational, 'a response to the demands of financial imperatives and business focus; the identity being eroded is that of professional and teacher' (p. 113). In comparison, the strategy adopted by priests sees the team as their primary focus. Page describes 'priests' still being dedicated to the moral purpose of further education, but they consider the best way to maximise student welfare and success is through effectively managing and motivating staff. This means that priests act as 'intercessors between lecturers and senior managers, translators of often incomprehensible and mysterious senior management decisions'. Within Page's typology the 'convert' is in 'institutional transition'. They are the FTMs who most readily identify themselves as managers, and prioritise managerial tasks over teaching and learning.

The final categorisation 'martyrs' is placed in the middle of the triangle equally exposed to each of the trialectic pressures. Managers adopting this position have the greatest amount of elasticity, and Page describes them as being 'dragged between foci, reactively addressing what is the current imperative' (p. 117). The model usefully develops an insight into the tension first line managers face in developing and shaping their identities within an environment of potentially conflicting trialectic pressures. It also exposes the impact of marketisation on FTMs, mediating between a neo-liberal output-focused ideology, and the values and beliefs of teachers.

Concluding comments

In relation to the central research question for this project, there was clear evidence of the influence of a wide variety of external factors on the formation and development of FE teachers' identities, in particular, the importance of organisational influences on an individual's agency to act. Participants adopted a range of strategies, which reflected their personal capacities, and responses to a variety of contextual dimensions (Priestly et al. 2015). The strategies reflected differing levels of agency including; innovation, mediation, resistance and compliance. Although there were some links between the nature of the organisational culture and the strategy adopted by the individual teacher, there was also evidence that some participants were able to enact their own Ti by resisting the effect of a managerialist culture. Some teachers achieved this by separating out the classroom environment, as a professional space, where they enacted their own sense of identity, away from the wider college environment where they felt less empowered.

This notion of organisational spaces is discussed by Lucas and Crowther (2016) in an FE context. They refer to the 'strategic action field' adapted from (Fligstein and McAdam 2012) of incorporation, where the dominant managerial discourse has meant FE colleges no longer focus on teaching as a central purpose. Teaching and learning as part of an education process has been reduced to a set of quantifiable outcomes. The strategic action field of incorporation controls what is focused on and valued within colleges, and they argue that in the case of FE this was the 'creation of markets, or quasi-markets' (2016: 584). They point to other areas such as professionalism becoming unorganised professional spaces, as there was 'no strategic interest sufficiently developed to manifest a shared understanding in a policy field. In other words, while the strategic action field (Incorporation) shapes some areas or fields it has very little influence or interest in others' (p. 584). This separation between the discourse of the market and professionalism is reflective of a separation between the classroom and the wider organisational environment. The unorganised social spaces outlined reflect the opaque nature of the institutions with a lack of unifying values with which to galvanise teachers.

There was also evidence of the impact of individuals' organisational role on their perception of the importance and priority given to teaching and learning. This was most clearly demonstrated in the narrative of Doug as a senior manager with his pragmatic view of the teaching role and Sandra, with a metaphor which was completely focused on the centrality of teaching and learning to the purpose of the organisation. These two opposing views symbolise FE since incorporation and resonate with Alison Wolf's comments regarding the relentless change that has impacted the sector and left it without a clear purpose. That said, the evidence in this study of teachers reclaiming their identities within the classroom environment demonstrates the potential for individual change and improvement within FE.

References

Ball, S. 2003. The teachers' soul and the terrors of performativity. *Journal of Education Policy* 18(2): 215–228.

Ball, S. J. 2007. *Education PLC: Understanding Private Sector Participation in Public Sector Education*. London: Routledge.

Ball, S. 2008. *The Education Debate*. Policy Press.

Barker, C. 2005. *Cultural Studies: Theory and Practice*. London: Sage Publications.

Beck, J. 2008. Governmental Professionalism: Re-professionalising or De-professionalising Teachers in England. *British Journal of Educational Studies* 56(2): 119–143.

Boylan, M. and Wolsey, I. 2015. Teacher education for social justice: Mapping identity spaces. *Teaching and Teacher Education* 46: 62–71.

Briggs, A. R. J. 2003. Finding the balance: Exploring the organic and mechanical dimensions of middle manager roles in English further education colleges. *Educational Management and Administration* 31(4): 421–436.

Coffield, F., Steer, R., Hodgson, A., Spours, K., Edwards, S. and Finlay, I. 2005. A new learning and skills landscape: The central role of the Learning and Skills Council. *Journal of Education Policy* 20(5): 631–655.

Colley, H., James, D., Diment, Kim. and Tedder, M. (2007). Unbecoming teachers: Towards a more dynamic notion of professional participation. *Journal of Education Policy* 22(2): 173–193.

Cote, J. and Levine, C. 2002. *Identity Formation, Agency and Culture*. New Jersey: Lawrence Erbaum Associates.

Davies, W. 2017. *The Limits of Neoliberalism: Authority Sovereignty and the Logic of Competition*. London: Sage Publications.

Day, C., Kington, A., Stobart, G. and Sammons, P. 2006. The personal and professional selves of teachers: Stable and unstable identities. *British Educational Research Journal* 32(4): 601–616.

Devine, P. A. Pearman, M. and Prior, D. 2009. *"Feelbad Britain." How to make it Better*. London: Lawrence and Wishart.

Fenwick, T. 2006. Escaping/becoming subjects: Learning to work the boundaries in a boundaryless work. In S. Billett, T. Fenwick and M. Somerville (Eds.), *Work, Subjectivity and Learning: Understanding Learning through Working Life* (pp. 21–36). Dordrecht: Springer.

Fligstein, N. and McAdam, D. 2012. Toward a general theory of strategic action fields. *Sociological Theory* 29(1): 1–26.

Gee, J.P. (2001). Identity as an analytic lens for research in education. *Review of Research in Education* 25, 99–125.

Gleeson, D., Davies, J. and Wheeler, E. 2005. On the making and taking of professionalism in the further education workplace. *British Journal of Sociology of Education* 26(4): 445–460.

Gleeson, D. and James, D. 2007. The paradox of professionalism in English further education: A TLC project perspective. *Educational Review* 59(4): 451–467.

Gleeson, D. and Knights, D. 2006. Challenging dualism: Professionalism in troubled times. *Sociology* 40(2): 277–295.

Hall, S. and O'shea, A. 2013. Common sense Neoliberalism. *Soundings* 55: 8–24.

Hamilton, M. 2007. Reflections on agency and change in the policy process. *Journal of Vocational Education and Training* 59(2): 249–260.

Hoyle, E. and Wallace, M. 2007. Educational reform: An ironic perspective. *Educational Management Administration and Leadership* 35(1): 9–25.

Jeffrey, B. and Woods, S. 1996. Feeling de-professionalised. *Cambridge Journal of Education* 26(3): 325–343.

Jephcote, M., Salisbury, J., Fletcher, J., Graham, I. and Mitchell, G. 1996. Principals' responses to incorporation: A window on their culture. *Journal of Further and Higher Education* 20(2): 33–48.

Jephcote, J, & Salisbury, M. 2008. Initial encounters of an FE kind. *Research in Post Compulsory Education* 12(1): 149–162.

Johnson, G. 2001. Accounting for pre-service teachers' use of visual metaphors in narratives. *Teacher Development* 5(1): 119–140.

Keltchermans, G. 2005. Teachers' emotions in educational reforms: Self understanding, vulnerable commitment and micro-political literacy. *Teaching and Teacher Education* 21: 995–1006.

Leitch, R. 2006. Limitations of language: Developing arts-based creative narrative stories of teachers' identities. *Teachers and Teaching: Theory and Practice* 12(5): 549–569.

Lucas, N. and Crowther, N. 2016. The logic of the incorporation of further education colleges in England, 1993–2015: Towards an understanding of marketisation, change and instability. *Journal of Education Policy* 31(5): 583–597.

O'Leary, M. 2013. Surveillance, performativity and normalised practice: The use and impact of graded lesson observations in further education colleges. *Journal of Further and Higher Education* 37(5): 694–714.

Page, D. 2011. Fundamentalists, priests, martyrs and converts: A typology of first tier management in further education. *Research in Post-Compulsory Education* 16(1): 101–121.

Priestly, M., Biesta, G. and Robinson, S. 2015. *Teacher Agency: An Ecological Approach*. London: Bloomsbury.

Randle, K. and Brady, N. 1997. Managerialism and professionalism in the 'Cinderella Service'. *Journal of Vocational Education and Training* 49(1): 121–139.

Robson, J., Bailey, B. and Larkin, S. 2004. Adding value: Investigating the discourse of professionalism adopted by vocational teachers in further education colleges. *Journal of Education and Work* 17(2): 183–195.

Sachs, J. 2005. *Teacher Education and the Development of Professional Identity: Learning to Be a Teacher*. London: Routledge.

Sfard, A. and Prusak, A. 2005. Telling identities: In search of an analytic tool for investigating learning as a culturally shaped activity. *Educational Researcher* 34(4): 14–22.

Shain, F. and Gleeson, D. 1999. '*Under new management*': Changing conceptions of teacher professionalism and policy in the further education sector. *Journal of Education Policy* 14(4): 445–462.

Smith, R. 2007. Of Duckers and Divers, mice and men: The impact of market fundamentalism in FE colleges post incorporation. *Research in Post Compulsory Education* 12(1): 53–69.

Smith, R. 2015. College re-culturing, marketisation and knowledge: the meaning of incorporation. *Journal of Educational Administration and History* 47(1): 18–39.

Stronach, I., Corbin, B., McNamara, O., Stark, S. and Warne, T. 2002. Towards an uncertain politics of professionalism: Teacher and nurse identities in flux. *Journal of Education Policy* 17(1): 109–138.

Vähäsantanen, K. 2015. Professional agency in the stream of change: Understanding educational change and teachers' professional identities. *Teaching and Teacher Education* 47: 1–12.

Viskovic, A. and Robson, J. 2001. Community and identity: Experiences and dilemmas of vocational teachers in post-school contexts. *Journal of In-Service Education* 27(2): 221–236.

Wolf, A. 2009. *An Adult Approach to Further Education*. London: The Institute of Economic Affairs.

Chapter 9

Character building
How accommodating is the FE Newbuild™?

Pete Bennett

This chapter addresses the 'architecturing' of the future both literally and metaphorically with specific reference to what the title calls 'the FE Newbuild™', the proliferation of newly built or considerably improved college campuses. The philosopher Martin Heidegger suggested that an essential relationship exists between ideas about 'dwelling' and 'abiding' (even 'building') on the one hand and ideas about 'thinking', even 'being' on the other: that who we are is intrinsically bound up with where we are situated (Heidegger, 1971: 143). He is particularly taken by a line from the German poet Hölderlin which simply states "man dwells poetically" further suggesting the situatedness of being human and also the potentially harmonic relationship between our 'abode' and notions of 'health and well-being' (*ibid.*). If education's proper subject might be expressed as various kinds of understanding surrounding being human and being alive, this might be a real fine place to start. It may be that this ur-act of 'inhabiting' is inextricably bound up with those developments of human potential sometimes called 'learning'. In fact a tentative hypothesis might suggest that we will 'work'/'learn' best when best accommodated, where 'best' implies 'most at home' since 'home' is that special name we give to places in which we are effectively accommodated.

On the face of it this bodes well for contemporary education, or at least the formal part of it. Though there have been significant differences of emphasis both the last Labour government and the subsequent Coalition have committed resources to improving the accommodation provided by schools and colleges whether this be part of the accelerated Academies programme or the 'does-what-it-says-on-the-tin' directness of 'Building Schools for the Future'. Thinking explicitly about Post-Compulsory Education provision in Birmingham and the surrounding Black Country, all of the major F.E. players have had major investment in 'bricks and mortar' (and especially glass and steel!). Within a decade the 'rolling stock' of local FE provision has been overhauled, enhanced or, most often, replaced. And what is not in doubt is that these building 'projects' project, making significant statements both aesthetically and ideologically. These 'grand designs' attest to the significance of PCE in our time, however else they are understood, not least that the 'Lifelong Learning Sector' is the biggest it has ever been and a player to be reckoned with. They are certainly 'grand' architecturally inviting inevitable comparisons with commercial corporate buildings or even cathedrals and temples (of learning?). This is interesting and a little out of kilter with the human proportions implicit in Heidegger's earlier formulation. Before these literally monumental constructions the human is all too easily lost to a feeling closer to 'awe' as exterior waterfalls and towering atria declare rather than invite.

It is the stated intention of this chapter to explore this apparent contradiction which may reference a tension at the heart of contemporary 'schooling' since 'the schooled society' now stretches significantly beyond schools from the cradle gravewards. Is it possible that objectively 'better' accommodation has failed to make the places we go to be educated more accommodating? The critical methodology I will use is admittedly both speculative and tentative based on theoretical models prompted by the work of Foucault and Lefebvre and on opportunistic observations rather than the systematic garnering of data from stakeholders. Thus it is not so much a review of research as a call for more significant and detailed examinations. Though the 'hunch' which prompted this writing hypothesised a building programme consolidating and extending the managerialist foundations of an FE sector servicing economic needs and soothing social ills, there is much here also to engender hope. As ever the resourcefulness of educator-learners and learner-educators engaging in rather than modelling educative experiences within these corporate knowledge foundries is simply inspiring. In the act of inhabitation, even in potentially uninhabitable spaces is the essence of participation, of criticality, of autonomy.

I have a fanciful notion, based on my experience as student, teacher and teacher educator that the key to a productive 'learning environment' is that it pass the '*Cheers*' test. The American sit-com, set in a bar, you may recall offered, in its theme song, the idea that "sometimes you want to go where everybody knows your name and everybody's glad you came!" The idea of a place that welcomes you for who you are and which promises active participation seems a pretty good starting point for anyone who wants to encourage learning or even contrive it. If our simplest ambition is to encourage our students to bring as much of themselves as they can into our classrooms, two things surely must follow. The first is that *we* do likewise and then that we work to create and maintain a space which makes these things more likely. In FE one problem is that the physical places in which we meet our students have unhelpful associations, stale smells of pedagogies past: they look and feel like places that were neither welcoming nor safe and then sometimes operate as if the greatest threat to public safety are the students themselves.

There is certainly a world of difference between the cosy refuge offered by *Cheers* and the declamatory rhetoric of the educational 'new build', between the modest and the spectacular and this is not entirely about scale. Guy Debord, who dubbed our contemporary *milieu 'The Society of the Spectacle'* does well to remind us that "The spectacle is the flip side of money" since in this case it might help to shed light on the character of these spectacular investments of time, spirit and, especially, money (Debord, 1967: 24). In an educational context where 'investment' has largely reconstituted itself as a loaded metaphor (where 'investments' are most often in 'people' or 'futures' or 'aspirations') it is as well to return regularly to the real 'bottom line'. Governments claim to be 'investing in education and on the whole we and they believe this to be the case (we 'buy' it) but looking more closely this may not be exactly where the money's going. The truth is, whatever your concerns about accountability or 'value for money' that capital projects at best spend their money 'in support of' education, enhancing the paraphernalia which may be thought to (but not proven to) further the educative act while 'education' remains rather difficult to 'reach'.

While material resources and the aesthetic impact of award-winning architecture will clearly have an impact, informing both the marketing and market, it would be naïve to see this explicit evidence of investment as unproblematic when judged by its educational outcomes. As critical and reflective practitioners we would do well to be both critical and reflective in the hope of unearthing a few simple and perhaps crucial questions. One such is the question of 'audience': what has the standard 'corporate splendour' refit to do with a core market of 16- to 19-year-olds?

It's a question that gets lost in the generic aesthetic appreciation/'shock and awe' engendered by so many of these 'spectacles' where the eager desire to meet the future and its apparent needs might be seen to skilfully divert attention from a more traumatic past and uncertain present. Just as once we were asked to swop local high streets for out-of-town megastores on the grounds that the latter were just significantly/objectively 'better' (newer, bigger, brighter) versions of the former so we are invited to bury the last fifteen years of FE beneath marble and glass as if it didn't happen. History though is not that easy to outrun even when absorbed by myth: it speaks through every architectural gesture. And here is such a reading, an interpretation.

"Look on my works ye mighty and despair"

The famous local lexicographer Samuel Johnson used to argue that most was revealed about a person by listening to them speak, by what they have to say and how this is being said. Applying this same model to the Lifelong Learning Sector opens up an interesting tension in terms of a sector charged with addressing a catastrophic skills shortage, emanating from poor achievement at school and meeting the needs of a cohort who for the first time are being 'required' to continue their unsuccessful educational journey presumably at a more conducive location and in a more appropriate register. How do we think these monumental structures seem to the 'hard to reach'? They certainly have 'volume' but can they hope to find an appropriate 'pitch'? It seems a very difficult match: the only precedent that comes to mind is the relationship between the 'wretched sinner' and the medieval cathedral, a dynamic more unashamedly based on power and hierarchy, an uncompromising and uncompromised path to salvation.

What I don't want to do at this point is to merely to demonise a power-hungry corporation but rather to consider the ways in which 'interesting' spaces communicate things about their identities, functions and relationships, whatever their intention. Obviously my initial reading is not the only one available and is presumably a way away from the colleges' own stated intentions. Nor is there any necessary problem with college buildings making powerful statements or even statements about power, certainly 'new builds' add status to a sector often dubbed the Cinderella sector and formerly occupying crumbling Victorian buildings or examples of seventies Brutalism. The philosopher Foucault reminds us that 'power' is not to be seen as a necessarily negative element, that it is productive rather than merely repressive but to be effective must be 'exercised' rather than 'possessed'. For Foucault power relations make connections and form relationships, surely a useful prompt for those genuinely interested in 'investing' in education. Power is a strategy that, for Foucault, creates and maintains relationships between what he dubs 'the sayable' and 'the visible', for example the conversations about/discourses of education on the one hand and the building we are raising to house them on the other (Kendall and Wickham, 1999: 49–50). What is said and just as importantly what it is possible to say both inside and about 'education' is played out in the structures we create for realising these notions. If the talk is of problems and deficit and compensation it is not surprising that we end up with elegant 'houses of correction'. And of course this is a complex process since the form of the visible does much to determine what it is possible to say within these visible 'technologies of learning'.

As what Foucault would term "a form of visibility", the college New Build™ is involved in a public conversation about education which Nick Peim has dubbed "the master myth of our time" (Peim, 2013: 32). Peim sees these institutions, "the machinery of education" he calls them, as dominating "both the built environment and the social experience" (Peim, 2013: 33). In doing so, they proclaim their "series of specific myths" as a simple cure for complex ills. The register (high declamatory) is relevant here since it 'registers' a significant if unnoticed shift of emphasis at the level of discourse, since myth is essentially a form of speech. The 'college' is properly a collective noun, denoting a community of scholars (teachers and students), a configuration that cannot ordinarily 'declaim', being inclined more to 'discuss' or 'debate'. The shift from this collective notion to an 'executive' notion is vital to our understanding of a contemporary FE in which the 'college' becomes a physical manifestation of the corporate 'structure', writ large in the landscape. And with the concept of 'corporation' comes all of the corporate superstructure; organisation, livery and ethos. And all this, bizarrely, at the very moment that the FE agenda is focused on those least well served by formal education, the 'client' formerly and briefly known as NEET on the way back from "ne'er-do-well". What will these newly 'christened' 'learners' find when they arrive at the security cordon at the nearly new local FE provider they are obliged to attend? At worst they will find that we have extended the school leaving age entirely to deal with those whose needs formal education has palpably failed to address and that this now merely continues in airier spaces. In fact, at worst, they will find colleges 'braced' for the challenge in the manner that once Roman soldiers on Hadrian's Wall prepared for the 'challenge' of Picts and Scots.

It would be easier to be less cynical if there was any evidence that we'd learnt some kind of lesson with these 'kids': my preferred tag since it is as kids that these 'individuals' (though more accurately largely disadvantaged 'groups') are first faced with the displacing *non-sequitur* which is an academic education predicated on somebody else's nation's curriculum. This is not a new problem but it perhaps needs some new solution. Since the emergence of an urban working class in the nineteenth century the two best answers have been either to not feel obliged to bother with people who show no inclination to benefit from formal education or conversely to create an economy which has meaningful work which allows these folks to flourish subsequent to a short spell in school. The current prescription of extended confinement in 'interesting' spaces coupled with more 'difficult' and opportunity-defining tests (where difficult really means more alien and irrelevant) seems unlikely to break the cycle of failure: I mean, of course, a cycle of failure for the system, for governments and, to some degree, even teachers.

You don't need Bourdieu to understand that both 'curriculum' and 'cathedral' are somebody else's dreams and that the more colleges resemble the interesting spaces of Art, the less well will they 'accommodate' their 'learners'. The painful truth is that if the first lesson you learn is that this place is not properly yours nor will ever be, then West Bromwich or Dudley or Wolverhampton will be just as much a prison as Denmark ever was to a Hamlet much more concerned to know who he is than 'accept his responsibilities'. We don't need Bourdieu because we have a rich social realist tradition which poignantly captures the reality without ever quite convincing us to change tack, in fact the opposite.

In 2018, Billy Caspar, Barry Hines's emblematic 'urchin' immortalised by Ken Loach and David Bradley in *Kes* will be retirement age. If fictional characters could critically reflect what would Billy, or more crucially Hines, have to say about prospects for the working-class 'runt' half a century on. In the early eighties, after spending the seventies taught by " belligerent ghouls in Manchester schools" Stephen Patrick Morrissey had this reflection:

> All I learnt was to have no self-esteem and to feel ashamed without knowing why. It's part of being working class, this pathetic belief that somebody else, somewhere, knows better than you do and knows what's best for you.
> (Fletcher, 2012: 93–94)

The stately pleasure domes of FE seem unlikely to be places where those forced to stay on, presumably as an extended punishment for their failure, will be consulted about what makes them tick or even what made them fail. Instead they'll be likely offered 'employability', a subject interestingly never offered the most employable, who find that degrees from the better universities fit this bill nicely. Meanwhile the unemployed and unemployable have their aspirations, or at least their eyes, raised by the promise of salvation.

This for Nick Peim is the most sinister aspect of the education myth, the notion, contrary to all evidence that education is "the key to social salvation". For Peim, the "glaringly obvious fact" is that "the apparatuses of education are clearly designed to reproduce inequality" (Peim, 2013: 33). And what more significant embodiment of this than the FE 'Grand Design', a modern *Titanic*, with courses at various levels to suit the public pocket and plenty of room in 'steerage'. For so many of these 'below deck' types, Peim opines that education is an offer than can be neither refused nor accepted. The desire though is to see these New Builds™ as department stores of education, stocked full with learning (or at least 'learners'), "the gift that keeps on giving" (Peim 2013: 38). Perhaps a metaphor too far? Meet the new structure, same as the old structure.

"The whole earth is a hospital, endowed by the ruined millionaire"

Peim is concerned with a process of representation long in the making which portrays those who lack education or fail to dance to its catchy tune as "being in need of reorientation, salvation, and realignment" (Peim, 2013: 38). In this story colleges are reconstituted as treatment centres or community learning hospitals, sanatoria of the soul. Here is the visible manifestation of a trend spotted by Zukas and Malcolm as early as 1999 which creates "the educator as psycho-diagnostician and facilitator of learning" in studied difference to the student, now dubbed 'learner', perhaps due to his or her imagined unwillingness to learn. Here "the role of the teacher is firstly to diagnose the learner's needs" and then "to facilitate their learning by using techniques, tools and approaches which meet those needs" (Zukas and Malcolm, 1999: 3).

'Diagnosis' and its family may have a lot to answer for in the context of contemporary FE as the focus of a deficit model of education in which students 'lack' and colleges 'treat' and 'fix', even 'cure'. In such a world, as Zukas and Malcolm prophesised, the student-learner is "an anonymous, decontextualized and degendered being" whose responsibility is to acquire skills (Zukas and Malcolm, 1999: 3). And what better place to 'process' needs than the ubiquitous anonymous, decontextualised and degendered 'complexes' that most colleges have become. Insensitive, even oblivious, to their surroundings, these acts of architectural auteurship scream 'otherness' and 'exclusivity' to those in need of familiarity and reassurance. In such a place the great divide theory is apotheosised with educators in every sense 'other' than student-learners with an emphasis on technologies of learning rather than communities of practice, organisation rather than culture, managing rather than engaging.

Like colonial warehouses which, with their decorated facades and impressive designations (India House, Orient House) give little indication of what lies beneath, so these new workhouses, clearing the streets of the urban poor (now "socially excluded"), give no outward indication of their role in "population management" (Peim 2013: 33). There is a Monty Python sketch about an architect charged with designing a new residential development whose previous experience has been entirely in designing abattoirs. Though the model he presents to the selection panel fits the bill, it only takes a couple of questions to reveal that a key driver of the design is the clean and effective disposal of excess blood. Similarly the New Build™ epitomises the neo-liberal agendas of FE's recent past: ask not what your college can do for you, rather ask what you can do for your college. These are models of power relationships as clearly as the diagrams of management 'structures' which are displayed on the internal walls and moreover these former models are more abiding (effectively permanent).

Roland Barthes famously proclaimed that "the city is a writing and he who moves through it is a kind of reader" (Barthes, 1986: 95): the New Build™ similarly. In the depersonalised environments offered by significant capital investment where 'hot desking' has given way to 'hot rooming' and most rooms seem to present as 'laboratories of learning', one might perhaps believe that learning can be manufactured and achievement guaranteed. Certainly this is not a model in which the so-called learner is required to bring very much of themselves. It is as if the residue of the last 'student' reinventions (as 'customers' or 'clients') has returned with a vengeance in buildings increasingly taking their aesthetic from retail parks. While we may on occasions think that colleges are places where education is bought and sold, the 'customers' of FE differ from retail customers in one important respect. Retail customers pay their money and collect their goods: that is their role: they are not required to engage and give of themselves to access their goods, their purchases are not obstructed by their attitude or effort. This is a long way from De Certeau's notion of the 'reader' furnishing the rented room of the text "with their acts and memories", filling the imaginative landscapes "with the forests of their desires and goals" (De Certeau 1984: xxi).

"The lunatics are taking over the asylum"

What cause then to hope? Clearly these 'airy spaces' are not all proving mausolea of the imagination and many will embrace the comfortably new over the even sentimentally inadequate old buildings which opened their doors to learning previously. Also students and teachers will and do find a way to make better (rather than 'proper') use of the facilities, addressing it like any other 'social product'. This is Lefebvre's term taken from his seminal publication *The Production of Space*, where he addresses 'space' as a social *product*, no longer "passive or empty" but rather "part of the relations and force of production" (Lefebvre, 2003: 208). As a Marxist reading of space it appears on the surface to offer little more than what we already have: culture and ideology are reproduced and redistributed.

However where Lefebvre is intriguing is in his explication of the ways in which space is socially appropriated by those who ostensibly lack ownership of it or dominion over it in spontaneous acts of resistance. Lefebvre raises and acknowledges some of the arguments explicated and implied within this chapter about the relationships between space and power, property and propaganda: in simple terms "It is bought and sold: it has exchange and use value" (Lefebvre, 2003: 208). In Marxist terms he accepts that "social space could be seen as a superstructure, as outcome of forces of production and structures", manifestations of the dominant mode of production, in this case, capitalism. However, Lefebvre cannot reduce space to a mere product, insisting rather that "space intervenes in production itself" and as such is "not located on this or that 'level' or 'plane' as defined by traditional hierarchies" (Lefebvre, 2003: 209). Space acts "unevenly, therefore, but everywhere".

In this way Lefebvre opens up the possibilities that space offers, speculating that it shares these qualities with only a couple of special elements: "Like time? Perhaps! Like language?" (Lefebvre, 2003: 209). So whatever the intentions of state sponsors or architects space acts as "effect, cause and reason, all at once" and "it changes with societies". And this promises much for an appreciation of the potential of the hitherto maligned Newbuild™ situated in a brave new FE desperate to expunge its past from the public record since for Lefebvre "The concept of space links the mental and the cultural, the social and the historical" (Lefebvre, 2003: 209). Context, as they say, is all.

Ask anyone who has enacted a 'Migration Plan' and taken possession of a bespoke Newbuild™ in the last decade and I suspect they'll bear witness to what Lefebvre calls "a complex process" and "a process that is gradual, genetic" (Lefebvre, 2003: 208). Lefebvre's model has three key operations:

- *Discovery*: (of new or unknown spaces, of continents or of the cosmos [metaphorically])
- *Production*: (of the spatial organisation characteristic of each society)
- *Creation*: (of *oeuvres*: landscape, the city with monumentality and décor).

(Lefebvre, 2003: 208)

While the contrast between 'landscape' and the 'city' may be rather less pronounced on most educational builds (though rarely entirely absent), no one across the West Midlands conurbation would doubt their "monumentality and décor": they are certainly vast and vain. They are also, like all spaces for Lefebvre, "complicated".

Lefebvre would question the direct connection between a space and its mode of production, challenging the clarity of messages about "the neo-liberal agendas of FE's recent past" in the spaces these produced. Rather Lefebvre finds that "There are discrepancies; ideologies are interpolated, illusions interposed" (Lefebvre, 2003: 209). In other words he observes the "dialectization of this static picture" with "everything in motion, in contradictions and transformations"

(Lefebvre, 2003: 213). In these contradictions possibility and potential persist unpoliced as "space exerts a curious logic" that "does not exclude (far from it) conflicts, struggles and contradictions, nor conversely, agreements, understandings, alliances" (Lefebvre, 2003: 211). In this dialectical interplay reside our hopes for a re-made FE sector and ironically so, given that as the economist David Harvey observes "One of the curious things about our educational system, I would note, is that the better trained you are in a discipline, the less used to dialectical method you're likely to be" (Harvey, 2010: 12).

These may indeed be places to learn but only if they're not places where learning is contained or even delivered. Rather they must be places in which learning and knowledge are discovered, produced and created irrespective of the posturings of policy and patronage. These Newbuilds™ are important contemporary texts and must be treated as such where 'readings' are active and not preordained. De Certeau wrote in *The Practice of Everyday Life* that "Today, the text is society itself. It takes urbanistic, industrial, commercial, or televised forms" (De Certeau, 1984: 167). Raymond Williams had argued twenty years before of the importance of studying systems of communication (chiefly public media systems) but also that "society is a form of communication, through which experience is described, shared, modified and preserved" (Williams 1962: 10). "We need to say what many of us know in experience", Williams argues, "that the struggle to learn, to describe, to understand, to educate is a central and necessary part of our humanity". For Williams "This struggle is not begun second hand after reality has occurred. It is in itself a major way in which reality is formed and changed". Perhaps if we can come to understand these Newbuilds™ as texts in our time we can begin to engage in a fundamental way with the way we live, and learn, now.

References

Barthes, R. (1986) "Semiology and the Urban", in *The City and the Sign: An Introduction to Urban Semiotics*, M. Gottdiener and A. P. Lagopoulos (eds), New York, 8 Columbia University Press, 7–98.
Debord, G. (1967) *The Society of the Spectacle*, London: Rebel Press.
De Certeau, M. (1984) *The Practice of Everyday Life*, Berkeley: University of California Press.
Fletcher, T. (2012) *A Light That Never Goes Out: The Enduring Saga of the Smiths*, London: Windmill Books.
Harvey, D. (2010) *A Companion to Marx's Capital*, London: Verso.
Heidegger, M. (1971) *Poetry, Language, Thought*, New York: Harper & Row.
Kendall, G. and Wickham, G. (1999) *Using Foucault's Methods*. London: Sage
Lefebvre, H. (2003) *Key Writings*, London: Continuum.
Peim, N. (2013) "Education as Mythology", in *Barthes' "Mythologies" Today: Readings of Contemporary Culture*, P. Bennett and J. McDougall (eds), Abingdon: Routledge.
Williams, R. (1962) *Communications (Britain in the Sixties)*. Harmondsworth: Penguin.
Zukas, M. and Malcolm, J. (1999) "Models of the educator in higher education", paper presented at the British Educational Research Association Conference, University of Sussex, Brighton, 2–5 September, www.leeds.ac.uk/educol

Chapter 10

"Feeding the monster"
Vocational pedagogy and the further education policy present

Donna Drew, Emma Love, Alan Davis and Rob Smith

Introduction

In England, the histories of colleges of further education are rooted in local communities within towns and cities. Prior to incorporation in 1992, these colleges were often called technical colleges – indicative of their role in providing post-16 educational courses more closely connected to employment than those offered by schools. Day release courses were on offer through which young people who were already in work were able to gain a qualification, often subsidised by their employer. A slow process of mergers, takeovers and (more recently, since Area reviews) closures has meant that the number of colleges has reduced from 427 to 325 in 2016 (AoC undated, 2017). International comparisons with the English context provides illuminating insights. In the US, the terminology used to describe vocational (or 'career and technical') education courses and colleges varies between states and institutions. To that extent, federal structures and state autonomy precludes a centralised definition or funding model which results in a patchwork provision that, by definition is attuned to local/state needs. That said, career and technical courses are perceived to carry a stigma and have experienced a reduction in funding comparable to English further education courses in the last decade (Jasper 2016). In Australia, the situation is different inasmuch as market arrangements and adjustments in funding have resulted in little change in the number of providers over the last two decades. The mix of colleges and smaller private providers appears to mirror the English context although Australia appears to have a much higher number of providers (Korbel and Misko 2016). Burke's research (Burke 2015) provides evidence for a decline in quality that maps against an overall decline in public funding.

In England in recent years, policymakers' interest in vocational education and, more specifically, vocational pedagogy has intensified. Major policy interventions in the last two decades include the introduction of General National Vocational Qualifications (1994), Entry to Employment (2003–2010), Train to Gain (2006) and the 14–19 Diploma (2008) among others. In addition, college teachers might be forgiven for believing that a reinvention of apprenticeships is the prerogative of every new government: in the last 15 years apprenticeships have twice been revisited and relaunched (Modern Apprenticeships [2001] and [new] Apprenticeships [2010]). Indeed, with the recent introduction of an employers' 'levy' (DfE 2017), apprenticeships have become the key policy vehicle recasting further education as a delivery system for producing 'employment-ready' (young) people to service the nation's economic needs.

This resuscitation of apprenticeships appears in large part to be a response to some heavy criticism about the relevance and effectiveness of vocational courses. Notably, in 2011, the Wolf report found that many young people were being "steer(ed) into programmes which are effectively dead end" (Wolf 2011: 8). It also commented on the funding-driven nature of vocational courses in FE:

> 14–19 education is funded and provided for (young people's) sakes, not for the sake of the institutions who provide it.
>
> (ibid. 8)

The report painted a picture of over-involvement on the part of government in colleges' curricula through 'micro-management' resulting in "repeated, overlapping directives, and . . . complex, expensive and counterproductive structures" (p. 9). Furthermore, the report criticised the information produced by further education providers and by implication central government and suggested that current (marketised) arrangements have led to cultures that do not produce neutral information in a clear and transparent way. Casting doubt on low level vocational qualifications developed by colleges that had no traction with employers, the report appealed for the qualification and funding systems to be "simplified dramatically". In 2013, the policy focus on vocational education again sharpened with the publication of the Commission on Adult Vocational Teaching and Learning report (CAVTL 2013; 9) which stressed the importance of "a clear line of sight to work" and the "two-way street" (between employer and educational provision) as key ingredients in delivering effective vocational pedagogy.

This chapter will draw on research data gathered from and with vocational teachers from colleges in the West Midlands in the years since these reports were published. It will look at the policy response to these reports and the impact in colleges of this response.

The present and presence – a conceptual framework

Lefebvre uses the terms 'presence' counterposed against 'the present' in his theoretical attempt to integrate space and time as important components of a critique of 'le quotidien' or everyday life (Lefebvre 2004).

> We must ceaselessly come back to this distinction (opposition) between presence and the present. . . . The present simulates presence and introduces simulation (the simulacrum) into social practice. The present (through representation) furnishes and occupies time, simulating and dissimulating the living. Imagery . . . succeeds in fabricating, introducing and making

accepted the everyday. A skilfully utilised and technicised form of mythification (simplification), it resembles the real and presence . . . but it has neither depth nor breadth nor flesh . . . presence is **here**. . . . With presence there is dialogue, the use of time, speech and action. With the present . . . there is only exchange and the acceptance of exchange, of the displacement . . . by a **product** (emphases in original), by a simulacrum. The present is a fact and an effect of commerce; while presence situates itself in the poetic: value, creation, situation in the world and not only in the relations of exchange.

(Lefebvre 2004: 47)

From this passage we can see Lefebvre presenting a picture of 'the present' as reality infused with and determined by ideology. The present displaces and substitutes itself for presence, and simulation (data, images, myths) underpin this displacement. Simulation here echoes the theorisation of Baudrillard and his notion of 'hyperrealities' (Baudrillard 1994) but develops it by situating it within bigger organisational and contextual frames. We will use 'the present' and 'presence' as a conceptual antithesis to illuminate the research data from the vocational teachers. 'The present' as we will use it in this chapter is a term that attempts to capture the mental construct of further education conjured into being by (neoliberal) government policy discourse and enacted in colleges that operates on the consciousness and through that the work of further education teachers. To that extent 'the present' is constituted of notions (given commonsense status), abstractions and generalisations that draw on the neoliberal imaginary (Fraser 1993) that currently shapes further education provision in England.

Policy context

In 2013, the Coalition government announced the introduction of new 16 to 19 Study Programmes. Study Programmes were the latest in a long line of policy interventions and initiatives intended to address the shortcomings of vocational education in England. As with other vocational policy initiatives in the past, Study Programmes were presented as an educational and training cure-all for a range of problems:

> By linking the education system much more closely to the world of work: with more relevant, respected qualifications, more employer influence over courses, and more focus on English and maths for all students, we are – at long last – ensuring that all young people, no matter what path they choose, get the best possible start in life.
>
> (Hancock 2013)

This speech by the then Skills minister presents the 16–19 Study Programmes as a necessary and long-awaited intervention that, superficially at least, appears to offer a clear and straightforward solution to a current and often long-standing problem.

Typical of announcements that contribute to further education policy in England, the launch of Study Programmes betrayed a worrying amnesia as regards the recent past. There is no mention of this being the latest attempt in a long list of half-successes and failures. The speech exemplifies the workings of further education policy discourse in the way it seeks to consolidate a seamlessness between the declared intention behind the policy (to ensure that all young people get 'the best possible start in life') and its enactment. The complexities of real-life experience in colleges as college staff respond to the policy and try to set up, recruit to and then sustain these new courses, are displaced and hidden. In this example, policy discourse concertinas time in such a way as to instantaneously enact the initiative. It isn't just that there is a gap between 'crude and simple' policy and "the 'wild profusion' of local practice" (Ball 1994: 10) but rather that one aspect of 'the policy' present in further education is that through its announcement, policy is magically enacted and this displaces the messy contingency of implementation in colleges.

Our research

This chapter comes out of a research project that addressed the burgeoning policy anxiety about "our failure to provide world-class vocational education" (Hancock 2013) on the part of the Coalition government (2010–2015). Central to our project was a belief that practitioners should be involved in research and writing about their own practice. This belief was a response to a perceived absence of practitioner voice in some of the recent policy literature (e.g. CAVTL 2013; Lucas *et al.* 2012). Much of that literature consulted with practitioners and absorbed their views but in most cases these views were not directly represented, *verbatim*. Nor were practitioners directly involved in undertaking or writing up the research. Our project differed on both counts. Built into the project was a research strand that aimed to build up an evidence base of *chalkface data* from this regional group of practitioners. Participants were given access to recent literature about vocational pedagogy and asked to relate this to their experience. Cultures of competition and accountability tend to isolate colleges and teachers from each other so one of the key social gains emerging from the project was the development of a community of practice of vocational teachers. Not only did this community of practice provide a network of mutually supportive individuals in which practice could be shared and new approaches developed, but we aimed to engage project participants in research and writing activities in order to counteract the unrealistic representations of FE that are a result of marketisation and policy rhetoric.

In these ways, the project involved the production of critical knowledge that (1) illuminated the lived experience of vocational teachers in FE and that (2) provided an under-narrative to the market-inflected data whose production is now a feature of work in colleges and which sustains further education's 'policy present'. The project's foregrounding of practitioner voices was not intended to champion a particular 'voice discourse' (Moore and Muller 1999). Instead, this project sought to represent data from a shared understanding of social reality as experienced in localised settings (see Young 2010: 24–34). In that sense, the representation of participants' experiences is an antidote to the simulations of further education produced by performance data as part of the current model of market accountability. Along with schools, hospitals, the police and other sections of the public sector that have had regimes of 'market accountability' forced upon them, the further education sector has developed cultures of managerialist positivism that prioritise favourable data above all other considerations. This approach to leadership and management has been described as follows:

> Managerialist positivism equates to the purposeful production and representation of data that deliberately excises inconvenient truths better to serve the interests of individuals/institutions acting within the 'fitness landscapes' of the marketised public sector.
> (Smith and O'Leary 2013: 246)

The simulations this data constitutes provide an example (in Lefebvre's terms) of 'the present' in further education colleges.

The findings

In this section we will present some of the findings from the research project and offer a commentary. We have divided the findings in a series of connected thematic areas to reflect the participants' main concerns.

Performance data

At the root of many of the issues raised by the vocational teachers in the project were current funding arrangements and their associated bureaucracy. While the teachers involved in the project had no objection to accountability, the data-driven cultures prevalent in their colleges were viewed as counter-productive. Instead of driving positive change, quality assurance processes and the data production associated with them were seen as alienating 'regimes of truth' (see Smith 2005) contributing to teachers' already onerous administrative burdens.

Tracking students' progress through regular assessments is an example of the kind of data-work that has come to feature so prominently in college teachers' duties. Marie talked about her college's use of an online tracking tool for individual students called 'promonitor':

> We have to do this thing on pro-monitor where basically we set all of these targets continuously: it's constantly monitoring.

Target setting for individuals is an aspect of the managerialist technology that ensures 'delivery' of the course objectives. That the process is supported by an online system contributes to a sense of centralised scrutiny and the pervasiveness of cultures of performativity. More than that however, there is an understanding that the simulations produced in this case by the promonitor tracking data is more important than the actuality of student progress. Jobs depend on the data being 'right' – whatever the state of teaching and learning.

According to project participants, 'quality' and administrative systems were undermining the very processes they were supposed to be monitoring. Teachers characterised this as finding themselves locked in a cycle of expending more and more time and energy to appease a leviathan with data, leaving less to focus on the real world the data was supposed to represent. As one participant put it:

> FE providers cannot quantify learning by bums on seats, student numbers and success rates. It now appears we are doing an injustice to our students, they are not statistics. These students chose to come to us for their learning.

The production of performance data in order to create these simulations of the productivity of vocational education was viewed as a gruelling inevitability, an aspect of their work that they referred to as 'feeding the monster'.

Funding cuts

Project participants reported that in the autumn of 2013 and 2014 college managers talked to staff about the need for increased 'productivity'. Productivity in this context is a term only made possible by the annually based funding of colleges. It is made visible by the performance data that teachers are required to produce. More than two decades of incorporation have resulted in an economisation of the consciousness of college teachers. This is a materialisation in thinking, *habitus* (Bourdieu 1977) and even disposition that is a feature of once-public-sector, now-marketised work under neoliberalism. One Media Studies participant, Lionel, stated:

> I have just been to a planning meeting and (this manager) is telling me we have got to work harder because of the cuts and so we've got to deliver this and that but we do that anyway.... One of the guys, a manager in the meeting said 'you're going to have to do more for less' and there was an implication ... that we could be teaching over 46 weeks of the year. But if we extend past 23 hours of teaching then the quality of the delivery is going to suffer ... it's suffering already because of the admin work we all have to do.

The episode recounted above or something like it probably occurred at staff meetings in FE colleges across the country in the summer and autumn of 2013 as a result of a cut to adult funding that meant a loss of 10% to some college budgets. In colleges, the kind of adjustment to timetables and to the curriculum on offer to students caused by reductions in funding is not a new phenomenon. In fact, college teachers in general are used to timetables being expanded and course hours being reduced on a year by year basis. It's important to understand that because of the grip of 'the present' the budget cuts can only intensify the necessity of 'feeding the monster'.

The passage also illustrates Lionel's concern about quality and how this is threatened by the imposition of increased productivity. This feeds into discourses about the 'flexible' FE teacher. Another participant, Marie, reflected:

> The rhetoric from managers now is not 23 hours contact time per week, it's that you are contracted for 37 hours per week, which leaves the situation open to interpretation.

It is a sign of the current breakdown in shared understandings between practitioners and policymakers that in FE colleges 'quality' has taken on a meaning that links it to the production of (often spurious) data. This is a prime example of 'the present' in further education: while the production of this performative data preoccupies and burdens teachers, the single most obvious impact on quality – the imposition of increased teaching hours on staff – is ignored. In the literature about vocational pedagogy, much of it published since 2008, it is extraordinary that there is no mention whatever of this contextual influence on the quality of vocational pedagogy brought about by the national reduction in college budgets.

Recruitment

According to the CAVTL report (2013) a consideration of the needs of potential students in conjunction with a knowledge of the demands of industry lay the foundations of successful vocational pedagogy. This positions enrolment and recruitment as crucial points at which colleges engage socially and educationally with students for the first time. Participants agreed that it was imperative that colleges help students to access a programme which reflects their interests to keep them engaged through courses that combine both theory and practice. However, during discussions amongst project participants, a very different picture of enrolment emerged in which recruitment was more about the college selecting the student – in some cases despite their interests.

> It's now a case of capturing the student, they are money. . . . Don't let them walk out of the door.
>
> (Diana)

Clearly, this was an area of college activity likely to have been influenced by the current funding crisis as, faced by reduced budgets, colleges went to great lengths to recruit as many students as possible. Diana's comment suggests that teachers were encouraged to recruit at all costs, irrespective of the 'industry demands' or 'learner needs'. This approach to recruitment is a clear example of the concerns raised in the Wolf report that "14–19 education is funded and provided for (young people's) sakes, not for the sake of the institutions who provide it" (Wolf 2011: 8).

But there is also a sense that this approach to recruitment undermines the status of vocational education in general. Vocational programmes can be seen (sometimes by FE teachers themselves) as a dumping ground for learners who are perceived as not academically able. This is one consequence of the continuing academic/vocational divide that is a structural feature of the English education system (Hodkinson 1989). Recruitment as represented in the contribution above consolidates this divide by objectifying students. In some instances, colleges that need to fill spaces on particular courses may steer young people in a particular direction but this is portrayed as students 'choosing' vocational subjects deemed as 'easy' to pass. Here, the FE market is seen to operate in favour of the 'producer' college and the student-consumer's choice is shown to be shaped by the needs of the college. This unequal, commercially inflected relationship is a result of the current funding regime. The aim for vocational programmes should be that learners eventually want to go in to that industry; if they are recruited to courses that do not interest them, then the whole process is short-circuited. If recruitment is guided by funding considerations and fails to balance students' interests with the needs of industry, then the real benefits to students, industry and to society at large will be lost.

Counter-productive policy intervention: the example of mandatory English and maths

In addition to the structural problems covered above, vocational teachers in FE colleges have also had to endure policy intervention that has impacted on their practice in detrimental ways. In the autumn of 2013, the introduction of a mandatory entitlement for all 16 to 19 Study Programmes to include English and maths had a dramatic impact on participants' work practices. This arose seemingly in direct response to an OECD report that according to Hancock:

> found that 16–24-year-olds in this country are among the least literate and numerate in the developed world.
>
> (Hancock 2013)

In response, the new 16–19 Study Programmes aimed to:

> ensure that students who don't get at least a C in English and maths GCSE by age 16 must keep on working towards them.

One project participant, Andy, went into great detail about how this had impacted directly on vocational tutors and their focus on vocational pedagogy:

> Little has changed with regards teaching in the vocational area, what *has* changed is tutors are now having to deliver maths and English. . . . (Vocational teachers') concern now is that success rates encompass both functional skills and their vocational area which is increasing stress levels. . . . Tutors feel that these areas should be carried out by specialists in that field. Imagine asking a maths or English teacher to teach construction! It wouldn't work! Yet here we are nearly three years down the line from the Wolf Report, with vocational tutors doing their best to teach maths and English . . . tutors are facing a huge challenge to get their students to achieve.

It is tempting to view these circumstances as an outcome of the Lingfield Report (BIS 2012) that removed the requirement for college teachers to have a teaching qualification. Lingfield's deregulation then can be seen as contributing not to raising standards or bolstering teachers' professional identity but rather, the reverse as diluting expertise and the importance of a subject specialist knowledge base:

> Why isn't the emphasis being directed at teachers who presumably hold degrees in these specialist areas? I believe the answer is not to train existing staff, but to employ specialists in this area to deliver quality. After all, you would not ask a maths teacher to build you a house.

Andy's contribution highlights a yawning gap between policy rhetoric and policy implementation: the disjunction between the exaggerated policy announcement and the reality of the changes as experienced by practitioners on the ground. The lack of congruity between the two, the superimposition of announced policy over the more complex, chaotic actuality (or 'presence') in colleges constitutes 'the present' for further education providers. In this case, Hancock's policy intervention with its "focus on English and maths for all students" through which the government is "at long last – ensuring that all young people, no matter what path they choose, get the best possible start in life", has translated into a scenario in which teachers have been forced to teach subjects in which they are unqualified. Andy also felt aggrieved that FE colleges were being forced to take remedial action in response to perceived 'failings' in the secondary sector:

> From previous experience and conversations with our students, it is clear that maths and English were not the most popular of subjects at school, especially maths. Now, (non-specialist) FE tutors are being expected to deliver in thirty six weeks what secondary education could not do in five years.

Andy's comments here point up once more the failings in the current model of accountability through funding that fragments students' educational narratives into chunks that are artificially viewed as somehow independent from each other.

Conclusions

Overall, the project revealed the way that vocational education policy initiatives to raise standards in vocational teaching and learning contributes to an already troubled landscape. While the latest reboot of apprenticeships is still bedding in, it is clear that the Study Programme policy initiative has failed to address the fundamental issues connected to the funding model and regimes of data-for-accountability. This has impacted on the ability of these reforms to gain real traction and bring about real change for the better in vocational education in England. The key issues in vocational education in England compare to those in Australian and the US contexts: funding levels, maintaining 'quality' and dealing with the stigma of lower status qualification routes all resonate. What's also clear is that market arrangements seem only to have exacerbated these problems.

The message from this particular research study is that the focus needs to shift away from seeking a philosopher's stone that can alchemise vocational pedagogy and provide the dramatic gains in quality sought by successive governments. While the existing funding arrangements (and cuts) continue, the constant flow of policy interventions will be deformed by the financial priorities of colleges operating within a quasi-market and the efforts of vocational teachers will continue to be undermined. Because of the continuous policy churn in colleges it seems appropriate to develop the notion of 'the present' to make it more reflective of the further education context. Policy change is so perennial and all pervasive that to talk of the *further education policy present* as a permanent feature of 'the present' as experienced by college teachers is warranted. The *further education policy present* is an aspect of the conditioning of teachers of vocational qualifications in further education. Simultaneously, it is a condition in itself: indicating that 'feeding the monster' – activity that feels futile and self-defeating and meaningless for both teachers and learners – has come to dominate the work and colonise the 'presence' of vocational teachers in colleges in England.

References

Association of Colleges (AoC). Undated. *College Mergers.* www.aoc.co.uk/about-colleges/college-mergers. 12.09.17.
Association of Colleges (AoC). 2017. *College Key Facts 2016/17.* www.aoc.co.uk/about-colleges/research-and-stats/key-further-education-statistics. 15.08.17.
Ball, S. J. 1994. *Education Reform.* Buckingham: Open University Press.
Baudrillard, J. 1994. *Simulacra and Simulation.* Ann Arbor: University of Michigan Press.
Bourdieu, P. 1977. *Outline of a Theory of Practice.* Cambridge: Cambridge University Press.

Burke, G. 2015. Funding, participation and quality in VET. Monash University Australian Vocational Education & Training Research Association (AVETRA) 2015 Conference Melbourne. www.lhmartininstitute.edu.au/userfiles/files/Burke%20AVETRA%202015%20Conference%20Paper%2023%20April%20Revision.pdf. 15.08.17.

CAVTL. 2013. *It's about Work: Excellent Vocational Teaching and Learning*, Commission on Adult Vocational Teaching and Learning. (LSIS, Coventry/BIS London).

Department for Education (DfE). 2017. *Apprenticeship Funding: How It Will Work*. www.gov.uk/government/publications/apprenticeship-levy-how-it-will-work/apprenticeship-levy-how-it-will-work. 06.08.17.

Fraser, N. 1993. Clintonism, welfare, and the antisocial wage: The emergence of a neoliberal political imaginary. *Rethinking Marxism*, 6:1, 9–23.

Hancock, M. 2013. *Matthew Hancock Speaks about Reforms to Vocational Education*. www.gov.uk/government/speeches/matthew-hancock-speaks-about-reforms-to-vocational-education. 07.08.14.

Hodkinson, P. 1989. Crossing the academic/vocational divide: Personal effectiveness and autonomy as an integrating theme in post-16 education. *British Journal of Educational Studies*, 37:4, 369–383.

Jasper, M. 2016. Accepting alternatives: Career and technical education should be embraced. *Harvard Political Review*. http://harvardpolitics.com/united-states/accepting-alternatives-career-technical-education-embraced/. 10.08.17.

Korbel, P. and Misko, J. 2016. *VET Provider Market Structures: History, Growth and Change*. Adelaide: NCVER.

Lefebvre, H. 2004. *Rhythmanalysis*. London: Continuum.

Lucas, B. Spencer, E. and Claxton, G. 2012. How to teach vocational education: A theory of vocational pedagogy. City & Guilds. www.educationinnovations.org/sites/default/files/How-to-teach-vocational-education.pdf. 15.11.17.

Moore, R. and Muller, J. 1999. The discourse of 'voice' and the problem of knowledge and identity in the sociology of education. *British Journal of Sociology of Education*, 20:2, 189–206.

Smith, R. 2005. Grecian urns and yellow cards – quality and the internalisation of the quasi-market in the FE sector [online]. *Journal of Critical Education Policy Studies*, 3:2. www.jceps.com/index.php?pageID=article&articleID=54. 15.08.17.

Smith, R. and O'Leary, M. 2013. New public management in an age of austerity: Knowledge and experience in further education. *Journal of Educational Administration and History*, 45:3, 244–266.

Wolf, A. 2011. *Review of Vocational Education, the Wolf Report*. www.gov.uk/government/publications/review-of-vocational-education-the-wolf-report. 16.08.17.

Young, M. 2010. *Bringing Knowledge Back in*. London: Routledge.

Chapter 11

Faith, apostasy and professionalism in FE

Joel Petrie

Introduction

This chapter will explore professionalism in English Further Education (FE). It will specifically consider the discourse that followed the "professionalism war": the dispute ostensibly between FE's then professional body, the Institute for Learning (IfL), and the sector's lecturers. An examination of the language of the subsequent reforms will suggest echoes of the long-standing use of religious metaphors in education and FE. It will consider if the prevalence of religiously metaphorical sectoral language may suggest the possibility of a "faith" or ideology which could be the basis of a shared professionalism; or whether professionalism is too contested by FE "apostates" to achieve any level of sectoral unanimity. Finally, it will be suggested the professionalism war represents an episode within a broader ideological struggle, suggesting that an alternative ideological position on professionalism is required: one that promotes and empowers lecturers via a model that embraces autonomy and fosters a democratic, collegiate ethos.

The professionalism context in English FE

The IfL was created in 2002, claiming to be an independent practitioner-led professional membership body. Membership was voluntary, and it attracted 266 subscribers in its first year (SET, no date). This limited professional interest in the new body may have reflected a sense that the IfL was encroaching (potentially deliberately and strategically) on the role of the sector's principal trade union Natfhe (National Association of Teachers in Further and Higher Education). Further, the IfL's stated emphasis on professionalism, divorced from key issues of industrial relations such as pay and conditions, was deeply problematic. For instance, Waugh had previously argued that re-professionalisation in FE would imply some sort of post 16 professional body which:

> precisely by focusing on "professional" issues in contradistinction to "industrial relations", would base itself on a definition of industrial relations

which the employers would like . . . [lecturers] to operate with – for example, harmony not conflict, a "right to manage" and separation of industrial relations from professional issues.

(Waugh, 2011: 23)

In addition, concerns were raised that the IfL might be too favourable to government agendas. Coffield's analysis of the IfL's ultimate demise is pertinent here:

Right from the start the IfL failed to establish itself as an independent organisation, free from government influence. It could not even get its own name right. Its core function was to further the development of tutors in FE, so it should have been called the Institute for Tutors or Teaching.

(Coffield, 2015a: 9)

Nevertheless, the sector's trade unions cautiously welcomed the introduction of a professional body, arguing for its potential role in countering:

the increasing deprofessionalisation in colleges. In the 1990s, an FEFC report exposed that only 1% of college budgets were spent on CPD, and a subsequent UCU survey reported that much CPD was irrelevant to members, with almost a half indicating that their employers were either not at all or hardly at all effective at supporting staff needs with CPD opportunities. . . . Moreover, a survey commissioned by the IfL itself underlined the ongoing blight of casual lecturing contracts with the associated inequality of access for agency and part-time lecturers to staff development opportunities.

(Petrie and Peutrell, 2015: 11)

The FE professionalism landscape in England shifted radically in 2007: parliamentary regulations were introduced which required FE lecturers to register with the IfL and within a year it had 200,000 members. In 2010 the government withdrew subsidised funding for membership, meaning lecturers would need to pay fees themselves. There was a very public campaign against the fees (Dennis, 2015; Rouxel, 2015), and an ostensibly independent review of professionalism in the FE and skills sector – *Professionalism in Further Education* (Lingfield, 2012) chaired by Lord Lingfield, which ultimately resulted in the revocation of the 2007 regulations, including mandatory IfL membership. By 2013, IfL membership had collapsed, and ultimately in October 2014 the IfL passed its legacy to the Education and Training Foundation (ETF).

Shortly before the publication of the Lingfield report the then minister with responsibility for the sector, John Hayes, proposed a modern "guild" approach within FE, with an associated emphasis on the rediscovery of "craft" as a dynamic of professional learning. He additionally stressed that the FE Guild needed to be an employer-led partnership (the IfL had at least rhetorically been committed to being member-led). Lingfield's report endorsed the establishment of the FE Guild, and further proposed an FE Covenant, which would provide:

> the place for the expression of a code of professional conduct and those many other matters of mutual interest across the sector which transcend anything that readily can be agreed between the individual employer and its staff. We see the Covenant as an important means towards securing the success of a Guild and something to which all Guild members should formally consent.
> (Lingfield, 2012: 4)

To an extent the proposal to establish an FE Guild came as no surprise to a sector subject to regular policy churn. Even before the establishment of the IfL educational ministers of all political persuasions had regularly reconfigured bodies responsible for aspects of FE professionalism with little regard for sectoral continuity or stability:

> In the period since incorporation such bodies have metamorphosed with dizzying regularity according to the whims of successive governments: the Further Education Staff College (FESC) and Further Education Unit (FEU) merged into the Further Education Development Agency (FEDA); this in turn became the Learning and Skills Development Agency (LSDA), which itself evolved into the Quality Improvement Agency (QIA) and the Learning and Skills Network (LSN); followed by the Learning and Skills Improvement Service (LSIS).
> (Petrie, 2015: 7–8)

Richardson (2005: 140) points out that medieval craft guilds had both occupational and spiritual attributes, pursuing pious goals as benevolent and religious societies. The quasi-religious language of the Hayes' Guild proposal with Lingfield's associated "transcendent" covenant was a new development, and is notable given that FE is in the main an avowedly secular sector. Ultimately the ETF absorbed the remaining functions of the IfL by establishing within its structure a new professional association – the Society for Education and Training (SET); and the notion of an FE Guild, with its historic and potentially exclusive professional connotations, was dropped. The proposal to establish an FE Guild is a footnote in the sector's history, but it nevertheless remains pertinent as an example of how religious metaphors often feature as part of the ideology of educational discourse, including in FE.

Religious metaphors in education and FE

Jauhiainen and Alho-Malmelin (2004: 459) argue that the increased significance of education 'is such a comprehensive phenomenon that in order to understand it analogies have been sought from one of the most ancient and "natural" products of human culture, religion'; and identify that education has been analysed in terms of ritual, ceremonies and symbolic objects, such as rites of passage, degrees and titles. Lumby and English suggest that 'a consideration of leadership and religion seems entirely *apropos* in understanding how leaders make meaning of their work and how they find the lessons of faith important in defining, guiding, and sustaining it' (2010: 85). However, they reject the potential criticism that such an analytical framework is intrinsically a matter of religious belief, arguing such an endeavour includes 'those of a less conscious religious bent who invoke meta-physical or faith-based metaphors in their work' (ibid.).

Lumby and English, quoting Pattison, argue that the only real tool leaders have is language, and that management's 'use of signs and symbols and their myriad manifestations in visions, missions, slogans, goals and objectives, evaluative systems, mediating disputes, planning, evaluating, and defining resources and costs and providing the motivation to develop and employ them are linguistically centred'; indeed 'the managerial "revolution". . . has been as much a rhetorical event as anything else' (Pattison, 1997, quoted in Lumby and English, 2010: 88–89). Pattison identified mystical metaphors deriving from apocalyptic, millenarian Christianity and its language: 'strategic planning . . . is a ritual' often resting on 'visions and missions that have little to do with reality and are not open for challenge or change' (Lumby and English, 2010: 90). Indeed

> it is not the quest for improvement and for perfection that appears quasireligious in nature, but the fact that they no longer appear open to question. As goals they have taken on the inviolacy of commandments and educational leaders are the priests.
>
> (ibid., 94)

Management activity is 'outright religious in content, scope and intensity . . . goals and processes have been shorn of obvious religious titles and practices, but remain nevertheless though with secular names' (ibid., 91).

Metaphors of values and faith have regularly informed the analysis of education outside the FE sector. Gottlieb and La Belle (1990: 9) argue that Freire's famous metaphor of liberation (in part through education) as childbirth can be seen as belonging to 'a system of Christian religious metaphors' he employs, which additionally include many other 'secularized religious metaphors' such as 'vocation', 'conversion', 'communion', 'incarnation', 'salvation', 'unveiling', 'naming' and even 'the word'. Illich characterised the school as a

> ritual of initiation which introduces the neophyte to the sacred race of progressive consumption, a ritual of propitiation whose academic priests mediate between the faithful and gods of privilege and power, a ritual of expiation which sacrifices its dropouts, branding them as scapegoats of underdevelopment.
>
> (Illich, 1974: 44)

More recently Biesta *et al.* identified, in relation to school teachers, that 'the comparative lack of discourses around purpose and values strongly suggest a disconnection between purpose and method, and an impoverishment in teacher discourses' (Biesta *et al.*, 2015: 635); and Ball famously argued that education reform brings about change in teachers' subjective existence, which represents 'the struggle over the teacher's soul' (Ball, 2010: 217).

According to Hansen the idea of vocation ("to call" from its Latin root *vocare*) 'has been used to describe both secular and religious commitments' (1994: 259). In a religious context a vocation might be a calling to serve the divine, treating life 'as a pilgrimage toward greater meaning and truth' (ibid: 259); whilst in a secular framework 'vocation denotes a person's conception of his or her life in terms of social mission . . . a strong and persistent disposition to be of service to others' (ibid: 259).

In a specifically post compulsory context Daley describes the vocational passion of students embarking on FE teacher training programmes; highlighting their 'love of subject and their need to make a difference to people's lives; they wanted to pass things on or pay things back, they discussed social justice and the love of working with people' (Daley, 2015: 13). But not all FE professionals would endorse the vocational metaphor, despite manifesting qualities that might be identified with it. For instance Gleeson *et al.* highlight that FE lecturers may explicitly reject the notion of vocation whilst expressing 'values and attitudes traditionally associated with professional commitment and engagement' (Gleeson *et al.*, 2005: 450).

Perhaps one of the longest standing metaphors associated with FE relates to its ability to offer second (or third or fourth) educational chances, in particular to students who may have been unsuccessful in their earlier schooling. There is something redemptive in this discourse, which mirrors the Christian tradition and this redemptive quality was articulated by Kennedy in *Learning Works: Widening Participation in Further Education*:

> It is further education which has invariably given second chances to those who were forced by necessity to make unfulfilling choices. It said "try again" to those who were labelled as failures and who had decided education was not for the likes of them.
>
> (Kennedy, 1997: 2)

However, FE's capacity to offer second chances, especially to adults, has been increasingly undermined by shifts in funding and government priorities:

> Further education provision, over the last decade or so, has moved from one where there was a strong focus on vocational, remedial, second chance or part-time learning for adults, either accredited or not, to one which has become a central and key provider of learning that is driven to meet the economic demands of the country.
>
> (O'Grady, 2013: 62)

The metaphor of transformation utilised to describe FE and lifelong learning has a resonance with faith-derived discourses. Of all the UK educational sectors FE's role and impact is described most in terms of social justice, hope and transformation. For Halpin 'education is essentially a future-orientated project concerned to bring about improvement, specifically *growth* in the learner's knowledge and understanding, successful teaching requires its practitioners to teach with hope in mind' (Halpin, 2001: 405–406). According to Jauhiainen and Alho-Malmelin 'faith in education refers to collective confidence – on both the individual and educational policy level – in the possibilities of education to advance the individual's living conditions, work career and status in society' (Jauhiainen and Alho-Malmelin, 2004: 461). FE is very regularly described in these terms:

> transformation in the context of [further] education is about providing an environment where learners flourish in democratic critical spaces based on respect; learners who have often been silenced and marginalised entering further education's landscape are offered choices and hope which streams into their personal and public journeys.
> (Duckworth and Smith, 2016: no page)

Perhaps the flip side of learning transformation is the current widespread anxiety that FE is facing a period of radical and damaging flux: a 'post-apocalyptic era' (O'Leary, 2016: no page) likely to be as turbulent as the post-incorporation age. Yet the sort of educational reform that resulted in incorporation and the recent area reviews may also be presented as a 'miracle cure, a kind of panacea for a wide variety of social ills and problems' (Jauhiainen and Alho-Malmelin, 2004: 462). It should be noted that metaphors such as transformation are also widely colonised by senior managers in FE to assert institutional values and promote organisational change: the lived experience of transformation that follows is often less than wholly positive for both staff and students if it entails redundancies, the closure of adult classes and an increasingly aggressive managerialism.

Corporate mission statements and institutional missions litter the FE landscape. Barry *et al.* argue that collective will in organisations is coupled to corporate objectives 'through the revelation of "vision" and "mission" – and faith sustained through restorative ritual and rite of passage' (Barry *et al.*, 2001: 89); in such organisations the appraisal can be viewed as a system of surveillance 'resembling the confessional' (2001: 92) promoting docile self-regulation. Employing a parallel metaphor Wilson similarly suggests that there can be 'a strong odour of the confessional box about the appraisal interview' (Wilson, 2002: 621). Simmons and Thompson describe official reports and policy on creative teaching and learning in FE as an 'evangelising discourse' (Simmons and Thompson, 2008: 604); and in their discussion of gendered leadership practices in FE, Kerfoot and Whitehead identify the visionary qualities of some managers, 'fuelled through and reified by the adoption of quasi-religious metaphors such as "evangelism" . . . [and] notions of vision, self-sacrifice, faith, self-belief and endurance' (Kerfoot and Whitehead, 2000: 194).

Boocock explores metaphors in his account of lecturer and manager motivation in FE: self-interested knaves and altruistic knights (2015: 173). Whilst not explicitly faith based these metaphorical characterisations assume or reject chivalric codes deriving from the Christian tradition as 'altruistically motivated professionals' or 'self-interested agents' (Boocock, 2015: 173). Page (2011) considers first tier managers in FE in quasi-religious terms, as fundamentalists, priests, converts and martyrs. Further, he discusses the hierarchical rise of FE managers in terms of emergence, with promotion operating as a kind of ordination: his participants describe fulfilling middle management duties 'before taking on the role officially; promotion (ordination) was merely a conferment of title on leadership practices they performed on a daily basis' (Page, 2011: 266).

The figure (Figure 11.1, ibid: 264) represents Page's quasi-religious typology of first tier managers, who are in his view members of a

> holy order, those who participate in the institutions of faith. Most critical here is the belief of the professionals within colleges, their faith that education and training is capable of acting as a transformative agent in the lives of their learners.
>
> (ibid: 263)

The foci of this typology (team, students and organisation) are emic, i.e. from within the social group, and from the perspective of the research subject; rather than etic, i.e. from outside the college, from the perspective of the observer. In the context of the dispute over FE professionalism perhaps an additional focus applies to lecturers: the sector itself.

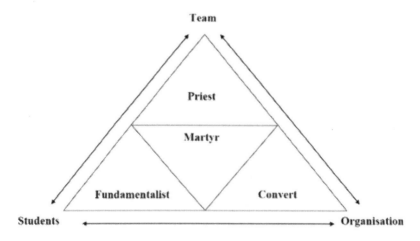

Figure 11.1 FTM model

Source: Page (2011)

Professionalism, faith and apostasy

The prevalence of religiously metaphorical FE language may suggest the possibility of a shared faith or ideology, which could in turn inform a common professionalism. However the evidence of the ideological dynamics of the "professionalism war" suggests that sectoral values are contested and far from universal. In 2015 his reflection on the 800th anniversary of Magna Carta led Coffield to 'produce a Bill of Rights for the teaching profession. . . . The thirteenth century barons insisted on 63 clauses, Martin Luther nailed 95 theses to the door of the church in Wittenberg' (Coffield, 2016: 85); and at his keynote at the inaugural *Tutor Voices* conference Coffield invited delegates (tongue firmly in cheek) to join him in nailing the Bill of Rights to door of the Education Ministry. This linkage to Lutheran reform may suggest a situation in which even when educators share a faith it may be at odds with institutional or governmental visions, rendering them sectoral "apostates".

Apostasy may be defined as the renunciation of a religion, or the adoption of beliefs contrary to those previously held. It may also be used metaphorically to describe the renunciation of nonspiritual values, and is used in this latter regard for the purposes of the discussion of professionalism and the fundamentally ideological nature of the IfL dispute. It should be noted that in the months preceding the crisis of confidence in the IfL, a UCU survey found that a majority of lecturers 'still favoured a professional body, but less than a fifth thought the IfL was fulfilling this role' (Petrie and Peutrell, 2015: 11). The IfL's demise was a key moment in the history of FE professionalism: sector apostates renounced a particular vision of professionalism in opposing the professional body, and as a result shifted and reformed canonical professional codes. However, apostasy brought with it unintended consequences, such as the revocation of the regulation requiring qualified teachers; and as Elliot suggests, those in powerful FE positions may actively stifle heretical opposition (2017: xxv). Rouxel points out that in the region of 130,000 of the IfL's 200,000 members boycotted the mandatory membership fee (a far greater number than Natfhe's then membership); representing 'the most widely supported industrial action seen in the FE sector since the incorporation of colleges' (2015: 134). Whilst the fee imposition sparked the dispute, wider professional concerns fanned the fire. The imposition of mandatory membership had been tolerated rather than embraced: membership was a kind of tithe, and when the government funding for its evangelical version of professionalism was withdrawn, the (unwilling) adherents to the IfL orthodoxy became apostates. Rouxel suggests that at its root the dispute represented 'a discussion about what FE is for' (2015: 131). Dennis too argues that opposition to the IfL entailed the articulation of a more democratic, critical professionalism; and represented a 'pronounced act of collective dissent by post-16 teachers in the UK' (2015: 70). The rejection of the IfL brand of professional membership and identity coincided with an emerging sense that a broader based professionalism was needed; and whilst the opposition was initiated by a policy requirement, the post-16 professionalism discourse it engendered broadened to issues of equity, inclusion and social justice (Dennis, 2015: 72).

As Tomkins (2010) points out, the history of the British labour and trade union movement is inextricably linked with Christianity; and according to the Labour Prime Minister Harold Wilson, it owes more to Methodism than to Marx. In this context, FE professionalism too may have a residual religious legacy; a heritage which would contradict Shaw's famous aphorism that all professions are a conspiracy against the laity (1911). Indeed in the current neoliberal context FE professionals are peripheralised, and hardly represent a priestly class collectively machinating against its lay congregations. Instead, in FE's current alienated state they may be non-conformists, if not Marxists: unwilling apostates in their own profession; but the successful opposition to the IfL may tentatively suggest the potential of collective ideological agency.

Conclusion

So where is the sector now in terms of faith, apostasy and professional autonomy? The broader aspirations for a more democratic, activist model of professionalism articulated by FE apostates at the height of the professionalism war, and elucidated by Taubman (2015) remain live, current issues. However, the landscape of FE professionalism itself is increasingly fractured: the days of the IfL's 200,000 strong professional membership are long gone; and its inheritor the ETF SET currently has only 15,000 members (SET, 2017). More recently the College of Teaching, a professional body seeking to attract mainly school teachers, has confirmed its intention to recruit from within FE. A former college principal suggests this could both render SET redundant and enhance FE teachers' status 'as members of a professional organisation that works across all education sectors. Teachers are teachers wherever they teach, and a College of Teaching – open to teachers across the board – is what's needed' (Evans, 2015: no page). It remains to be seen how this will play out, but there may be a sectoral move towards greater unity, manifested in the 2017 decision by the NUT (National Union of Teachers) and the ATL (Association of Teachers and Lecturers) to form the NEU (National Education Union), which could prefigure a genuinely cradle-to-grave educational trade union.

Meanwhile trade union concerns in relation to professionalism continue to be reflected in regular conference motions to UCU (University and College Union) – the successor to Natfhe – which consistently argue that attempts to 'professionalise the FE sector often adopt a deficit analysis: assume we are not professional; lack a democratic ethos; and promote managerialist, neoliberal policies' and call for a notion of professionalism that is 'democratic, representative, egalitarian, campaigning, and non-mandatory . . . [and] independent of government, employers and bodies representing colleges; and capable of challenging them all' (UCU, 2015: no page). Indeed *Tutor Voices*, a grassroots professional association, was established by lecturers with these proposed characteristics

(Coffield, 2015b: 11). Page's typology of front line FE managers suggests categories including fundamentalists, priests, converts and martyrs, with the further possibility of evangelists, prophets and atheists. The lesson of the FE professionalism war may be that the apostasy of FE lecturers makes them, by and large, closer in faith terms to Quakers, Shakers and Anabaptists.

References

Ball, S. (2010). 'The teacher's soul and the terrors of performativity.' *Journal of Education Policy*, 18(2), 215–228.

Barry, J., Chandler, J. and Clarke, H. (2001). 'Between the ivory tower and the academic assembly line.' *Journal of Management Studies*, 38(1), 87–101.

Biesta, G., Priestly, M. and Robinson, S. (2015). 'The role of beliefs in teacher agency.' *Teachers and Teaching: Theory and Practice*, 21(6), 624–640.

Boocock, A. (2015). 'Knaves, knights or networks: Which assumption of manager motivation should underlie further education policy?' *Research in Post-Compulsory Education*, 20(2).

Coffield, F. (2015a). 'Resistance is fertile: The demands the FE sector must make of the next government.' Keynote at New Bubbles Conference, 26th March 2015. Thistle Hotel, London Heathrow.

Coffield, F. (2015b). 'A cause worth fighting for: Tutors voices.' Keynote at Tutor Voices Inaugural Conference, 26th September 2015. Northern College, Barnsley.

Coffield, F. (2016). 'Teachers as powerful, democratic professionals' in Coffield, F. and Higgins, S. (eds.) *John Dewey's Democracy and Education: A British Tribute*. London: IOE Press.

Daley, M. (2015). 'Why teach? Not afraid to dance' in Daley, M., Orr, K. and Petrie, J. (eds.) *Further Education and the Twelve Dancing Princesses*. London, Trentham.

Dennis, C. (2015). 'Locating post-16 professionalism: Public spaces as dissenting spaces.' *Research in Post-Compulsory Education*, 20(1), 64–77.

Duckworth, V. and Smith, R. (2016). 'Further education: Transforming lives and communities.' Online. http://transforminglives.web.ucu.org.uk/2016/06/20/stories-of-transformation/ [accessed 26/11/16].

Elliot, G. (2017). 'Preface' in Daley, M., Orr, K. and Petrie, J. (eds.) *The Principal: Power and Professionalism in FE*. London, Trentham.

Evans, S. (2015). 'New professional bodies for FE under fire over "lack of coherent thinking".' Online. www.tes.com/news/further-education/breaking-news/new-professional-bodies-fe-under-fire-over-lack-coherent [accessed 28/07/17].

Gleeson, D., Davies, J. and Wheeler, E. (2005). 'On the making and taking of professionalism in the further education workplace.' *British Journal of Sociology of Education*, 26(4), 445–460.

Gottlieb, E. and La Belle, T. (1990). 'Ethnographic contextualization of Frieire's discourse: Consciousness-raising, theory and practice.' *Anthropology and Education Quarterly*, 21(1), 3–18.

Halpin, D. (2001). 'The nature of hope and its significance for education.' *British Journal of Educational Studies*, 49(4), 392–410.

Hansen, D. (1994). 'Teaching and the sense of vocation.' *Educational Theory*, 44(3), 259–275.

Illich, I. (1974). *Deschooling Society*. London: Calder and Boyars.

Jauhiainen, A. and Alho-Malmelin, M. (2004). 'Education as a religion in the learning society.' *International Journal of Lifelong Education*, 23(5), 459–474.

Kennedy, H. (1997). *Learning Works: Widening Participation in Further Education*. Coventry: FEFC.

Kerfoot, D. and Whitehead, S. (2000). 'Keeping all the balls in the air: Further education and the masculine/managerial subject.' *Journal of Further and Higher Education*, 24(2), 183–201.

Lingfield, R. (2012). *Professionalism in the Further Education* (The Lingfield Report). London: DBIS.

Lumby, J. and English, F. (2010). *Leadership as Lunacy: And Other Metaphors for Educational Leadership*. London: Sage.

O'Grady, A. (2013). *Lifelong Learning in the UK*. London: Routledge.

O'Leary, M. (2016). Private communication.

Page, D. (2011). 'Fundamentalists, priests, martyrs and converts: A typology of first tier management in further education.' *Research in Post-Compulsory Education*, 16(1), 101–121.

Pattison, S. (1997). *The faith of the managers: When management becomes religion*. London: Cassell.

Petrie, J. (2015). 'How Grimm is FE?' in Daley, M., Orr, K. and Petrie, J. (eds.) *Further Education and the Twelve Dancing Princesses*. London, Trentham.

Petrie, J. and Peutrell, R. (2015). 'Unprofessional bodies?' *Post 16 Educator*, 79 (April–June 2015), 11–14.

Richardson, G. (2005). 'Craft guilds and Christianity in late-medieval England: A rational-choice analysis.' *Rationality and Society*, 17(2), 139–189.

Rouxel, D. (2015). 'Dancing in plain sight' in Daley, M., Orr, K. and Petrie, J. *Further Education and the Twelve Dancing Princesses*. London, Trentham.

SET (Society of Education and Training). (no date). 'The history of IfL.' Online. https://set.et-foundation.co.uk/about-us/ifls-legacy/ifls-history/ [accessed 28/07/17].

SET (Society of Education and Training). (2017). *Annual Review: Highlights of 2016–17*. London: ETF.

Shaw, G. B. (1911). *The Doctor's Dilemma*. London: Constable and Co Ltd.

Simmons, R. and Thompson, T. (2008). 'Creativity and performativity: The case of further education.' *British Educational Research Journal*, 34(5), 601–618.

Taubman, D. (2015). 'Reframing professionalism and reclaiming the dance' in Daley, M., Orr, K. and Petrie, J. (eds.) *Further Education and the Twelve Dancing Princesses*. London, Trentham.

Tomkins, S. (2010). 'The Christian tradition of politics.' Online. www.theguardian.com/commentisfree/belief/2010/apr/09/christianity-politics [accessed 28/07/17].

UCU. (2015). 'UCU Congress 2015.' Online. www.ucu.org.uk/congress2015#MOTIONS [accessed 13/04/15].

Waugh, C. (2011). 'The meaning of "reprofessionalisation".' *Post 16 Educator*, 2 (March–April 2011), 22–24.

Wilson, F. (2002). 'Dilemmas of appraisal.' *European Management Journal*, 20(6), 620–629.

Section III

Creativity and resistance

Chapter 12

The experience of Ofsted
Fear, judgement and symbolic violence

Catherine Gallagher and Rob Smith

Introduction

England shares many of the neoliberal features of education policy that can be seen in, for example, Australia and the US. To that extent, there are similar debates about teacher 'performance' and accountability (see Marshall et al. 2012; Darling-Hammond and Hyler 2013; Cochran-Smith et al. 2012) and about university involvement in teacher education (Smith et al. 2015). In England, the vexed issues of teacher accountability and the role of HEIs in teacher education crystallise in the function and workings of the Office for Standards in Education (Ofsted). Geographical considerations may mean that while the US and Australia both have a patchwork of different overseeing bodies, in England, Ofsted is *the* sole national mechanism for enforcing market accountability in relation to 'teacher performance' and accountability in schools and colleges. In addition to this, recent educational policy in England (DfE 2016) signals how the place of university-based teacher education has become contested which makes Ofsted's role in overseeing teacher education programmes in universities all the more significant.

Neoliberal dependence on so-called performance data positions Ofsted as an enforcer of the *doxa* of technical rationality that marketised forms demand. The underpinning emphasis in regulation relies on 'thin equity' (Cochran-Smith et al. 2016: 4) that positions teachers as a key variable in learners' educational outcomes at the expense of a perspective that takes broader social factors into account. But issues of social justice to one side, this chapter will focus on Ofsted's enforcement role and, using Bourdieu, will theorise how Ofsted delegates 'pedagogic authority' through inspection and legitimates and models 'symbolic violence' through authoritative judgement.

In England, all further education colleges produce performance data on an annual basis in order to continue to draw down public funding. This data forms part of the accountability mechanisms that have historically attached to marketised public sector organisations. Data is amassed centrally by government to give an overall picture of 'productivity' and 'standards' and to inform target setting. Locally, market position for individual colleges depends more critically on the judgement of an external market regulator. Ofsted carries out inspections across England in order to ensure the 'robustness' of performance data and to maintain standards in schools, colleges, nurseries and other children's services. These inspection visits last several days. Ofsted presents itself as having a mission to 'help providers that are not yet of good standard to improve, monitor their progress and share with them the best practice we find' (Ofsted 2014A), to raise standards and 'drive improvement . . . for all learners' (Ofsted 2014B). Ofsted's role also extends to inspecting teacher education courses for further education teachers. Inspections contribute to market data as they culminate in the publication of an overall grade for the performance of the institution in question. In this way, Ofsted not only acts as an external and supposedly objective judge of the quality of provision, it also provides 'market information' supposedly to influence consumer choice.

This chapter draws on the experiences of university and college teacher educators from a partnership made up of one university and eight colleges in the West Midlands of England. These experiences were collated to form a body of data gathered during an inspection of initial teacher education (ITE) courses for college teachers in March 2013.

The national context

According to the neoliberal view, education has a central role in human capital production (Becker 1993) and this has led to an increase in government focus on the way in which teachers are educated. Between 2010 and 2014, university-based models of teacher education were undermined by Michael Gove, Secretary of State for Education (see Mansell 2013). Gove was outspoken in his views about HE-led teacher education, calling his opposition The Blob (see for example Robinson 2014) and he introduced an inspection regime of teacher education programmes in which Ofsted's judgement was linked to future funding. This assault on 'ideological' teacher education culminated in the introduction of a more 'robust' framework by Ofsted (running from Sept 2012 – June 2014) which scrapped the 'satisfactory' judgement and replaced it with 'requires improvement'.

In relation to ITE courses, to complicate the situation further, the publication of the Lingfield Report (BIS 2012) removed the requirement for college teachers to be qualified *as teachers*. Whether college staff needed to be qualified as teachers was left to principals to decide.

Theory

Bourdieu and Passeron see symbolic violence as an integral aspect of power relations in educational settings:

> Every power to exert symbolic violence, i.e. every power which manages to impose meanings and to impose them as legitimate . . . adds its own specifically symbolic force to those power relations.
>
> (Bourdieu and Passeron 2013: 4)

In what some may view as an overly deterministic view, Bourdieu and Passeron see education as reproducing the power relations of a given society and position pedagogic actions and through those the role of teachers, centrally in the reproduction of the existing social order. Their thinking equates pedagogic action with 'symbolic violence' inasmuch as it is the imposition of a 'cultural arbitrary' (ibid. 5) in the interests of a particular group or class. Bourdieu and Passeron see legitimacy or pedagogic authority as a necessary aspect of this process and view the process as 'invisible' to both teachers and learners.

Leaving a discussion of how critical pedagogy sits theoretically outside this operation of symbolic violence to Chapter 3, this chapter will focus on the key role of teacher education in the reproduction of the social practice of further education. In the discussion that follows, we will develop a commentary about one Ofsted inspection to provide a sense of how a centralised market regulator can act as a mediator of government policy. In doing this, we will present inspections as events/sites of struggle over pedagogic authority.

The partnership inspection

Despite deregulation, the partnership courses involved in the inspection that is the focus of this chapter were running in several different colleges and remained an important part of the university's ITE provision. The focus was on the university as having a central role in designing and administering the courses. The inspection was announced by a phone call asking staff to supply all the performance data of the previous three years with a commentary on trends. The lead inspector also asked for a list of all students' names, their subject specialisms and placement addresses so that observations could be carried out. On the following Monday, six inspectors travelled to different colleges in the partnership while the lead inspector came to meet the course leaders at the university. Over the next three days, the lead inspector held report back sessions each evening at 5pm at the university to provide insights into inspection findings so far. On the final Thursday morning, there was an 'information-giving' session at which the lead inspector offered headline findings.

The next section will draw on data (in the form of written reflections and notes) as gathered by the teacher educators during and in the immediate aftermath of the partnership inspection.

Measuring learning

The partnership's position on grading course in this case was unusual as it did not adhere to Ofsted's grading framework of using the assessment labels 'outstanding', 'good', 'requires improvement' and 'inadequate' to student teachers or their lessons. This appeared to be an obstacle for the inspection team as its frame for analysis and commentary on students' progress was not there to draw upon. In the absence of a series of grades to measure progress, the courses being inspected were structured around a personalised critical dialogue between personal tutor, mentor and student that mapped across students' journal entries, observations, academic coursework and action planning. But seemingly the inspectors found the depth, nuance and detail evidenced by this dialogue to be less effective at providing the teacher educators or the students with an insight into their progress than 'clearer' grades.

Measuring learning became a theme during the inspection. According to participants' notes, the final grading session provided a series of comments on this theme.

> There is a lack of evidence of trainees understanding what level they are at.

And:

> There's a nagging concern about trainees being aware about how they are performing as benchmarked against best practice in the sector.

Underpinning these statements is a view of learning that involves steady and measurable progress from one 'level' to the next, like stairs on a staircase with each stair being the same height. Ofsted's paperwork does not include any definition of learning as a calibrated process and this was not the partnership's view of how learning is structured but clearly Ofsted's role as centralised regulator requires such a definition. Apart from the reliance on the discredited notion of 'best practice' (see Coffield and Edwards 2009), here the *use* of grading is conflated with providing students with a national overview of where they stand in relation to the practice of other (outstanding, good, requires improvement, inadequate) teachers. The implicit message is of a need to adopt a normative, officially sanctioned approach. This connects to the focus on 'a lack of evidence' revealing how the enforcement of the inspection operates at two levels: first, it assesses evidence but second, it polices what counts as 'evidence' in this way asserting a culturally arbitrary typology. This assesses the partnership as needing to focus not just on delivering high quality teacher education, but on creating evidence of this in a form deemed acceptable.

The same issue re-surfaced in another feedback session:

> It is not clear that the University tracks students' progress throughout the year.

This notion of 'tracking progress' suggests a similarly linear view of learning. The inspectors required numerical data as evidence of tracking. The store of qualitative evidence of students' growing awareness and development that was a cornerstone of the course was invalidated because no numerical summary of progress was available.

One of the college teacher educators described a discussion with an inspector in the following way:

> The inspector stayed for the whole lesson which was two hours and at the end . . . she whispered to me, "Can we have a chat?" . . . The next hour and a half was an extraordinary occasion because the inspector proceeded to try every way she could to extract from me any negative comments about the non-grading of observations (and) communications with the university partnership. . . .
>
> On the Wednesday she held a lunchtime meeting with the team including our line managers. She pursued the same agenda. . . . It must have been frustrating for her because . . . I have no problem with giving verbal developmental feedback and I do have my doubts that giving any person a "number" makes their teaching any better or worse from year to year.

Grading then is an important part of the approach and in our analysis this links to (1) the (admittedly crude) shorthand idea that grading creates a sense of comparable standards across institutions and (2) it provides a speedy comparative shorthand. The grading of students epitomises the symbolic violence wrapped up in assessment. Symbolic violence in grading operates through the imposition of an 'objective' grade, a 'labelling' (Becker 1973) that has as its focus not the learning and development of the student, but instead, a connection to an external matrix of value for the purposes of providing market data.

But the inspection in this case moved beyond asserting a metrics-based norm; it also attempted to model assessment as a social practice and through that to provide a template for social relations between teacher educators and students – as the next section will outline.

Modelling symbolic violence and pedagogic authority

The partnership approach to observation and providing feedback also surfaced during the inspection visits. One HE colleague recounted:

> This was a positive experience and we had a 3 way discussion . . . (student, inspector, tutor). I gave the usual reflective feedback and when I finished (the inspector) agreed with the points. . . . He then offered feedback to the student and started with 'I think you will be a fantastic teacher'. . . . Then he asked the student about how the feedback was given – in which he felt my reflective questioning was 'long winded' and that the student might prefer me to 'get to the point'. . . . (I concluded that feedback is very much a non-negotiated method with Ofsted as I imagine they have a grade and thus a discussion is not needed?)
>
> Ofsted approach – short and to the point: 'You're fantastic and here are some points that could be developed'. . . . My approach: 'Let's talk about your teaching and learning and where do we want it to go? What else would you need to do to become the teacher you want to be and what do your learners need?' I think the difference is that we want teachers to have

ownership over who they are as teachers. Ofsted's approach is that 'we tell you what sort of teacher you are' and it is non-negotiable and static.

The passage is important because the focus is on *how* the assessment is communicated. The difference in approach here is rooted in a different view of how learning works and how knowledge and power interact. The Ofsted approach can be characterised in Bourdieusian terms of pedagogic authority: the tutor is required to undertake the role of authoritative judge. The observation process is an important opportunity to assert that authority. The assessor is the infallible judge, capable of absolute and objective judgement. This carries with it a set of assumptions about power and knowledge. There is no sense of co-construction of meaning and the knowledge travel is strictly one way (and presumably believed to be objective). This can be viewed as a normative intervention aimed at shaping the relations between students and teachers as well as its tone. The imposition of meaning provides an explicit example of symbolic violence as a cultural and pedagogic practice.

Authoritative judgement

On the third day, the Lead HMI reported that the partnership could not be 'outstanding' because the sample students that had been observed were 'not universally good or better'. This phrasing suggests that, as signifiers, the categories depend on their relation to each other rather than on any connection to a signified reality. It was pointed that the course had three months to run, time enough for the students observed to improve; according to participants, the reply was:

> The student observed this morning will never be a good teacher.

This definitive (and summative) statement prompted the question: do the inspectors take account of the different rates at which students learn? – which was answered in the affirmative. What was worrying here was that the lead inspector appeared entirely ignorant that the force of his comments was nudging the teacher educators towards the kind of 'gaming' that has become prevalent in marketised educational settings. There was a lack of awareness that to achieve 'improvement' might involve the adoption of an admissions policy that discriminated against applicants from lower income/social class and People of Colour (PoC) backgrounds in favour of white middle-class students. This would mean diluting a commitment to a widening participation agenda.

Ofsted's high stakes regulatory power: how did we get here?

The blinkered fixation on performance data is a key area of weakness. The following passage from Ofsted's Annual Report of 2013 illustrates the problem:

> Getting quality assurance and performance management right are core to improving the quality of teaching and learning. Where procedures were ineffective at improving teaching . . . managers typically failed to use data on learners' performance to identify areas of provision with weaker teaching.
>
> (Ofsted 2013)

The passage demonstrates a lack of understanding of the gap that has opened up in colleges (and schools) nationally between performance data and good (or outstanding) teaching and learning. Worryingly, there is also a failure to understand that the emphasis on data has led to a generation of teachers who have been effectively trained in manipulating it and that this activity is prioritised by managers at the expense of a focus on real teaching and learning.

Ofsted is not as it claims to be an 'independent and impartial' body (Ofsted 2014a) but rather is there to model symbolic violence: to train teachers to adopt a legitimised disposition of assessment and authoritative judgement. This amounts to policing cultural compliance and the penalising any educational institution that fails to pay lip service. Ofsted's approach is best encapsulated in the term 'managerialist positivism' (Smith and O'Leary 2013). This is an ideological position which underpins new public management (NPM), a data-driven approach that has taken hold in the public sector. Managerialist positivism actively disregards context, insisting instead that everything can be measured and compared in a straightforward way across different contexts.

Fear, technical rationality and habitus

It's difficult to underestimate the dread that fills teachers when contemplating the arrival of Ofsted in their school, college or university. The short notice period of two days designed to make inspections more 'robust' means the fear of Ofsted inspections now blights whole academic years as colleges and schools are left hanging in anticipation of the call that announces an imminent inspection. Fear is an everyday aspect of the college teacher's lifeworld. Fear is embedded in their practice, is a constitutive part of their professional identity and fear is at the core of the model of change that Ofsted embodies, how it operates to bring about change.

> We are afraid of what we cannot control, dominate, calculate, anticipate and plan: everything that slips through the net of rationality. Not for nothing, in cultural contexts in which the fragility of reason is an essential note, fear increases significantly. We mistrust its power to deliver us from evil. We have ceased to believe in traditional religion, but also in the potential of modern reason.
>
> (Torralba 2011: 59)

The quotation above sees fear as arising from the irrational features of our hypermodern conditions. This begins with the enforcement of one set of 'rational' procedures over another. In the current system, achievement data is taken as *the* measure of performance within the so-called market. This reduction of complex social and intellectual activity into numerical data (and often a single unifying 'grade') is a necessary feature of a marketised system that relies on comparison, competition and the publication of market data to bring about improvement. While damaging in the sense that it works against the interests of learners and clearly erodes public trust, this self-interested manipulation of performance data for institutional ends also produces the conditions for the growth of fear.

Fear operates in different ways in the playing out of the procedures of technical rationality in colleges. First, teachers are required to be complicit in the production of performance data. The requirement is straightforward: poor performance data leads to course closure and potential redundancy. But fear also operates at a deeper level and Ofsted's role highlights this. The opening up of a fissure between the simulations offered by crafted performance data and the real, lived experience of educational interactions and their complex social outcomes is disruptive of any sense that reason connects to the meaning of teachers' work.

The Bourdieusian concept of habitus is helpful here. The notion of habitus explains the norms, practices and ways of thinking that operate as norms in order to reproduce particular social conditions (Bourdieu 1994). The habituation that underpins the meaning of the term extends, importantly, to physicality: the repetition of bodily movements, repeated activities and, we would argue, affective states and dispositions.

From this we can see that Ofsted's role is to affirm the simulations, the market truth as it were, that are key aspects of the legitimisation of the marketised further education landscape. The necessity of legitimising these simulations involves promoting assessment 'events' that will yield appropriate data to support an entire edifice sustained by symbolic violence. The core of the function of Ofsted is legitimisation: the modelling and insistence on a specific form of pedagogic authority.

Concluding thoughts

The first point to make about the above inspection is that the analysis has enabled us to move well beyond the crude assumption of there being any direct relation between the inspection and any 'improvement' in the ITE offered by the partnership. The 'the implementation of (a) public summative evaluation' (as noted by Cochran-Smith et al. 2016: 3) was merely a part of the symbolic violence visited upon the ITE partnership that positioned it within the external marketscape. The summative judgement in this case was powerful in (1) shaping future funding possibilities and (2) influencing public perceptions. Its power lay solely in the potential for damage. That assertion fundamentally undermines the policy assumptions underpinning the monolithic Ofsted regime: that inspections lead to improvement.

Ofsted's role is complicated by the rapidity with which inspections are carried out. The production of market data necessitates velocity (Virilio 2006, 2012) and risks a superficial model that reproduces expectations similar to *Pygmalion in the Classroom* effect (Rosenthal and Jacobson 1968). The grades (with their veneer of objectivity) are an integral aspect of pedagogic authority but despite that, Ofsted's modelling suggests that the grades awarded to individual colleges are less important than the encounter with authority represented by the inspection. Viewed through that lens, inspection is a disciplinary event that attempts to coerce providers into adopting the centrally prescribed cultural practice of symbolic violence. Inspections are vital events in conditioning the habitus of teachers which means fear is an essential affective element in the legitimisation of neoliberal norms.

Positioning symbolic violence and fear at the heart of an analysis of Ofsted enables us to outline the principles of some meaningful alternatives. First and foremost this may require a re-examination of the purposes of further education (Biesta 2013) and a shift away from market-orientated cultures. Then, if we want to improve standards of teaching and learning through the involvement of a national agency, that body needs to shift its focus away from surface data and engage fully with the contextual issues and narratives of each institution inspected. In other words, such a body needs to be working with and alongside teachers, not managers. While Ofsted's focus continues to centre on such reductive and unreliable data and leadership and management in response focuses on promoting corporate cultures that ensure such data is favourable, learning and teaching will always take second place.

Finally, and perhaps most importantly, we need to re-examine the place of fear in the current system. If the improvement of learning and teaching in colleges requires learning, then we need to ask ourselves:

Is fear the best way of bringing about changes for the better in our colleges?

References

Becker, G. S. 1993. *Human Capital: A Theoretical and Empirical Analysis with Special Reference to Education*. London: University of Chicago Press.

Becker, H. 1973. Labelling theory reconsidered. In Becker, H. (Ed.). *Outsiders: Studies in the Sociology of Deviance* (pp. 177–212). New York: Free Press.

Biesta, G. 2013. *The Beautiful Risk of Education*. London: Paradigm.

BIS. 2012. *Professionalism in further education*. Final Report of the Independent Review Panel Chaired by Lord Lingfield. Department of Business, Innovation and Skills. Report available at: www.bis.gov.uk/assets/biscore/further-education-skills/docs/p/12-1198-professionalism-in-further-education-final, accessed 22.08.2017.

Bourdieu, P. 1994. Structures, habitus, power: Basis for a theory of symbolic power. In Dirks, N., Eley, G. and Ortner, S. (Eds.). *Culture, Power, History: A Reader in Contemporary Social Theory* (Chapter Four, pp. 155–199). New Jersey: Princeton University Press.

Bourdieu, P. and Passeron, J.-C. 2013. *Reproduction in Education, Society and Culture*. London: Sage.

Cochran-Smith, M., Piazza, P. and Power, C. 2012. The politics of accountability: Assessing teacher education in the United States. *The Educational Forum*, 77(1), 6–27.

Cochran-Smith, M., Stern, R., Sánchez, J., Miller, A., Keefe, E., Fernández, M. B., Wen-Chia Chang, W., Carney, M., Burton, S. and Baker, M. 2016. *Holding Teacher Preparation Accountable: A Review of Claims and Evidence*. Boulder: National Education Policy Center.

Coffield, F. and Edwards, S. 2009. Rolling out 'good', 'best' and 'excellent' practice: What next? Perfect practice? *British Educational Research Journal*, 35(3), 371–390.

Darling-Hammond, L. and Hyler, M. 2013. The role of performance assessment in developing teaching as a profession. *Rethinking Schools*, 27(4), 1–5.

Department for Education (DfE) 2016. *Educational excellence everywhere*, available at: www.gov.uk/government/uploads/system/uploads/attachment_data/file/508550/Educational_excellence_everywhere__print_ready_.pdf, accessed 12.08.17.

Mansell, W. 2013. Cambridge academics baffled by teacher-training shake-up. *The Guardian*, Monday 29 April 2013, available at: www.theguardian.com/education/2013/apr/29/teacher-training-universities-schools-direct, accessed 16.12.14.

Marshall, G., Cole, P. and Zbar, V. 2012. *Teacher performance and development in Australia*. Australian Institute for Teaching and School Leadership, available at: www.aitsl.edu.au/docs/default-source/default-document-library/teacher_perf__dev_aus_aitsl.pdf?sfvrsn=8, accessed 10.01.17.

Ofsted. 2013. *The Report of Her Majesty's Chief Inspector of Education, Children's Services and Skills: Further Education and Skills*, available at: www.ofsted.gov.uk/sites/default/files/documents/ar201213/Ofsted%20Annual%20Report%20201213%20FE%20and%20Skills.pdf, accessed 09.11.16.

Ofsted. 2014A. *Who We Are What We Do*, available at: www.ofsted.gov.uk/about-us, accessed 09.11.16.

Ofsted. 2014B. *Raising Standards, Improving Lives: (Ofsted) Strategic Plan 2014 to 2016*, available at: www.gov.uk/government/uploads/system/uploads/attachment_data/file/379920/Ofsted_20Strategic_20Plan_202014-16.pdf, accessed 02.01.14.

Robinson, N. 2014. *Michael Gove: Battling the Blob*, available at: www.bbc.com/news/uk-politics-26008962, accessed 22.08.17.

Rosenthal, R. and Jacobson, L. 1968. Pygmalion in the classroom. *The Urban Review*, 3, 16–20, available at: www.uni-muenster.de/imperia/md/content/psyifp/aeechterhoff/sommersemester2012/schluesselstudiendersozialpsychologiea/rosenthal_jacobson_pygmalionclassroom_urbrev1968.pdf, accessed 02.01.14.

Smith, E., Yasukawa, K. and Hodge, S. 2015. Australian VET teacher education: What is the benefit of pedagogical studies at university for VET teachers? *TVET@Asia*, 5, 1–15, available at: www.tvet-online.asia/issue5/smith_etal_tvet5.pdf, accessed 23.07.17.

Smith, R. and O'Leary, M. 2013. New public management in an age of austerity: Knowledge and experience in further education. *Journal of Educational Administration and History*, 45(3), 244–266.

Torralba, F. 2011. The essence and forms of fear in hypermodernity. *Journal of Contemporary Culture*, 6, 56–67.

Virilio, P. 2006. *Speed and Politics*. Los Angeles: Semiotext(e).

Virilio, P. 2012. *The Administration of Fear*. Los Angeles: Semiotext(e).

Chapter 13

Identity and autonomy in lifelong education

Victoria Wright and Theresa Loughlin

In this chapter, we critically engage with our experiences as observers. We have both had roles that involved grading the lessons of colleagues. We have also worked as teacher education tutors and observers for a number of years. Our current roles and experience is as teachers on a full-time pre-service PGCE (Postgraduate Certificate in Post Compulsory Education) course for teachers in further education settings taught in a university. Our chapter is a 'mosaic' (McLuhan, 1962: 65) as we share and contrast some of our lived experiences while also teasing out some distinctions between observations as part of a quality assurance system and teacher education observations.

Policy and practice review of graded and ungraded models

In a critique of graded lesson observations, Gleeson et al. (2015) reflected on the normalizing influence of Ofsted: "Teachers are encouraged to tailor what they do in the classroom during their graded observations to ensure that they comply with prescribed notions of 'good' or 'outstanding' practice, notions that are largely determined though not explicitly defined by Ofsted. (Gleeson et al. 2015: 83)" Ofsted's shift away from grading individual teachers' lessons is yet to be fully realized in the sector. In the Times Educational Supplement, Exley (2015) reported on tentative communication from Her Majesty's Inspector Phil Romain on this point: 'if training providers and colleges have "good reasons" to continue grading lessons internally, Ofsted does not want them to stop doing so'. Anecdotally, in our role as tutors, we are both aware of dual approaches to quality assurance where the provider has run a graded lesson observation process alongside more developmental approaches. This perspective is echoed by O'Leary (2016: 1) who reflects that 'this shift in [Ofsted] policy has not necessarily been matched by parallel shift in practice in many circles'. A number of shifts are included in the recent book edited by O'Leary (2016). In one chapter, Taylor (2016) (in O'Leary, 2016: 17) reports on "an initial move away from the graded approach and whilst making a significant transition from 'feeling like a number' was still perceived by many staff to be a form of 'numbers by colours'."

i.e as a process that required persistence, transparency and continued adaptation of underpinning processes to support the development of trust in the observers and the process itself. (Taylor 2016: 19)

Our discussion of observation and observation feedback naturally engages with core themes of teaching and learning and with notions of grading and measurement, teacher development and subjectivity. Any talk of lesson observations is complicated by the word 'quality'. Coffield and Edward (2009: 388) commenting on the notions of good, best and excellent practice, explain:

> a vibrant democracy needs an open-ended approach to 'good practice', which remains within the control of reflective and learning professionals, which remains sensitive to constantly changing local contexts, and which provides the resources to deal appropriately with the complexities involved in its identification and dissemination.

Our chapter focuses on students entering the teaching profession through completion of the one year PGCE. In Page's 4R model (in O'Leary, 2016: 71), such teachers are in the 'Receptive: Stage 2' where 'it's probable that teachers will engage with more observations than at any other time in their career'. Our writing tunes in to the need to develop an ethically informed and critical approach to experiences of observing.

Our autobiographies

We came to the role of 'quality' observer via different routes. This will be explained through our autobiographies. We both observed colleagues we knew within our own curriculum areas, and colleagues we did not know across other departments. These experiences will form part of our discussions into the complexities of observing and giving observation feedback.

Theresa

While both the quality observation and Initial Teacher Education (ITE) processes require teaching sessions to be observed, descriptive accounts of the respective key requirements of each may offer insights into both. While both require 'paperwork' much else is particular to one or the other whether this be criteria based on 'professional standards' (ITE) rather than Ofsted grade criteria (quality) or statement feedback (quality) rather than dialogue (ITE). While Initial Teacher Education might stress the importance of self-evaluation and reflective review through the ministrations of a subject mentor, the quality observation might be constituted by a surprise visit from a superior (occasionally accompanied by an external consultant) and intent on passing a significant judgment.

There are clearly some similarities but the two models are fundamentally different: a scientific managerial (quality) perspective contrasting with a values-based ethical (teacher education) perspective. If we look at the 'quality' observation process there is a definite link to the managerial role of observing teaching and learning, having to make a 'judgment' using the Ofsted grading criteria (Ofsted, 2015: 40). For some individuals, this process can be detrimental to their ongoing development (O'Leary, 2013); their graded outcome can also contribute to the outcomes of their department and overall organization Ofsted outcome, so in effect presenting a multilayered dilemma (see Figure 13.1).

If we compare this to the teacher training/education observation process, there are some similarities in the preparation of the paperwork requirement: some sort of lesson planner is required for both detailing learner profiles and information about 'impact' and targets to promote differentiated outcomes. The process here though becomes less judgmental, positioning professional practice in terms of the professional standards (Education and Training Foundation, 2014). The feedback is more dialogic: acknowledging individuals' progress whilst identifying areas for continued improvement. There is also an underpinning community of practice (Lave and Wenger, 1991) to support the process through a range of peer/colleague support.

I have experienced the observation process from a number of perspectives: as a teacher educator, a 'quality' observer and as line manager. The scope of these different roles has contributed to my sense of a dichotomy of professional obligations, the creation of a divided 'persona'. On the one hand, as a teacher educator, the role is one of nurturing and cultivating new promising teachers; on the other as a 'quality' observer, I felt concerned about the more scientific judgment of measuring an individual's performance and its possible consequences (Smith and O'Leary, 2013).

I experienced the observation process of in-service teachers as the sector underwent reforms to include the Further Education National Training Organisation standards (FENTO, 2001), the precursor of the legislated 2007 Workforce Reforms, which required all teachers in FE to obtain a teaching qualification. For some individuals, having their teaching and learning observed, was part of either an 'invitation' or 'invasion' into their classroom environment. I always tried to position myself as supportive for individual 'transitions' and ongoing development, but at this early stage of my career as an observer, I found I was having to manage a duality of roles (Sachs, 2001).

In 2007, the requirement to hold a teaching qualification became mandatory and the establishment of the Institute for Learning (IfL) provided the catalyst for staff development departments in some colleges to become central providers of initial teacher education/training. The observation requirements became firmly embedded with the use of a series of Professional Standards (currently, Education and Training Foundation, 2014).

Having been involved in the 'quality' observation process from its infancy, the methodology has evolved significantly in terms of the measurability of performance against a set of judgments. Early observational models were encouragingly supportive, celebrating 'best practice' and rewarding Grade 1 teachers with the opportunity to become 'Advanced Practitioners' or 'Learning Coaches'. They also provided a developmental dialogue about areas for improvement and staff development needs. But gradually observations became more aligned with 'performance management' (Smith and O'Leary, 2013; Ball, 2002) sometimes with whole organization or curricular 'observation weeks' being organized with a three-week notice period.

Ofsted graded statements changed in 2009 and there was a definite shift in emphasis in what constituted a Grade 1. Any observation awarded this grade had to be out of the ordinary with teaching, learning and assessment showing 'impact'. This meant I would have to seriously justify awarding any Grade 1's as the tone of the policy was that they would be scrutinized. The other significant change was in the Grade 3 and 4 statements, an individual judged to be an 'ok' teacher – a Grade 3/'satisfactory' in the 2001 criteria – would now, under the new 2009 criteria, be deemed 'requires improvement'.

So what impact did this have? Across the sector more performance management and 'capability' measures (Ball 2010) came into play, individuals judged a Grade 3 were now referred to a 'Learning Coach' to move this grade towards a 'good' Grade 2. Shifting the standards raised the stakes for new and experienced staff alike.

Victoria

In contrast to Theresa, I began conducting 'quality' observations before I became a teacher education tutor. In my first 'quality' role, I felt very powerful grading fellow teachers. My sense was that a Grade 1 was unattainable. It was mystical, to be revered by colleagues who received it, although dismissed by other colleagues. Of course, the grade itself contributed to a data set: this was one of the evidence bases on which the teachers, the teams, the departments, the institution was graded. I thought that a Grade 1 lesson would have to capture a moment, that particular moment, in which everything came together. I would have to observe/watch really carefully so that when I saw it, I could confidently grade it.

Later in my career, I held dual roles of 'quality' observer and teacher education tutor. In my teacher educator role, I am used to developing habits in my student teachers: they must be able to rationalize their approaches, reflect on (and in practice), evaluate and take action to support their development. In internal 'quality' observations, I was not asked to develop those habits in my colleagues. Those observations were framed by the quality measurement (at that time, the grade) that it would generate. I am reminded, in the writing of this, of that complicity therefore between the knowing observer and the knowing teacher who recognized that their grade is more than them as teachers and that the lesson is a performance, boundaried by the teacher's expectations of the observation process. In the following diary extract I share some of my observer expectations as a PGCE teacher.

A teacher education observation (January 2017)

> *Reflecting while drafting a chapter for the Identity and Autonomy book, sitting at the kitchen table and knowing that observation and feedback are things that I still want to write about.*

At this moment, I'm looking ahead and feeling slightly worried because my students haven't yet booked in for their Observation Four with me which I know should happen (in most cases) on their first block placement teaching practice (which yes, they're now on). And I'm thinking back to the 'journey' some of them have taken. . . . I remember the expectations I have of their Observation Four (conducted jointly by a university mentor and subject specialist placement mentor). Do they know my expectations?

I've been working with them each Wednesday all day, during Semester One. They have a good knowledge of me. I've gone through the lesson observation criteria at various points including of course when I did their first observation. . . . I have also emphasized, as we do in other modules across the course, the place of the Education and Training Foundation standards (ETF, 2014) in their development. Those standards are also referenced throughout their action plan in an ongoing record through the time of the course.

So what are my expectations? I have the PGCE observation criteria in my head because I've worked with it so many times. It's about trying new things, having a range of approaches, making sure everyone is included, embedding English/Maths/Technology. It's about having a teacher presence in which the classroom and students are managed and the work stimulates and stretches. And the ETF standards are of course easily mapped to that, with a focus on motivating students to achieve, securing and updating their own skills, and meeting sector priorities. In the mix of all of that, there are *my* expectations for them.

My expectations revolve around seeing, being a witness to their development. I want to see how much they have developed from Observation One to Observation Four. I want to see that they are going to get to the end of the course, as if the progress I see in that observation hour (our observations are one hour) will be a sign that such progress will get repeated throughout Semester Two. I want to see increased confidence as a teacher, more scanning and prompter management of the whole group and of the individuals within the group. I definitely want to see some new approaches and some risk-taking. I want to feel comfortable in their classrooms. I'd really like to enjoy the lesson. I'd also like to feel proud of them, thinking: look, I played a part in that (while knowing of course that there are a lot of people playing a part in 'that').

> Warning: this diary extract was written as unedited stream of consciousness.
> (16/01/17)

So, what are some of the differences between a teacher education observation and a 'quality' one?

Theresa has already teased out some of the distinctions between quality and teacher education observations. As teacher educators, we not only support the students progressing through their required observations, we also provide a platform for dialogic evaluation and reflection on their (student teacher) 'performance' to prepare them for employment. This resonates not only with our core values but also with the Education and Training Foundation standards (ETF, 2014) within which our teachers must work, e.g.

> '1   Reflect on what works best in your teaching and learning to meet the diverse needs of learners
> 2   Evaluate and challenge your practice, values and beliefs'.
>
> (ETF, 2014: 3)

In our observations, we know what stage individual student teachers are at on the PGCE course. We think about our knowledge of them when we observe them: how much prior teaching experience they have got, how many lesson observations they have had, to what extent they are able to self-evaluate. We negotiate specific action points to support them in their development. Those action points are recorded and monitored by them as they progress through the year. As teacher educators, we are also looking ahead to the progress that must be achieved by the end of their course. We signpost them to the future, to when they will be qualified. As Warford (2011: 254) comments (in his reframing of the Vygotskian concept of ZPD; Zone of Proximal Development, as Zone of Proximal Teacher Development):

> In applying prolepsis to teacher development, teacher educators should acknowledge and validate candidates' prior experiences of teaching and learning, while employing the future tense in discussing new lenses through which they will consider the same phenomena.

'Prolepsis' is described in the paper in the following way:

> a technique called prolepsis, which involves teaching in a way that 'assumes (or pretends) that the learners know more than they actually do'.
>
> (van Lier, 2004: 153, in Warford, 2011)

We would reframe that assumption in order to contextualize it to our practice and recognize that our ways of working depend on the stage the student teachers are at. However the basic premise that we will, as observers, be trying to reaffirm/establish or draw out their experience, is valid. We are supporting them in developing the tools they will need to survive the 'quality' observation process they will face when employed.

Our experiences of being observed

At this point in our 'mosaic' (McLuhan, 1962: 65), we want to share some of our own experiences of being observed, with a view to re-emphasizing the contextual nature of observation as lived experience. We also reflect, more teasingly perhaps, on what is seen to be judged most effective, previously Grade 1.

Sharing our experiences:

Victoria

It's inspection time.

I worked as an English lecturer in a further education college. The inspector came in to my classroom to observe me teaching a second year A-Level English Literature class. From memory, I think we were discussing a coursework text at the time: Atwood's *The Handmaid's Tale*. I remember that we all, myself and the students, were openly enjoying the text. We had a very good rapport with each other and, very helpfully, they all co-operated well with each other in the class discussion.

The scene is set therefore: we like our work, we like each other, the students are in discussion groups and I am going round, monitoring, adding/stretching, and then I will do a review. I am sharing this particular observation because for the first time, I laughed when I heard the feedback (provided by my programme manager). The inspector had been very positive (I thought over-zealous) about the group dynamic and the discussions that they had observed. My instant reaction, to laugh, was simply an honest recognition that I'd had very limited influence on that. I was pleased, of course, but I was very clear in my own mind that I had not explicitly 'done' anything. How could their judgement be perceived as a comment on my performance?

My perception was that, essentially, the students had invited me in to their learning community. I happened to be the lucky tutor who had a very nice group of students, all keen to achieve in the subject area. I also thought that it had been representative of lessons I typically had with that group, and very much because of the group themselves rather than due to any particularly strong influence that I had on them.

Theresa

One of my examples of observation feedback and not achieving a Grade 1 outcome was when I was told I had contravened a 'college policy' of 'no food or drink' in classrooms. Whilst I did not want to be seen to flaunt the rules and more importantly health and safety regulations, I had negotiated with the adult student group that drinks could be brought into the classroom as long as that did not contravene health and safety policy. I was graded 2 (old currency) and almost faced disciplinary procedures.

On another occasion, it was noted and commented on that one of my students was checking their mobile phone whilst in class. That college like many others, had made and most likely still does maintain a policy of 'no mobile phones in classrooms'. My counter argument was that the particular group being observed were studying a level 7 Diploma in Management on a part-time basis and were in fact senior operational and strategic managers in their own organizations. The timing of the class and therefore the observation was around the time of a shift change back at their base, the individual needed to check that there were no issues. As 'good' practice would state, I had negotiated with the student group at the beginning of their course that mobile phones could be kept on silent and that if they needed to deal with an urgent issue, they could step outside the classroom to take or make a call. I was graded 2 (new currency).

Becoming an outstanding teacher: meeting expectations

In this section, we highlight the impact of contextual variables on the role of the teacher. We critically engage with a mechanistic approach that seeks to measure and to provide a set of terms through which an outstanding teacher can be identified. Drawing on Ofsted vocabulary, what does it mean to be 'outstanding'? Is it maintainable, and at what cost?

The diagram below demonstrates the ever-increasing expectations on teachers in colleges in England. It illustrates how teachers are having to stabilize the internalized requirements not only of their individual subject specialist pedagogic knowledge and where that fits into the department in which they work, but also how that then connects with their organization's targets and overall goals. This ultimately feeds into external-facing performance data: the Ofsted reports, learner experience and satisfaction surveys, meeting legislative requirements, learner safeguarding and ultimately shaping public perceptions.

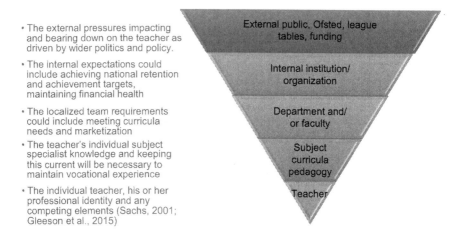

Figure 13.1 An inversion model of the requirements on a PCE teacher

Students on the PGCE course are also working to a number of expectations: those of their placement mentor, our expectations as university mentors, the expectations of the institutions in which they are placed (informed by internal and external stakeholder and quality processes), and their own expectations as to what it means to be an effective teacher. In Engeström's (2001: 138) depiction of expansive learning in the context of cultural historical activity theory, he emphasized: 'In important transformations of our personal lives and organizational practices, we must learn new forms of activity which are not yet there'. Warford (2011: 254) echoes that sense of 'employing the future tense in discussing new lenses through which they will consider the same phenomena' in relation to teacher educators working with their students.

Using Engeström's (1987) term 'community', we would recognize that students are entering a community of teachers under particular influences (the influence of the placement and university mentors and colleagues, the influence of the placement context and PGCE course expectations, etc.). In relation to the application of the community of practice model, Wright et al. (2017) cite Lave and Wenger's (1999) guidance that 'Viewpoints from which to understand practice evolve through changing participation in the division of labour, changing relations to ongoing community practices, and changing social relations in the community' (24).

Our students are preparing to be teachers in the context and timeframe of the PGCE course. During this time, they are also focused on their future aspirations; to become a future teacher in the sense of gaining employment in the sector and potentially to become the teacher they envision/ed. In ecological learning terms, as expressed by Jackson (ND): 'Our individual ecologies provide the contexts in which we create meaning from our lives'. Jackson (2017: 27) presents a model for learning ecology in which he defines the process as the achievement of: 'proximal goals informed by distal goals'. Our students' proximal goal is to obtain the PGCE PCE qualification. Their distal goal, as already indicated, is to be an effective teacher. That goal is informed by expectations that might come from previous educational experiences, i.e. teachers whose approaches they enjoyed, and perhaps teachers whose approaches they did not enjoy. Throughout their teaching practice experience, they are becoming a member of a community of practice of teachers, using the tools of a teacher (specification, lesson plan, etc.) and learning to talk as a teacher (recognizing the values, rules, discourse).

Final thoughts from Theresa on working with pre-service students

My previous role as a teacher educator working with in-service teachers, was one that required an approach that supported individuals who were not only managing busy teaching schedules and wider responsibilities as employed teachers, but were immersed in their teacher identity from day one of the course (see Figure 13.1). As a teacher educator with PGCE students attending university full time, there is a sense of them developing their teacher identity, acknowledging how theory is then put into practice, of them trying out for the very first time how to teach, have a voice and presence, command respect from student groups, plan and assess effectively for individual needs. I am in constant conversations about their teaching and placement developments through an online reflective blog and discussions with their subject mentors. The student group foster a 'community of practice' blog to share 'incidents' both critical and those all-important successes, feelings of elation as well as devastation when things may not have gone to plan. The most privileged part of my current role is the nurturing and cultivation of these new teachers in finding their teacher identities; how to manage working relationships and communication processes with placement mentors and colleagues and then presenting themselves in job applications and interviews.

Summary

Our starting points have been our involvement with the distinct entities of 'quality' and 'teacher education' observations. We hope to have illustrated some of the ways in which our professional identities have been variously developed and constructed by our observation experiences. In collaborating on this chapter, the model (tentatively explored) that emerged for us both reflected how the two roles (of quality monitor and teacher educator observer) are merging with the latest (ETF) professional standards. The model (depicted below) also seeks to illustrate what we observe in our work: the ever-increasing requirements for new student teachers to be 'ready' to teach from day one and be prepared within their probationary year (first year post teacher education qualification) to be observed on numerous occasions, sometimes up to a further eight times.

So how is our model (Figure 13.2) evolving and moving us forward? The challenges we face are linked to the 'judgmental' versus the 'developmental' role of the observation process. Our value base is one of developing individuals to be the best they can be whilst working within the Education and Training Foundation standards (2014). In the trainees' first probationary year, the goal from the organization's perspective is likely to revolve around contribution to high grade outcomes (both student success rate and, in quality and inspection terms, strong observation profile), i.e. in a graded quality assurance process, to ensure they achieve a minimum of Grade 2 (Ofsted, 2015 'Good'); anything less than that could mean that they may not be employed beyond their probation.

To conclude, we would recognize that there is a desire to embrace a new order in the observation process, one that moves away from a 'quality' model of individual performance to a more developmental approach that can foster (O'Leary 2014) the sharing of practice and learning from each other. It is this approach that best supports our student teachers in entering employment as it provides safe spaces for them to share their learning as teachers. The tension

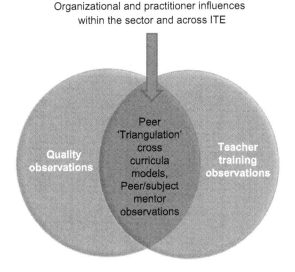

Figure 13.2 Emerging model of both quality and teacher training observations

between the developmental and quality observer roles has been and will continue to be demanding. But in keeping with O'Leary's (2013) philosophy (as a predicted framework for colleges), the observation of teaching, learning and assessment should remain: 'professionally enriching' and that it is 'most effective . . . when it prioritises the growth of tutors' professional learning and skills and empowers them to become active agents in the construction of their own professional identity, learning and development' (O'Leary, 2013: 9).

References

Ball, S. (2002) *Teachers' lives and careers*. East Sussex: Routledge Falmer Press.
Ball, S. (2010) The teacher's soul and the terrors of performativity. Available at: www.researchgate.net/profile/Stephen_Ball6/publication/232916965.pdf Accessed 25th October 2015.
Bronfenbrenner, U. (1979) *The ecology of human development: Experiments by nature and design*. Cambridge: Harvard University Press.
Coffield, F. and Edward, S. (2009) 'Rolling out "good", "best" and "excellent" practice: What next? Perfect practice?' *British Educational Research Journal*, 35(3): 371–390.
Education and Training Foundation (2014) Professional standards for teachers and trainers-England. Available at: www.et-foundation.co.uk/supporting/support-practitioners/professional-standards/ Accessed 15th November 2016.
Engeström, Y. (1987) Learning by expanding: An activity-theoretical approach to developmental research. Available at: http://lchc.ucsd.edu/MCA/Paper/Engestrom/expanding/toc.htm Accessed 8th October 2013.

Engeström, Y. (2001) 'Expansive learning at work: Toward an activity theoretical reconceptualization.' *Journal of Education and Work*, 14(1): 133–156.

Exley, S. (2015) Don't stop grading lesson observations, Ofsted tells providers. Times Educational Supplement. Available at: www.tes.com/news/further-education/breaking-news/dont-stop-grading-lesson-observations-ofsted-tells-providers Accessed 30th January 2017.

Further Education National Training Organisation (FENTO) (2001) Standards for teaching and supporting learning in further education in England and Wales. Available at: http://dera.ioe.ac.uk/4191/1/Standards%2520for%2520teaching%2520and%2520supporting%2520learning%2520in%2520%2520FE.pdf Accessed 15th June 2017.

Gleeson, D., Hughes, J., O'Leary, M. and Smith, R. (2015) 'The state of professional practice and policy in the English further education system: A view from below.' *Research in Post-Compulsory Education*, 20(1): 78–95, http://dx.doi.org/10.1080/13596748.2015.993877

Jackson, N. (ND) Lifewide learning and education: An ecological perspective. Available at: www.normanjackson.co.uk/uploads/1/0/8/4/10842717/lifewide_learning_an_ecological_perspective.pdf Accessed 30th January 2017.

Jackson, N. (2017) 'An ecological perspective on exploring and exploration.' *Lifewide Education Magazine*, 26–32. Available at: www.lifewideeducation.uk/uploads/1/3/5/4/13542890/lifewide_magazine_18.pdf

Lave, J. and Wenger, E. (1991) *Situated learning: Legitimate peripheral participation*. Cambridge: Cambridge University Press.

Lave, J. and Wenger, E. (1999) 'Learning and pedagogy in communities of practice' pp. 21–33 in Leach, S. and Moon, B. (eds.) *Learners and Pedagogy*. London: Paul Hill Chapman.

McLuhan, M. (1962) *The Gutenberg galaxy: The making of typographic man*. London: Routledge and Kegan Paul.

Ofsted (2015) Handbook for the Inspection of Further Education and Skills. January 2015, No. 120061. Available at: www.gov.uk/government/publications/handbook-for-the-inspection-of-further-education-and-skills-from-september-2012. Accessed: 13th December 2017.

O'Leary, M. (2013) Developing a national framework for the effective use of lesson observation in further education. *Project Report for UCU*. Available at: www.ucu.org.uk/media/6714/Developing-a-national-framework-for-the-effective-use-of-lesson-observation-in-FE-Dr-Matt-OLeary-Nov-13/pdf/ucu_lessonobsproject_nov13.pdf Accessed 31st May 2017.

O'Leary, M. (2014) *Classroom observation: A guide to the effective observation of teaching and learning*. Oxon: Routledge.

O'Leary, M. (ed.) (2016) 'Reclaiming lesson observation as a tool for teacher learning introduction' pp. 1–9 in *Reclaiming lesson observation: Supporting excellence in teacher learning*. London: Routledge.

Sachs, J. (2001) 'Teacher professional identity: Competing discourses, competing outcomes.' *Journal of Educational Policy*, 16(2), 149–161.

Smith, R. and O'Leary, M. (2013) 'New public management in an age of austerity: Knowledge and experience in further education.' *Journal of Educational Administration and History*, 45(3): 244–266.

Taylor, L. (2016) 'Somewhere over the rainbow: Transitioning from performative to informative models of observation' pp. 13–24 in O'Leary, M. (ed.) *Reclaiming lesson observation: Supporting excellence in teacher learning*. London: Routledge.

Van Lier, L. (2004) *The ecology and semiotics of language learning: A sociocultural perspective*. Boston: Kluwer Academic

Warford, M. K. (2011) 'The zone of proximal teacher development.' *Teachers and Teacher Education*, 27: 252–258.

Wright, V., Loughlin, T. and Hall, V. (2017) 'Lesson observation and feedback in relation to the developing identity of student teachers.' *TEAN Journal*, 9(1), 100–111.

Chapter 14

Subverting the pseudo-science of inspection with research-informed practice and pedagogic principles
An ungraded approach to the evaluation of teachers

Matt O'Leary

Introduction

Few areas of practice have caused as much debate and discontent amongst teachers in colleges and schools in recent years as that of lesson observation, particularly graded observations and the way in which they have been used as summative assessments to rank teachers' classroom performance. Recent research in the field has recounted the normalisation of graded lesson observations over the last few decades, highlighting Ofsted's hegemonic influence and control over education policy and practice (e.g. O'Leary 2013; Gleeson et al. 2015). At the same time, they have been critiqued for embodying a pseudo-scientific approach to measuring performance, as well as giving rise to a range of counterproductive consequences that ultimately militate against professional learning and teacher improvement (e.g. Edgington 2016; O'Leary and Wood 2016).

Lesson observation has a longstanding association as a multi-purpose mechanism in education, playing an important role in the training, assessment and development of teachers throughout their careers. In recent years though, it has come to be viewed quite narrowly by policymakers, inspectors and employers in colleges and schools in England as an assessment tool for monitoring and measuring teacher performance. This policy position exemplifies a core maxim of the epistemology and methodology of neoliberal approaches to accountability and teacher improvement that have dominated the English education system over the last three decades. A maxim that attempts to measure all forms of human activity, epitomised in the oft-quoted saying that 'you can't manage what you can't measure', or, in this case, 'you can't improve what you can't measure' (McKinsey and Company 2007: 38).

Graded lesson observations exemplify what Ball (2012) refers to as the neoliberal 'moral technologies' used to engender a culture of institutional performativity. Ball describes performativity as 'a form of hands-off management that uses comparisons and judgements in place of interventions and direction' (p. 31). Whilst comparisons and judgements are certainly inherent to graded observations, they are also a form of intervention as they involve observing teachers' practice and decisions being made about the professional capabilities of those teachers based on what the observer witnesses during the observed lesson. There are parallels here to the French philosopher Michel Foucault's discussion of the 'examination'.

Foucault (1977: 184) uses the notion of the 'examination' to exemplify a mechanism that measures performance through the 'power of normalisation', which 'imposes homogeneity but individualises by making it possible to measure gaps'. In this case, the 'homogeneity' referred to by Foucault is regulated by the need for observed lessons to conform to specific assessment criteria of what constitutes good or effective practice, along with the inclusion of the thematic priorities of others' agendas (in recent years English education policy has prioritised specific areas such as: embedding English and maths, equality and diversity and 'safeguarding' into observed lessons). Those that are able to demonstrate this normalised practice are deemed members of a homogenous community, whereas those outliers whose assessed performances reveal 'gaps' are required to undergo additional training and (re)education to ensure that they meet the appropriate standards when they are next observed. But this so-called process of standardisation is a spurious one that oversimplifies the complexity of teaching and teachers' work as others have argued (e.g. O'Leary and Wood 2016). It leads to a reductive view of the process of teaching, which assumes that all aspects of classroom practice can be uniformly identified, categorised and assessed in predictable and proportionate ways. This same reductive view is enshrined in Ofsted's inspection framework.

Contextual background to the inspection

Unlike the vast majority of other university ITE providers in England, the post-compulsory education (PCE) department at the University of Wolverhampton (UoW) did not use graded observations on its programmes. The underlying rationale for adopting an ungraded approach to the assessment of its student teachers did not emerge arbitrarily but was developed collaboratively over a sustained period of time. This approach was underpinned by a core set of principles and shared understandings about the purpose and value of the PCE ITE programmes, as well as being informed by empirical research into the use and impact of lesson observations in the further education (FE) sector and ongoing discussions with its partners and student teachers. For those readers who may not be familiar with the policy landscape at that time, it is important to stress that the UoW's approach was considered as maverick by some as it went against the grain of normalised models of observation. The team was therefore aware that the PCE programme would be subjected to heightened scrutiny and interrogation by Ofsted when it was announced that all of the UoW's ITE programmes were to be inspected in March 2013, especially given that both its primary and secondary programmes used graded observations.

The tone was set from the moment the inspection team arrived on the first day. The lead inspector's opening gambit was to ask the PCE management team to rate the quality of its programmes against Ofsted's 4-point scale.[1] Visibly disgruntled that the team had chosen not to apply this grading scale in its self-evaluation document (SED),[2] despite the fact that providers were not obliged to do so, the lead inspector seemed determined to assert his authority from the outset and in so doing echoed the McKinsey report maxim referred to earlier when he commented that he found it 'extremely difficult to demonstrate evidence of progress' without using some kind of numerical scale. So this inevitably begs the question, why did the partnership decide to go against the grain and adopt this stance?

It is important to emphasise that resistance to embracing Ofsted's 'dominant discourses' (Foucault 1980) and normalised practice was not based on any wilful refusal to comply or obey their authority as the regulators of quality for ITE provision, but driven by more fundamental concerns regarding the legitimacy and reliability of Ofsted's assessment framework and the subsequent impact of that on teachers in training. Needless to say the partnership's epistemological and methodological positioning did not sit easily with the inspection team as it presented them with certain challenges that they were unaccustomed to.

Evaluating the 'performance' of teachers

It was a strongly held view across the partnership that the use of a metrics-based approach was neither the most appropriate nor the most effective means of fostering student teachers' development, nor indeed of measuring the level of performance required for them to meet the 'pass' threshold criteria of its programmes. The partnership staff comprised largely experienced teacher educators who were comfortable and confident of being able to make judgements about the progress and performance of their students against the pass/fail assessment framework used on the programmes. In some ways this might be considered akin to the notion of 'fitness to practise' used by other professions such as health, though not in the form of a reductive checklist of a set of competences to be crudely evidenced during observations as was the case with the application of observation assessment criteria in most institutions. Instead, the partnership's criteria were used more as a shared frame of reference of multi-layered elements that could be drawn on flexibly and interpreted in a contextually specific way to capture the holistic richness of professional practice. In short, the assessment criteria sought to encapsulate the core knowledge, skills, behaviours and attitudes expected of these student teachers to demonstrate their professional capabilities to practise as independent teachers.

This 'fitness to practise' was initially mapped against the professional standards in use at the time in the FE sector (LLUK 2006) and subsequently against the Education and Training Foundation's (ETF) revised standards (ETF 2014). As the PCE partnership had been actively engaged with these standards through year-on-year collaborative work to revise and refine their application to its ITE programmes, a shared ownership of the assessment by those working on the programme had emerged over time and was subject to ongoing refinement. In contrast, it was not felt that the Ofsted 4-point scale could be applied with the same rigour, reliability and meaningfulness to assess students' attainment as the partnership's existing assessment framework and criteria, whereby students were either judged to have satisfied the criteria or not. Whilst all those teacher educators working on the programmes were clear as to what constituted a pass/fail and were confident in applying these criteria with a high degree of accuracy and consistency, the same could not be said about the interpretation and application of Ofsted's 4-point scale. There were three key reasons as to why this was the case and why the partnership was determined to defend its position on this during the inspection.

First, the criteria used to assess student teachers on its programmes were the product of years of intense, collaborative work of those teacher educators, during the course of which those involved had crafted and taken ownership of the criteria in such a way that they were able to engage with and apply the criteria meaningfully. Second, Ofsted's 4-point scale was/is purely a ranking system rather than an assessment framework with an accompanying set of contextualised criteria. What this meant in practical terms was that specific grade descriptors were so generic and vague to be worthless as an assessment tool, thus increasing the level of observer subjectivity. And third, a growing trend was beginning to emerge across the sector of links made between the grades awarded during observations and evaluative judgements of the professional competence and performance of individuals per se. Or to put it more simply, teachers were being labelled as 'grade 1/2/3/4' teachers, despite claims by institutions that it was the lesson that was being graded and not the individual. Witnessing the impact of such practice on experienced practitioners' professional identity and self-esteem, this was something that the partnership was mindful of not subjecting its student teachers to so early on in their careers.

In their study into the grading of student teachers on teaching practice placements in Scotland, Cope et al. (2003: 682) found that the success of such practice depended on 'a clearly reliable and valid system of assessment of the practice of teaching' and concluded that 'the evidence available suggests that this does not currently exist'. This is not a phenomenon specific to observation as a method of assessment, but reflects widely held beliefs among key researchers in the field of assessment such as Gipps (1994: 167), who argued three decades ago that 'assessment is not an exact science and we must stop presenting it as such.' The danger, of course, is that the inherent limitations of practice such as numerically grading performance are often overlooked and the resulting judgements are given far more weight and authority than they can realistically claim to have or indeed deserve. Thus one of the consequences of applying systems like graded observations is that the grade carries with it an absolutist judgement about the individual teacher's classroom competence and performance that belies the isolated and episodic nature of the observation itself. In the case of performance management observations that typically occur on an annual basis in most FE providers, this means that teachers carry with them the label of their allocated grade for at least a year until they are observed again, as evidenced in findings from the largest study into lesson observation in FE and the English education system in recent years (UCU 2013).

Prioritising teacher development

The UoW's ITE programmes were/are built on a developmental philosophy in which the student teacher's growth was/is prioritised. Staff working on the programmes were/are committed to helping their students to develop their pedagogic skills and subject knowledge base. It was therefore their belief that judging them against a performative, numerical grading scale of 1–4 would compromise that commitment and jeopardise the supportive focus of the teacher educator and mentor's relationship with their students. The partnership also benefited from being involved in and discussing the latest research into lesson observation as one of the university members of staff specialised in this particular area.

As mentioned above, recent research into the use of graded observation in FE revealed how it had become normalised as a performative tool of managerialist systems fixated with attempting to measure teacher performance rather than actually improving it. The teacher educators and mentors in the PCE partnership saw their primary responsibility as that of helping to nurture their student teachers as effective practitioners rather than having to rank their performance according to a series of loaded labels (i.e. 'outstanding', 'inadequate', etc.) that were principally designed to satisfy the needs of external agencies such as Ofsted within the marketised FE landscape. This emphasis on measuring teacher performance was also seen as responsible for what Ball (2003) refers to as 'inauthenticity' in teacher behaviour and classroom performance during assessed observations. This is typically manifested in the delivery of the rehearsed or showcase lesson as the high stakes nature of such observations results in a reluctance to want to take risks for fear of being given a low grade. Teachers are thus aware of the need to 'play the game', which can result in them following a prescriptive template of 'good practice' during assessed observations. Yet being prepared to experiment with new ways of doing things in the classroom and taking risks in one's teaching is widely acknowledged as an important constituent of the development of both the novice and experienced teacher (e.g. IfL 2012).

Furthermore, findings from two separate studies on observation in FE revealed some of the distorting and counterproductive consequences of grading on in-service teachers' identity and professionalism (e.g. O'Leary 2013; UCU 2013). Staff in the PCE partnership at the UoW, many of whom were FE teachers themselves, were determined to protect their student teachers from such consequences during their time on the programme. This did not mean, however, that they avoided discussing the practice of grading teacher performance with them or confronting some of the challenging themes and issues associated with it. On the contrary, this was a topic that was addressed explicitly through professional development modules and wider discussions about assessment and professionalism as part of the ongoing critically reflective dialogues that occurred between teacher educators, mentors and students throughout the programme.

Developing critically reflective teachers

The university's PCE ITE programmes were/are underpinned by the notion of critical reflection. Brookfield (1995) argues that what makes critically reflective teaching 'critical' is an understanding of the concept of power in a wider socio-educational context and recognition of the hegemonic assumptions that influence and shape a teacher's practices. The PCE partnership viewed the use of graded observations as an example of one such hegemonic assumption. Thus the purported outcomes of graded observations (i.e. improving the quality of teaching and learning, promoting a culture of continuous improvement amongst staff, etc.) were not necessarily the actual outcomes as experienced by those involved in the observation process itself. Added to this was the thorny issue of measurement.

During the inspection, it became apparent that the PCE partnership's ungraded approach was problematic for Ofsted. When the lead inspector was directly asked at a feedback meeting with the partnership if the use of a grading scale was considered an obligatory element of being able to measure teachers' progress and attainment, he categorically stated that was not the case nor did Ofsted prescribe such policy. However, this was subsequently contradicted in the final report with the statement that as the partnership did not grade, it was considered 'difficult to measure student progress from year to year or the value that the training added in each cohort'. In spite of the presentation of a wealth of interwoven sources of qualitative evidence (e.g. tutor/mentor/peer evaluations, self-evaluations, integrated action/development plans, critically reflective accounts) illustrating these student teachers' journeys throughout their programmes of study, the inspection team was reluctant and/or even unable to conceptualise the notion of improvement unless the outcome was expressed in the form of a number. One possible explanation for this may be because reading such qualitative accounts is more time consuming and much less straightforward than relying on the reductive simplicity of allocating a number to something, however spurious that number might be. Another explanation may be that the ontological, epistemological and methodological positioning of the inspectorate's assessment framework predisposes it to a conceptual intransigence when it comes to evaluating teaching. This reveals the extent to which 'managerialist positivism' (Smith and O'Leary 2013) has become an orthodoxy and Ofsted its agent of enforcement. Notwithstanding these challenges, the partnership team was resolute in defending its practice and emphasised how the broad range of evidence captured in the combination of formative and summative assessments provided a rich tapestry of these student teachers' progress and attainment throughout the programme and ultimately one that was more meaningful than the allocation of a reductive number.

Developments since the inspection

In the year following the inspection, Ofsted announced a policy shift, recommending the discontinuation of the grading of individual lessons observed during inspections (Cladingbowl 2014). I was directly involved in discussions with Ofsted's National Director for Schools at that time, Michael Cladingbowl, about this policy shift prior to its implementation. A position paper written by the Ofsted Director for Schools explained the rationale for the change in policy:

> Like many others, I have strong views about inspection and the role of inspector observation in it. I believe, for example, that inspectors must always visit classrooms and see teachers and children working. Classrooms, after all, are where the main business of a school is transacted. It is also important to remember that we can give a different grade for teaching than we do for overall achievement, particularly where a school is improving but test or examination results have not caught up. But none of this means that inspectors need to ascribe a numerical grade to the teaching they see in each classroom they visit. Nor does it mean aggregating individual teaching grades to arrive at an overall view of teaching. Far from it. Evaluating teaching in a school should include looking across a range of children's work.
>
> (Cladingbowl 2014: 2)

There is no doubt that Ofsted's decision to remove grading from individual observations during inspections was met with widespread approval by teachers. This reaction was unsurprising given how graded observations had become one of the most controversial areas of practice for the profession in recent years (e.g. O'Leary and Brooks 2014). Yet the timing of Ofsted's shift in position was interesting, as it arguably occurred at a point when the inspectorate was eager to improve its public image by engaging more with the teaching profession in the wake of growing criticism of its credibility and legitimacy as a regulator of quality and standards in colleges and schools from the profession itself and even the Secretary of State for Education at the time.

Three years have passed since this shift in policy, but the extent to which it has led to the kind of substantive change in observation practice in colleges and schools anticipated by the profession remains unclear and unconvincing to date. Whilst there have been some encouraging developments reported across sectors (e.g. O'Leary 2016), many teachers maintain that Ofsted's decision to remove grading has failed to result in a meaningful shift in the mind-sets of senior managers and leaders as to the underlying use(s) and purpose(s) of observation, reinforcing the idea that its use as a form of summative assessment is a dominant, deeply engrained practice that has proven resistant to change. But given the popularity of Ofsted's policy shift and mounting research evidence in the field of observation highlighting the shortcomings of performative approaches, it begs the question as to why change has not happened more quickly and on a wider scale.

Changing thinking and practice that has become normalised and engrained over decades does not happen overnight and invariably takes a long time. And sometimes no matter how compelling the evidence presented, some people remain resistant to change. There are those who have become institutionalised into associating observation with a performance ranking exercise, regardless of the purpose or approach. They are either unable and/or unwilling to conceptualise the use of observation outside of a performative context and see an umbilical link between classroom performance and attempts to measure it. Thus simply asking observers not to grade lessons any more without addressing the more fundamental issue of how they conceptualise and carry out their role in practice becomes little more than a superficial change.

As I made clear to Ofsted's Director in our discussions at the time, a change in policy does not necessarily equate to a change in practice and/or thinking. It was clear to me that this change in positioning had not been thought through carefully by Ofsted and was, in reality, little more than window dressing as well as an attempt to placate a disgruntled profession. Furthermore, it remains a policy decision that is fraught with inconsistencies and contradictions.

Despite declaring graded observations as no longer being fit for purpose in inspections, Ofsted continues to grade teaching, learning and assessment as a whole against its 4-point scale in inspections. Surely if the grading of individual lessons has been deemed unnecessary and inadequate, why should it be any different for making an overall judgement? In a similar vein, whilst it defends its decision to scrap graded observations from inspections, when asked what its stance is on those institutions that continue to grade, it contends that senior managers and leaders in colleges/schools are free to determine their own policies and it is not in Ofsted's remit to tell them what (not) to do. It is ironic but equally contradictory that an agency that has played such a central role in shaping the education policy agenda over the last twenty-five years should revert to adopting a position of neutrality on this matter. Such a position suggests a lack of clarity and confusion as to its role and remit. It cannot be denied that Ofsted has had an indelible impact on the discourse and cultures of teaching and learning in colleges and schools since the 1990s but what has become apparent is that its inspection methodology is out of touch with what we know about capturing and promoting effective teaching and learning.

Notes

1 The 4-point scale used for Ofsted inspections at the time was as follows: 1 = outstanding; 2 = good; 3 = satisfactory; 4 = inadequate.

2 The self-evaluation document (SED) was a self-assessment report that all ITE providers were required to complete and submit to Ofsted at the end of each year. It represented an important source of evidence and reference tool for the inspection team before and during the inspection.

References

Ball, S. J. (2003) The teacher's soul and the terrors of performativity. *Journal of Education Policy*, 18(2), pp. 215–228.

Ball, S. J. (2012) *Global Education Inc.: New Policy Networks and the Neo-Liberal Imaginary*. London: Routledge.

Brookfield, S. D. (1995) *Becoming a Critically Reflective Teacher*. San Francisco, CA: Jossey-Bass.

Cladingbowl, M. (2014) *Why I Want to Try Inspecting without Grading Teaching in Each Individual Lesson*, June 2014, No. 140101, Ofsted. Available at: www.ofsted.gov.uk/resources/why-i-want-try-inspecting-without-grading-teaching-each-individual-lesson Accessed 23/8/2016.

Cope, P., Bruce, A., McNally, J. and Wilson, G. (2003) Grading the practice of teaching: An unholy union of incompatibles. *Assessment & Evaluation in Higher Education*, 28(6), pp. 673–684.

Edgington, U. M. (2016) Performativity and the power of shame: Lesson observations, emotional labour and professional habitus. *Sociological Research Online*, 21(1), 11. Available at: www.socresonline.org.uk/21/1/11.html. Accessed 27/5/2017.

Education and Training Foundation (ETF) (2014) *Professional Standards for Teachers and Trainers in Education and Training – England*. Available at: www.et-foundation.co.uk/wp-content/uploads/2014/05/4991-Prof-standards-A4_4-2.pdf. Accessed 03/11/2016.

Foucault, M. (1977) *Discipline and Punish: The Birth of the Prison*. Harmondsworth: Penguin.

Foucault, M. (1980) *Power/Knowledge – Selected Interviews and Other Writings 1972–1977*. Brighton: The Harvester Press.

Gipps, C. (1994) *Beyond Testing: Towards a Theory of Educational Assessment*. London: Falmer Press.

Gleeson, D., Hughes, J., O'Leary, M. and Smith, R. (2015) The state of professional practice and policy in the English further education system: A view from below. *Research in Post-Compulsory Education*, 20(1), pp. 78–95.

Institute for Learning (2012) *Leading learning and letting go: Building expansive learning environments in FE*. London: Institute for Learning.

Lifelong Learning UK (LLUK) (2006) *New Overarching Professional Standards for Teachers, Tutors and Trainers in the Lifelong Learning Sector*. London: LLUK.

McKinsey & Company (2007) *How the World's Best Performing School Systems Come Out on Top*. Available at: www.mckinsey.com/clientservice/socialsector/resources/pdf/Worlds_School_Systems_Final.pdf. Accessed 10/12/16.

O'Leary, M. (2013) Surveillance, performativity and normalised practice: The use and impact of graded lesson observations in Further Education Colleges. *Journal of Further and Higher Education*, 37(5), pp. 694–714.

O'Leary, M. (Ed) (2016) *Reclaiming Lesson Observation: Supporting Excellence in Teacher Learning*. Abingdon: Routledge.

O'Leary, M. and Brooks, V. (2014) Raising the stakes: Classroom observation in the further education sector. *Professional Development in Education*, 40(4), pp. 530–545.

O'Leary, M. and Wood, P. (2016) Performance over professional learning and the complexity puzzle: Lesson observation in England's further education sector. *Professional Development in Education*, 43(4), pp. 573–591.

Smith, R. and O'Leary, M. (2013) New public management in an age of austerity: Knowledge and experience in further education. *Journal of Educational Administration and History*, 45(3), pp. 244–266.

University and College Union (UCU) (2013) *Developing a National Framework for the Effective Use of Lesson Observation in Further Education*. Project report, November 2013. Available at: www.ucu.org.uk/7105. Accessed 11/12/2016.

Chapter 15

Teaching an old dog new tricks
Developing instructor and teacher identities in a military context: a conversation

Steve Coleby and Stuart Smith

The purpose of this chapter is to reflect the experiences of teacher/instructor and instructor/teacher leaders (formally and informally) at a potentially important moment in the development of training and education within the military context, here the RAF. The main setting for the work discussed is the Defence School of Aeronautical Engineering at RAF Cosford. Here over an extended period both initiatives from the instructors themselves and the larger organization and a productive collaboration with a local university (Wolverhampton) has raised the profile of the 'teacher trade' with more instructors getting externally recognized qualifications and the attendant 'conversations' that this implies. Though also prompted by the attentions of Ofsted, this has resulted in an almost unprecedented way in a heightened interest in matters pedagogical and in the commitment of various individuals across the organization to exploring the issue of 'instructor development' across the trajectory of a five-year 'tour'. These 'creative conversations' are not without difficulties as this chapter will show: the default remains a 'command' model of education where 'teaching' often seems synonymous with 'telling'. However, in the period we've recently lived through across the sector, this is a broadly familiar context.

The chapter takes the form of a conversation between two committed teachers and teacher educators who represent different ranks and experience but each offer both a critique of the prevailing situation and an appreciation of the value of developing more effective instructor identities. The dialogue works through a number of 'takes':

Who do you think you are?

STU: I am currently a Flight Lieutenant in the Royal Air Force and my 'branch' is education. I am nominally an educator.

STEVE: One may be forgiven for not associating the Royal Air Force (RAF) with an academic or educational environment with. It is for example commonplace to hear when I am asked the question "What is it that you do?" the response; "Oh you're in the RAF, are you a pilot?"

I am not a pilot. An engineer once told me "You can teach a monkey how to fly, but you can't teach them how to fix a plane!" By trade I was trained as an Avionics Technician through an Advanced Modern Apprenticeship Scheme, spending many years working on Front Line Aircraft in every corner of the globe, in just about every condition and environment imaginable. This story really starts though when I was promoted and 'moved' into an Instructor 'role'.

Tell us a little more about the context

STEVE: This is a very different account of teaching observations made in the largest Aeronautical Engineering environment in the country: in fact, one so well regarded it now trains Armed Forces Engineers from the Middle East with the potential in the near future of other European countries' forces too. It is also a context with its own traditions and at times we can appear to be speaking our own language. This is a guarded language by and large, protected by steel barbed-wire fences and a steely-eyed armed guard at our main gates. One of these 'guarded' terms, and the focus of this piece, is 'instructor'.

'Instructor' is usually used to identify a specific type of teaching work directed at RAF 'folk' (engineers, chefs, administrative staff, regiment, intelligence branches, police though perhaps not pilots!). The RAF instructor is employed solely on their prior experience and relevance to a specific trade, suggesting that this 'teaching work' is barely considered. Like the government's Teach Direct scheme, if you 'know' it you can obviously teach it.

STU: When I first started my educational journey reflection was not something that I had considered, practiced or understood but I jumped in feet first. This was a truly enlightening experience which has sent me on my journey to BA (Hons) and now a piece of work for a book, unimaginable when I started my RAF career. It begs the question: "how did that happen?". I often ask myself and the answer is both infinitely complex and stunningly simple. In a way this is what my research and subsequent work in the past year has been moving towards, in fact the whole process of becoming a critically reflective practitioner. I recall the first piece of work:

The conversation was taking place on a wet and windy day in the north of Scotland, it was an Royal Air Force base and I had just completed my first teaching lesson. One of my old friends and a young mechanic had walked with me to the crew-room for a well-deserved brew, the bitter cold of the beginning of winter meant we were not hanging around. The conversation went "you are very good at this teaching stuff, have you been doing it long?" followed be me informing them that this was my first lesson solo (not something I had planned to inform the students). They both said at the same time "you should consider this as a career, best teaching I have received."

I had never considered this but this conversation did echo in my mind for some months. Was I really cut out to be a teacher? Could I actually do the job well? This role was in the versions I had accumulated through my 'education', daunting, as people act on your very word and your word is the gospel (in some cases).

Dickens captures this version well in *Hard Times*:

> The speaker, and the schoolmaster, and the third grown person present, all backed a little, and swept with their eyes the inclined plane of little vessels then and there arranged in order, ready to have imperial gallons of facts poured into them until they were full to the brim.
> (Dickens, 1995: 4)

I have grown from low-achieving school student, to airman in the Royal Air Force, to Instructor, to Training Officer and now today, teacher, educator, instructor. This why I feel I can, with some credibility discuss the 'idea' of 'the instructor' and the creation and development of 'them', because this word needs making flesh, within a military context. It would seem from a distance that there is an expectation that the military will develop the perfect teacher with discipline already in abundance and a sound engineering background:

What are the issues then?

STU: The interesting part of this is that we may well have the best teachers among our engineers at Cosford, but we just don't know. We do have a highly motivated set of engineers and in some the potential to be very good teachers. This is unfortunately where we meet an *impasse* as we do not identify the best nor unlock the potential they may possess. In fact I believe we stifle the ability for them to break out and improve. This is no different to many companies or agencies or educational establishments but it does present a basic problem to those looking to improve the quality of our 'instruction'. Teaching capacity is an investment, it is not taught in weeks but developed with experience and time.

The fact is we have some very talented people and we do not allow them to grow. We have very good engineers from numerous trades and we require them to be in the college for a five-year tour. This should allow them to develop the necessary skills and use their first line (aircraft) experience to enrich the training, but only if we allow them to fully explore these opportunities. We do not explore the depth of their desire or motivation to become a teacher/instructor, thinking instead of performance indicators and the demands of the 'processing' of recruits.

Nevertheless I would suggest that this is in fact how many people fall into teaching, particularly in vocational areas. My experience is that a large percentage move onto teaching after gaining the enrichment of life and work in whatever field they chose and teaching appeared.

STEVE: The RAF of course has an inherent interest in providing "Excellent" training. "Respect, Integrity, Service and Excellence" form the core ethos of the RAF drilled into its personnel from their first inspirational view of the recruitment video to their last day of active service. Excellence in all we do; therefore the way in which we educate should be no different.

Context though in this case has much more purchase than policy. The reality of what these young trainee engineers may be expected to do is daunting: responsibility for the maintenance and upkeep of multi-million pound aircraft (to look at it materialistically) and the safety of the pilot, navigator or hundreds of personnel boarded on the large transport aircraft focuses the mind rather. Keeping the aircraft in the sky with the ability to land safely is the overall goal. Forget not of course that intertwined somewhat ironically with safety, is the successful ability to be able to drop some precision weapons exactly when and where they are needed. Travelling at Mach 1 at 30,000ft dropping a bomb onto a moving target takes some complicated calculations, and of course some of these young engineers will soon be tasked to maintain and functionally test these systems to ensure that when needed, they work. The ability to destroy the enemy with such impressive technological aids is the side of the RAF that does not appear all too often in the recruitment videos.

When something goes wrong with an RAF aircraft, it is big news. From the tragic loss of the life on-board the Nimrod aircraft in 2006, to the two recent fatal Red Arrow Hawk aircraft incidents failure never goes unnoticed. When the RAF has an accident, it is global news. Therefore it must be blatant logic to train these engineers as effectively as possible to prevent events like the aforementioned recurring. It must surely be of critical importance, and of course, interest.

How do you train instructors then?

STEVE: I was sent to RAF Cosford to teach new RAF engineers the basics of working on aircraft. Those readers who have ever fixed a car using a Hayne's Manual may have a vague idea of just how complex aircraft engineering could be. There is the mind-numbing extrapolation and understanding of engineering policies and governance, the in-depth levels and quantities of aircraft documentation and the control and use of hand tools before the young engineer is even allowed anywhere near an aircraft: topped off with the obligatory multiple choice exam that must also be passed before progression. From there it is a basic understanding of mechanical and avionics systems, before progressing on to work on live, running aircraft and their immediate pre- and post-servicing. (Very much like a daily MOT).

The content of the course that is delivered realistically should not be news to any instructor employed to teach it. As previously mentioned; an instructor is taken on by previous experience just like at a secondary school. This is however where problem number one reveals itself.

STU: So how do we develop this individual to become the teacher that will deliver this enriched and vitally important training, given that the military is an inherently dangerous place and the training is vital to save lives? You may think that we would give instructor training that would replicate a system similar to that of an educational organization, and that this training would be in high demand by the newly promoted and posted engineers. The simple answer is *no*. We give them a few weeks training and throw then in the deep end (without a buoyancy aid!). We give them some rudimentary training that covers the basics such as 'pose-pause-pounce'[1] a process for delivering a question to the students, PowerPoint as a visual aid and documentation that stands as tall as the instructor. And despite the protestations of excellence, this applies seemingly to the trained not the trainer: in my recent study a manager stated "The RAF wants 60% pass rate, not excellence", and "it's not our job to raise standards".

These are the kinds of barriers to improvement seen also elsewhere: achievement is defined by who passes the test, the trainees feel that they are fully prepared and the engineer-educator feels that attempts to genuinely raise standards are futile in the face of merely statistical understandings of 'quality'. This is a carrot guarded by a stick motivationally speaking.

STEVE: It is a mandatory pre-requisite that the instructors employed are experienced in the trade that they will be expected to deliver. Consideration however of the specific character or extent of the experience appears to have not been given. There are those who have worked on helicopter fleets and never touched a fast jet since their own training. There are those on fast jets who have never touched a helicopter since their training. There are those who have only worked on large transport aircraft and never touched a fast jet or a helicopter. Then there are those who have worked in maintenance bays and never touched any type of aircraft. There are newly promoted individuals (the current minimum rank to be an instructor is Corporal) and there are individuals who are coming to the end of their career.

I from experience can certainly testify that despite my service and skillset developed and enhanced through time and practice, I was ill-prepared to actually 'teach' these things to a classroom of sixteen teenagers or young adults. That requires something rather different. A facility to communicate or even a desire to teach might have been a better place to start. However, the RAF is clear at least that the instructor *role* is temporary. In the eyes of the military; the individual asked to fulfill this role puts on this identity lightly, their 'trade' remains foremost. In my case it was made clear that I was to see myself as an Avionics Technician on 'Instructional Duties'. This causes a few problems.

Inevitably there are those who want to be instructors, though none can join the RAF with the desire to be an instructor. This is where a noticeable divide exists between a teacher and an instructor. It is not a *trade* that can be applied for, likewise there is no academic pre-requisite required to fulfill this role. This of course is very unlike a primary school teacher for example who must hold as a minimum an Honours Degree, or a teacher in a Further Education college required to hold a Certificate in Education. The academic understandings of pedagogy, the proven ability to teach are unrecognized in favour of an experiential version of 'subject knowledge' supplemented by a Suitability Interview carried out by engineers.

STU: The shift of emphasis came with the support of a local H.E.I. which offered both in-service teacher education and the opportunity to 'top up' to a degree. As already stated we had experienced engineers from numerous trades who have an abundance of the newest and most relevant experience, also the drive and determination that new and keen individuals potentially bring. Then we get the academic system to 'whet their appetites' and provide meaningful civilian qualifications. However, allowing instructors to become trainee teachers both in and alongside their job roles has implications not only for the quality of discussion around a new idea; 'pedagogy'. And getting instructors to reflect, read and research means they are likely quite quickly to explore the here and now, considering for example Secondary school Deputy Head Joe Kirby's observation that "The understandable reaction of new trainee teachers to such ineffective ITT provision is frustration and resentment" (Kirby, 2013). As my own research revealed, instructors did not feel adequately trained to carry out the role and that they did not feel prepared to start to instruct. Even if we (the management of training at RAF Cosford) consider that the instructor is trained enough to carry out the role, this becomes a mandate at least to develop them further.

What about a longer term strategy for development?

STU: This is crucial as we then start to discover how we can develop the instructor.

The crux of the issue is a little more obvious and will need a complete rethink surrounding who delivers this training and how it is delivered. An engineer in the RAF, as in other aeronautical environments, works to a schedule that is strictly controlled so that what is being completed on the aircraft is carried out correctly every single time. The current system reflects this by instituting a procedure (based on PPP [Pose – Pause – Pounce] and powerpoint that ensures that the information will always be available to trainees and requires little training for the trainer. This model is a 'Command' model, a process model that acknowledges only transmission and 'channel noise' while ignoring 'mediation' or even participation: "it's not our job to raise standards".

Now I am not saying that the training is insufficient or does not meet the requirements; we have enough checks and balances in the system to make sure of that. But the training could be much more exciting and motivational to young individuals who are at the start of a career that will take them round the world and at times into danger and more efficiently focused on learning and thinking rather than processing and progressing. It is also important that we do not lose the valuable instructors who find time to invest in their teacher roles and are discovering how this system might be developed.

This is not a change to be initiated by student outcomes, which are unproblematic, but rather by the establishment of a teacher education ethos which values the identity 'teacher' and requires in return a commitment to reflection and research. Discovering in these 'acceptable' ways that instructors do not feel supported to perform the role or feel suitably trained created an opportunity for action but also a platform on which 'instruction', instructing' and instructor' could be discussed. My own research epitomized the potential in the response of one participant: "If there were time or sufficiently qualified instructor supervisors who could then coach the delivery staff then the monitoring would have a much more meaningful place within CPD, until this changes it is just a hoop to jump through once a year."

The instructors have to be motivated to further develop and given support and time to carry this out. It must not be seen as directed or required but an opportunity to be grasped.

STEVE: Prompted by movement above and below (Ofsted have taken a progressively greater interest) the RAF is further encouraging the development of their teaching methods and delivery styles. A multi-million pound project has been recently piped into the engineering training at Cosford as well as a push to enhance instructional teaching techniques to fall in line more with modern learning styles and "blended learning" techniques. Whilst the desire and vision is admirable, there is a glaringly obvious deficiency that threatens its impact: the instructors, who are seen by the larger project merely as a clear conduit.

The RAF will deliver their own bespoke training to ensure the instructor is suitably trained and prepared and this training may have little truck with 'modern learning styles and "blended learning" techniques'. Changing shape, length, acronyms (of course) and accreditation, the Defence Train The Trainer (DTTT) is the only mandatory course required before being allowed to teach the trainee engineers. Rather short (one may lament) at two-and-a-half weeks, the course is designed to give the instructors basic delivery, a basic understanding of learning styles and a bit of confidence in the classroom. There are invariably other local procedures that an instructor may be supported by, for example an instructor may be required to watch a lesson a specified quantity of times before delivering it. But there is no further training offered to assist the instructor in how to create an effective, conducive lesson. My own journey took me via a Certificate in Education to Qualified Teacher Status and a degree but not from the foundations provided by DTTT but rather by realizing there was so much I needed to know.

And the future?

STU: I currently work away from RAF Cosford and this has allowed me to get a perspective from a different area within the RAF. My work takes me to an aircrew environment of pilots, navigators, tactical directors and mission commanders. The aircrew at RAF Waddington, and indeed the whole of the Royal Air Force, have a completely different culture (I use culture deliberately as it is a culture that all within this 'fellowship' follow religiously) to development and professionalism. It stems from the initial training they receive and how this training is built upon to make sure we have suitably trained professionals within the service that work with civilian counterparts on a day-to-day basis. The observation of performance is the norm and happens on a regular basis (daily in some cases, monthly at least). It allows for the individual to be confident to complete their role, it also highlights what improvements can be made. No fear is apparent within the culture and for a transparent development portfolio to be produced. The process is simple and allows for a record of tasks completed and development opportunities to be highlighted, the benefits both up and down the chain of command allows for confidence for all in the role and the management of these roles.

With a lack of fear I have seen how competencies are developed and improved. This is encouraging since flying a multi-million pound aircraft around the world leaves limited opportunities to get it right.

The key is to create a culture in which development is focused on what people do and what they want to achieve. Without this, CPD can become a 'poison chalice'. To motivate people and not provide them with the opportunity to develop further and expect them to grow is complete madness, but we are relying on the good will of our instructors to carry this development banner. The cost of this type of development or tailoring the type and style of development is not negligible but the benefits are incalculable. Historically, when times are hard, the first thing that is removed is the training, which in itself is a symptom of the real problem. The opposite has to be the case. As we reduce in numbers we will need more suitably qualified personnel that have the capacity to deliver more and this sort of CPD will enhance these abilities. It will also give us appropriate growth on the initial investment. If the training is not right at the start of a journey it will never improve, in the way bad habits learnt during the time you learn to drive with your parents have a knock on effect later.

STEVE: The key is to see instructing for what it is, when effective: 'teaching' and to see teaching as a vital multi-departmental trade, which like any other trade needs to be 'learnt' (i.e. requires a substantial investment of time and expertise). Currently 'instructor' is a role either imposed or casually taken on. In all other contexts desire is assumed but here it must be fought for and that process starts with the kinds of professional conversations that go on in other trades and with a lesson observation regime that is developmental rather than a performance against a pre-populated checklist. These habits are hard to break and only by seeing them as such will proper progress be made.

STU: The military also have a habit of attaching rank with the standard or level of work required; in reality it may be the lowest rank that has the most ability. We consider that the instructor will just happen. Fundamental cultural change will allow for the full development and assist the improvement and encouragement of the people we rely on. It should not be pushed or expected and the voice of the instructor should not be ignored but listened to and reacted upon.

This situation is not at crisis at present but with the reducing cost and manpower we will have to be smarter in our support and training, not removing it in the name of continuous improvement. John F. Kennedy once said "The Chinese use two brush strokes to write the word 'crisis.' One brush stroke stands for danger; the other for opportunity. In a crisis, be aware of the danger – but recognize the opportunity."

(Juritzen, 2009: 10)

Note

1 This is the 'mirror-signal-manoeuvre' of military instruction. The instructor poses a question, waits for the appropriate interval and then picks on someone!

References

Juritzen, P. (2009) *Yes We Can: The Leadership Challenge in a Recession*. Saga Real: AS.
Dickens, C. (1995) *Hard Times*. London: Penguin Books.
Kirby, J. (2013) Why isn't our education system working? Accessed on 13/9/2017 at Pragmatic Education at https://pragmaticreform.wordpress.com/2013/04/27/system/

Chapter 16

Constellations of practice

Lou Mycroft and Kay Sidebottom

Posthumanism: "how newness enters the world" (Rushdie, 1991: 394)

Don't let the abstract put you off. Few of these concepts were familiar to us a few years ago. Although interested in research – and certainly pedagogically experimental – we defined ourselves after Gramsci as 'philosophers of praxis' (Mycroft, 2016) and, as busy teacher educators, had not ventured into any deeper waters of philosophical theory outside the pages of *Sophie's World* (Gaarder, 1995). We may have seen ourselves as pioneers of social purpose education (Mycroft and Weatherby, 2017) but we were confined within structures, systems and processes that we could not see or see beyond, even as they frustrated us. We were experiencing another Gramscian concept, "cultural hegemony" (Glassman, 2012), colluding in our own imprisonment by accepting the way things were. Brodkey (1996: 75) writes that, "The only way to fight a hegemonic discourse is to teach ourselves and others alternative ways of seeing the world." Our gaze opened up when we discovered a new lens: that of posthuman thinking.

Posthumanism moves beyond the social constructs of the Enlightenment, which gave so much to the world and at the same time laid down the structures which confine our thinking today: including a human ideal resembling Vitruvian Man (picture him in all his privilege). Enlightenment thinking classified the world into the taxonomies we still operate within – and endlessly replicate. At the time, this period rich in scientific and philosophical advance promised 'enlightenment' for all who paid sustained and rational attention to their education; several centuries later equality is still a distant dream and the Vitruvian human 'ideal' remains globally dominant, through oppression and colonialisation 'othering' all those who do not – can not and will not – fit its pattern. Braidotti's (2013) reading of 'posthuman' equates with 'post-Vitruvian', envisioning a world beyond the hierarchy of identities it precipitated. A different kind of humanity, where we are technologically **media**ted (the word 'media' is no accident; it changes us) and non-human actors such as animals, artificial intelligences and 'things' (Bennett, 2010) are studied for the clues they give us about how we collectively shape the world (Taylor, 2016).

The rhizome: community as curriculum

Looking at the world through a posthuman lens is addictive; once you start deconstructing what's around you, the possibilities are infinite. Our starting point was to question conventional patterns in education and how they were shaped by structures designed for another age. The botanical metaphor of the rhizome appealed to us: persistent, subversive and unpredictable, rhizomes (think buttercups) make their way underground, appearing only where conditions are right for them to flourish. Rhizomatic working has energy, it brings an activist focus by tunnelling its way out of the flowerbed, crossing disciplines and refusing to differentiate between gardens and wasteland: it is essentially democratising, revealing unseen demarcation lines before breaching them. Taylor describes the potential of rhizomatic practice to "generate more (not less) of life" (2016: 24) and Cormier has spent the past decade operationalising it under the strapline, "the community is the curriculum" (2008), most notably with the Massive Open Online Course (MOOC) 'Rhizo14', which both inspired and warned us about the challenges of 'rhizomatic' as a concept and how a rhizomatic future could operate (Mackness, Bell and Funes, 2016). Unlike Deleuze and Guattari we welcome metaphor as a navigational device when charting unfamiliar concepts (Mackness, Bell and Funes, 2016); imagery and stories have been helpful where the literature talks about instruments as 'nodes' and 'assemblages'.

The metaphor 'constellations' came from the practical, activist, cross-disciplinary art of Basis voor Actuele Kunst (BAK) Utrecht. This contemporary art network aims to join diverse practitioners together through creative and playful reimaginings of society in order to "grasp and influence our rapidly changing times" (Hlavajova and Sheikh, 2016: 34). In an education system where (A) stars are manifest and increasingly meaningless (Draper, Houghton, Read, Bird and Tatten, 2016) the energy and beauty of the metaphor appealed to us and we claimed it for our work.

Affirmative politics: reaching beyond places of pain

In rhizomatic working, 'teams' are not forever, projects are time-limited and the work becomes the organisation, rather than the organisation being the work. People come together in 'constellations of practice', gathering around shared drive and energy for a limited period of time (and potentially working in several constellations at once). This manner of working is sometimes described as 'nomadic', with the nomad following the path of the rhizome (Wray, 1998 cited in Mackness, Bell and Funes, 2016). The process opens up spaces (in an educational context) for 'pedagogies of air' (Barnett, 2007), where teachers and students can take flight and direct their own paths in ways which are freed from conventional norms and patterns.

So far, so Utopian. But powerful forces hold the status quo in place and rhizomatic practice is still subject to pressures of 'othering' from those clinging on to privilege and power, not least to those of us trying to operate within formal structures. Braidotti (2013) usefully explores Spinozan principles of *potentia* and *potestas*, to help rhizomatic practitioners walk the tightrope of working differently in traditional spaces. *Potestas* she defines as 'politics as usual', meaning not (necessarily) party politics but the exercise of hierarchical power; conventionally defined as 'leadership'. *Potentia* is a politics of hope (Mycroft and Weatherby, 2017), opening up spaces for thinking and working together differently. It contains within it the notion of 'affirmation', direct from Spinoza (Braidotti, 2016), which respects the history of standpoint politics, whilst at the same time encouraging a move beyond the places of pain that drive them, to a post-identitarian future. *Potentia* alone sounds enticing, but we live in a world of power hierarchies where we need to temper the mix with *potestas*, in order to have any impact.

Cartography – drawing our own map

Constellations of practice are underpinned by dense and sometimes impenetrable theory. An exhortation to read Deleuze and Guattari (2013) in the original French sounds an indulgence warning for busy activist educators who are also raising children and caring for elderly relatives. And an argument between participants who tried to impose theory and those who resisted it nearly scuppered Rhizo14 in its third week (Mackness, Bell and Funes, 2016). Dive in if you wish – we do, from time to time, mindful of the dangers of operationalising a concept with only a superficial grasp of theory. You'll find a world of nomad war machines, smooth and striated spaces, lines of flight, territorialisation/deterritorialisation, becoming-minoritarian . . . every time we closely study a concept we have new, activist ideas so it's work worth doing. But we are also nomadic in that we don't believe any theory is fixed; Deleuze and Guattari simply gave us concepts thirty years ago that make sense to us to work with today, they may have been visionary but they had no crystal ball.

Another connected metaphor, that of cartography, affords us the opportunity to create our own philosophical map, which we operationalise concept by concept into our practice, playing fast and loose with the rules (we remember being told on Twitter that we had not created a community of practice after Lave and Wenger (1991), because we were involved in its genesis, therefore it was an exercise of our power). In the Braidottian sense, cartography maps what it means to live at this moment in time and is "a theoretically based and politically informed reading of the present" (Braidotti, 2013: 164). We know that our maps are never the finished work.

Constellations in action

As teacher educators, our challenge was to create and contribute to constellations of practice whilst operating within the constraints of both an organisation and a tightly regulated sector. We were relatively autonomous professionals, with freedoms that were impossible to imagine in the "exam factories" (Coffield and Williamson, 2011) of many of the people we were working with, so our variation of rhizomatic learning, the Community of Praxis (Mycroft, 2016) operated across freely available 24/7 social media blended with face-to-face opportunities which were focused on making the most of physical connection and our time together. The people who 'met' in these spaces were tutors and students, graduates and fellow travellers, critical friends connected nationally and globally on platforms of equality.

What we hoped was to bring *potentia* into spaces of political domination: the prisons, community centres, public sector organisations, charities and private training companies that formed students', colleagues' and our own workplaces. If posthuman is rethinking what it is to be human, we wanted to rethink what it was to be an educator and thus to explicate and subvert the alienating methods of production we were all engaged in, whilst being mindful of Hafez's warning against the limits of subversion (Hafez, 2015; Mycroft, 2016). We knew there would come a point where we could push no further, but we wanted to do what we could. The joy was to find others out there, working in similar ways. We will go on to outline just some of these 'constellations' and the ways in which they have afforded new lines of flight, disrupting and deterritorialising fixed patterns of education (Deleuze and Guattari, 2013).

#UKFEChat

Founded by Sarah Simons, #ukfechat is a shifting constellation of further education professionals who join a weekly Twitter chat and come together – largely self-funded – for a conference each year. This hugely successful network would not define itself as posthuman but it models rhizomatic principles in its vital, affirmative approach, open to all, promoting teacher agency and rightly describing its operations, in the face of complex theory, as uncomplicated at the point of access (Simons, 2015). Although 'led' by Simons, an enthusiastic bunch of fellow travellers offers an effective level of distributed leadership.

Leicester unconference

Also on Twitter (a huge driver of professional agency for each of us), a chance conversation led to a one-day 'unconference' between the students of two teacher education programmes, in Barnsley and Leicester. The remarkable thing about this was both that it happened quickly and it was completely unfunded; a rarity in the further education sector. Without arguing for less funding in further education, this ensured freedom from bureaucratic red tape. The constellation shone briefly; brought diversity to both study groups, led to lasting professional friendships and was, from the start, an opportunistic one-off, rich in opportunity with no need to formalise or repeat.

Tutor Voices

Tutor Voices is a campaigning constellation run by further and adult education professionals. It has a 'Bill of Rights' (Petrie, 2015) but no budget or organisational structure, operating rhizomatically across freely available social media and the educational press. It arose out of a group of people who were brought together to write a book (Daley, Orr and Petrie, 2015), communicating during and after that process via initially a hashtag, then a blog and then an informally crowd-funded conference to launch the movement. Its energies ebb and flow around ideas; its leadership is distributed and non-hierarchical. Sometimes it stagnates; other times it flourishes and we have learned not to force engagement; when an issue ignites the Tutor Voices 'members' they step up to the plate, ready for activism.

Snow day

On a day when it snowed heavily, a college was closed. Students and tutors co-created a rhizomatic 'pop-up' 'course' (or constellation), to explore the topic of the day which by happy chance was 'Exploring your digital footprint' (Mycroft, 2015). Every member of that group participated, including students and tutors who weren't due to attend physically; via outward-facing social media it attracted real-time national and international interest. The 'pop-up' idea was later absorbed into a co-constructed digital resilience programme (Longden, Monaghan and Mycroft, 2016). More than a year later, the session topped the end of course evaluation, described by students who were by this time digital experts, as some of the most memorable and effective learning of their lives.

Identities

The only conventionally funded example presented here, Identities was a project which brought together art and reflexion, to explore intersectionality. Notably – and rhizomatically – the method of expressing intersecting identities through art was 'accidental', arising from one of the facilitators encountering a single poem (We Are Poets, 2013). It resulted in a constellation of educators from across the North of England curating and producing artwork which represented the cross sections of their 'places of pain' (TeachNorthern, 2015); follow-up coaching explored post-identitarian activism.

Posthuman pedagogy

In our practice, pro-social pedagogies are combined in constellation with digital engagement and resilience training, to provide stimuli for critical thinking and strategic action. Digital domains are laden with *potentia* and therefore form an essential part of the mix; as is explicating the meta-narrative around its annexation by *potestas*: data-mining and algorithmic manipulation. The Deleuze and Guattari vision remained *niche* until Web 2.0 technology made it possible to "work collaboratively in a shared space" (Gauntlett, 2011: 39). Although the markedly international Rhizo14 showed it was possible to create totally online constellations (Mackness, Bell and Funes, 2016), our experience is that face-to-face engagement can add depth and purpose, without compromising flexibility. We have effectively used pro-social pedagogies such as the Thinking Environment (Kline, 2009) to build community and strong, respectful, challenging relations which feature genuine diversity of opinion and endure online.

We emphasise the physicality of these times by avoiding digital (time for that when we are not together) and incorporating regular 'thinking walks'. What is remarkable about these sessions is their post-identitarian approach to diversity; although standpoint-based 'places of pain' may be explored, ultimately the definition of diversity which drives the pedagogy is 'being present as yourself' in community with others. We have further explored this palpable sense of 'belonging' in work around the Prevent Strategy (Thornton and Sidebottom, 2017), which created its own rhizomatic off-shoots, online and nationwide.

The Community of Praxis flourishes because an 'anti-hero' (Wilson, 2013) approach to distributed ideas of leadership is expected and nurtured by coaching, rooted in an absolute belief in the equality of teachers, students (and everyone) as thinkers. Whilst it's impossible to deny the power relations inherent in any hierarchy, our belief is that the way students are 'othered' by teachers is the most damaging feature of education today. Unpoliceable, because they are not always visible (imagine a subset of the Snow Day group meeting in a cafe far away from tutors) rhizomatic constellations force a sharing of leadership and provide a fertile environment for co-production.

Our experience of the Community of Praxis goes back nearly a decade, to a time before the influential work of Reddy (2016), when we were literally scorned out of the room at teacher education conferences for talking about our 'unprofessional' Facebook pedagogy. In all that time, hands on hearts, the digital spaces of the online community have never been abused and we believe that practice principles arising from a value of equality are at the heart of that level of mutual respect. Alongside the experience of learning to be autonomous, self-efficacious students, there is also the opportunity to grow resilience, digital and otherwise (Longden, Monaghan and Mycroft, 2016); a new world skill which stands alongside problem-solving, curation, enterprise and the application of creativity as being necessary to social progress and the future of work (Bregman, 2014).

Our work is, after all, social justice education and whilst a core of values cannot be assumed, the explication of values can be encouraged and common ground territorialised. There are paradoxes at play: that the freedom of the rhizome needs the boundaries provided by a values-based behaviour manifesto to be able to thrive; that facilitation is necessary to ensure people are cognisant of the tensions inherent in rhizomatic, *potentia* working, in a *potestas*-dominated world. Constellations of practice are never neat; energies are often unexpected and progress messy and tangential. To find joy in this, rather than risk and fear, is a challenge in the educational system (Hughes, 2015).

Conclusions

To develop agency as teachers and other identities out in the world takes resilience and drive: theirs/ours and that of the people who facilitate them/us. We have come to believe that traditional systems of education compound inequality and breed passivity and resistance. Advanced capitalism in its single-minded pursuit of fiscal growth has squeezed *potentia* energy – the spirit of life Spinoza called *zoë* (Braidotti, 2013) – out of education by removing its social purpose in favour of the economic imperative. The intentional and explicated subversion of the structures of capitalism (and its counterweight, the Marxist legacy), via rhizomatic constellations, enables binaries and borders to be transcended, however briefly, to let in the new.

Intentionality is important. We are not experimenting on students, colleagues and critical friends, we are experimenting *with* them and they need to be fully in the picture if they are to be present as themselves; our post-identitarian definition of diversity. A final piece of posthuman theory to introduce here is the notion of 'becoming'; that 'otherness' can be overcome, finally, by what Deleuze and Guattari (2013) described as the anti-fascist process of liberating oneself from dominant power structures. Constellations of practice contain the possibility of anti-fascist working, as long as they don't hang around too long after the work is done, to become reterratorialised, or incorporated back into the 'machine'.

We didn't expect constellations of practice to be as powerful as they are, and as beloved as they have become, to people who have had the opportunity to work and study that way. A genuine partnership between empirical experimentation and the slow absorption of theory, developing rhizomatic practices has brought us surprises along the way. For example, our experience of art as a thing 'that does' was unexpected, arising as it did out of a single poem, accidentally encountered. This poem (We Are Poets, 2013) has continued to resonate through a number of constellations, enabling an exponential number of students to explore their intersecting identities each year.

None of these constellation examples is particularly complex and the only thing that stops more people from operating in this way is a dominant discourse founded in the essential inequality of hierarchy and fundamentally committed to 'control'. In their uncompromising equality and commitment to fresh and diverse thinking we believe rhizomatic constellations can be genuinely revolutionary because they grow agency in places where agency has forgotten to grow – in a patronised student population and a depressed teaching one. As long as the work remains the organisation, and constellations avoid incorporation into the 'machine', they retain the spirit of *zoë* and offer us genuinely new ways of rethinking education.

In increasingly divided times globally, Spinoza's affirmative politics, forged in another turbulent era, drive us and the ways of working which have emerged from studying his essential vitalism and which provide vehicles for the activism of many. In writing this chapter we returned to an early constellation – The Identities Project – and experienced yet again the joy and liberation of discovering a new way of working which counters the alienating methods of production we find ourselves trapped within. To paraphrase ourselves (Sidebottom and Mycroft, 2015), constellations of practice allow us to explore,

> how we, as educators, balance along the boundaries, wanting to slip Into the cracks but not sure how.

References

Barnett, R. (2007). *A Will to Learn: Being a Student in an Age of Uncertainty.* Berkshire. Open University Press.
Bennett, J. (2010). *Vibrant Matter: A Political Ecology of Things.* London. Duke University Press.
Braidotti, R. (2013). *The Posthuman.* Cambridge. Polity Press.
Braidotti, R. (2016). *Don't Agonize, Organize.* E-Flux Blog. 2 November. Online https://conversations.e-flux.com/t/rosi-braidotti-don-t-agonize-organize/5294
Bregman, R. (2014). *Utopia for Realists and How We Can Get There.* London. Bloomsbury.
Brodkey, L. (1996). *Writing Permitted in Designated Areas Only.* Minneapolis. University of Minnesota Press.
Coffield, F. and Williamson, B. (2011). *From Exam Factories to Communities of Discovery.* London. Institute of Education.
Cormier, D. (2008). *Rhizomatic Education: Community as Curriculum.* Online http://davecormier.com/edblog/2008/06/03/rhizomatic-education-community-as-curriculum/
Daley, M., Orr, K. and Petrie, J. (2015). *Further Education and the Twelve Dancing Princesses.* London. Trentham Books.
Deleuze, G. and Guattari, F. (reissue 2013). *A Thousand Plateaus.* London. Bloomsbury Academic.
Draper, C., Houghton, J., Read, B., Bird. D. and Tatten, J. J. (2016). A socially inclusive A-star is only possible through the understanding of black holes. *Forum: Thinking the Yet to be Thought,* 58(3), 339–344. http://dx.doi.org/10.15730/forum.2016.58.3.415
Gaarder, J. (1995). *Sophie's World: A Novel about the History of Philosophy.* London. Orion Books.
Gauntlett, D. (2011). *Making Is Connecting: The Social Meaning of Creativity, from DIY and Knitting to YouTube and Web 2:0.* Cambridge. The Polity Press.
Glassman, J. (2012). Cracking Hegemony: Gramsci and the Dialetics of Rebellion in Eckers, M., Hart, G. and Kipfer, S. (eds.). *Gramsci: Space, Nature, Politics.* London. John Wiley. Pp. 239–257.
Hafez, R. (2015). Beyond the Metaphor: Time to Take Over the Castle in Daley, M., Orr. K. and Petrie, J. *Further Education and the Twelve Dancing Princesses.* London. Trentham Books.
Hlavajova, M. and Sheikh, S. (2016). *Former West: Art and the Contemporary after 1989.* Cambridge, MA. MIT Press.
Hughes, J. (2015). Frivolity as Resistance in Daley, M., Orr, K. and Petrie, J. *Further Education and the Twelve Dancing Princesses.* London. Trentham Books.
Kline, N. (2009). *More Time to Think.* Great Britain: Fisher King Publishing.

Lave, J. and Wenger, E. (1991). *Situated Learning: Legitimate Peripheral Practice.* Cambridge. Cambridge University Press.

Longden, A., Monaghan, T. and Mycroft, L. (2016). Opening the Arms: The FAB project. *InTuition.* Spring 2016.p.17

Mackness, J., Bell, F. and Funes, M. (2016). The rhizome: A problematic metaphor for teaching and learning in a MOOC. *Australasian Journal of Educational Technology*, 32(1).

Mills, C. W. (1959). *The Sociological Imagination.* New York. Oxford University Press.

Mycroft, L. (2015). *Footprints in the Snow.* Online https://teachnorthern.wordpress.com/2015/01/21/footprints-in-the-snow/

Mycroft, L. (2016). Northern College and the philosophers of praxis. *Forum: Thinking the Yet to be Thought*, 58(3), 415–420. http://dx.doi.org/10.15730/forum.2016.58.3.415

Mycroft, L. and Weatherby, J. (2017). Spaces to Dance: Community Education in Daley, M., Orr, K. and Petrie, J. *Further Education and the Twelve Dancing Princesses.* London. Trentham Books.

Mycroft, L. and Weatherby, J. (2017). Social Purpose Leadership: A New Hope in Daley, M., Orr, K. and Petrie, J. *The Principal: Power and Professionalism in Further Education.* London. Trentham Books.

Petrie, J. (2015). Opinion: Tutor Voices will be a strong, democratic and professional voice for the sector. *Times Educational Supplement.* 5 September.

Reddy, S. (2016). *Facebook Pedagogy and Education in Apprenticeships.* ALT-C Blog. Online https://altc.alt.ac.uk/blog/2016/08/facebook-pedagogy-and-education-in-apprenticeships/#gref

Rushdie, S. (1991). *Imaginary Homelands: Essays and Criticism 1981–1991.* New York: Penguin.

Sidebottom, K. and Mycroft, L. (2015). *Falling Between the Cracks.* TeachDifferent Identities Blog. https://tdidentities.wordpress.com/

Simons, S. (2015). UKFEchat proves the power of being part of a community. *Times Educational Supplement.* 29 September.

Taylor, C. (2016). Close encounters of a critical kind: A diffractive musing in/between new material feminism and object-oriented ontology. *Cultural Studies – Critical Methodologies*, 16(2), 201–212.

TeachNorthern. (2015). *TeachDifferent: Identities.* Online https://padlet.com/teachnorthern/1o5tjeqff8qg

Thornton, K. and Sidebottom, K. (2017). Prevent as an opportunity to educate out hate. *FE News.* 15 March.

We Are Poets. (2013). *I Come From.* Online https://vimeo.com/54291012

Wilson, R. (2013). *Anti-Hero.* Clore Social Leadership Foundation. Online www.cloresocialleadership.org.uk/userfiles/documents/Research%20reports/2012/Research,%20Richard%20Wilson,%20FINAL.pdf

Wray, S. (1998). *Rhizomatic-Nomadic Resistant Internet Use.* Online www.thing.net/~rdom/ecd/rhizomatic.html#RESISTANT

Chapter 17

'The Marriage of Heaven and Hell'

Discourses of autonomy and reason in further education

Kirstie Harrington

> *Rintrah roars & shakes his fires in the burden'd air;*
> *Hungry clouds swag on the deep.*

So begins the poet and illustrator William Blake's visionary work *The Marriage of Heaven and Hell*, Blake's bold attempt to make sense of public life in the last decade of the 18th century. Conceived formally as an imitation of biblical prophecies, it is Blake's most influential political and philosophical thesis. Blake is concerned by contemporary man's loss of autonomy due, in his analysis, to Reason. He starts with the presentation of the argument in which 'Rintrah' (believed by some to be Blake himself) rages against the fact that man has allowed himself to be drawn from his rightful path of spiritual freedom, experience and autonomy, in favour of the safer route offered by 'Reason', to the detriment of his individuality. The 'safer route' may prove a fruitful path of analysis also: 'safety' is a key prop of the current educational dispensations.

For Blake, in his 18th-century context, it was the mantras of religion which were responsible for laying down the rules by which the thoughts and actions of mankind were governed and measured, enslaving humanistic thoughts and desires which in the poem Blake defines as "energy". Thus in the poem Blake contradicts the common understanding of the words 'Heaven' and 'Hell' by defining Heaven as housing those individuals who reject all forms of systematic control instead choosing to follow the path of their own energy and senses while Hell is the dwelling place for those who have allowed their energy to be stilled by embracing systems of control created by others: *Jerusalem's* 'dark satanic mills' of course were churches!

Looking at the systems of control that exist today, almost three centuries on, it must be said that Blake's poem continues to offer a prophetic warning of the dangers in embracing and believing in systems that promise enlightenment at the cost of an individual's 'soul'. Comparisons can be made between the controlling force of religious doctrine that aggravated Blake, and the governmental systems that are employed in modern times to restrain and frustrate individual autonomy. Blake's poem has in this way provided the foundation stone for my research into the potential loss of professional autonomy among

FE teachers together with the potential erosion of core educational purposes that has resulted in the lack of development of personal autonomy in human beings. This has become increasingly problematic within 'further education' (FE) today: it is often attributed to the systematic 'marketisation' that commands this educational area.

Like Rintrah I could roar and shake my fires but, in fact, I am sitting, reflecting and wondering whether I really want to be part of this after all. As if reading my mind, Elizabeth Atkinson (2003) sums up my thoughts:

> What for goodness sake is my problem? My problem is this: I don't believe in any of this stuff; and I don't believe in the requirement to believe in it. And worse, I don't believe in what I am doing to maintain, perpetuate and reproduce it.
>
> (Atkinson and Satterthwaite, 2003: 6)

I am disillusioned with what I see around me and am tired of fighting against the hammer that is constantly trying to smash my well-rounded educational beliefs very firmly into a square hole.

Body and soul: the purpose of education within FE

> Education should make people ungovernable.
>
> (Peter Barnes)

It seems that post compulsory education (PCE) is clouded in confusion concerning its purpose. Teacher roles within FE are a case in point. These 'learning and teaching' practitioners must endure the scrutiny of their professional performance, standards and abilities, while jumping through hoops to comply with corporate procedures in the hope that their efforts, support, encouragement and beliefs will make a difference to the lives and futures of the students they are teaching. There are also those that who have come to internalise these corporate systems due to becoming desensitised over time to their calling by the market structures that now govern FE and which now have become acceptable norms. It is also likely that to some, teaching as a vocation in its original sense has been replaced by 'vocational' in terms of its modern definition and that teaching in FE to these individuals is seen as 'just a job no different to any other'.

Society is also confused about the purpose of FE, and seems to have the preconception that future employment is dependent on participation in FE and on the participation *of* FE. This may be due to the generic 'Operation Mindcrime'[1] of Reason that promotes the theory that participation in PCE will increase personal life chances socially, vocationally and economically. It must be said that for some sections of society this preconception is based on personal experiences which may have been the case in previous decades, when more opportunities to enter employment existed. These beliefs are passed on through generations so that for many the chance of gaining employment by participation in FE is absolute. The controlling power recognises these societal beliefs and adds strength in making it central to policies that are created for FE. Opportunities for an improved life style and greater wealth are dangled like a carrot in front of people as the motivating factor for educational purpose. Reason employs FE as the solution to fixing the broken-down society that exists in Britain today with the added expectation of shouldering blame for being the cause of the problems when solutions are not found.

The controlling powers see only one purpose for education, that is: the national economic project. This argument is advanced by Avis (1997) who examines economic policy of the Conservative government of the late 20th century to define how FE has become instrumental in the training of a highly skilled workforce that is seen to be imperative to "national competitiveness" in the global economy. Avis discusses through analysis of employment, education and training policy, how reforms have: "been aggressively nationalist in its commitment to a British supremacist view of global competition".(Avis, 1996: 3) Avis argues in support of the argument that true educational purpose of the development of "intellectual innovation" has been removed by the current FE corporate structures:

> A form of cultural degradation is being visited on the nation as the dead hand of business managerialism drains its educational institutions of intellectual vitality.
>
> (Avis, 1997: 3)

He also examines how 'globalisation' of the economy and the erosion of 'education' in FE has gone unquestioned and become accepted as the norm for cultural thinking.

The current system not only serves to produce a compliant labour force but can also be seen as a measure for dealing with school leavers who cannot access higher levels of study or employment on leaving school, by enrolling them onto meaningless generic work skills programmes of study such as 'skills for working life and citizenship', thereby creating a 'holding pen' for a percentage of the population that ensures unemployment figures are maintained at manageable levels. Nelson and O'Donnell (2012) comment on this making reference to Hayward and Williams (2011: 12) who are critical of "pseudo-vocational programmes that act as little more than warehousing for young people with few options at the age of 16". College managers are persuaded that their primary concerns are with the economic success of their own enterprise, following the rules of state control and disregarding any consideration of what the argument states to be true educational purpose. College managers are reminiscent of circus clowns performing a chaotic 'balancing act': "The inescapable double bind is that they disseminate chaos in the course of earnestly trying to do what the technologies of normalizing power ask of them" (Little, 1993: 119).

It is little wonder with the confusions surrounding FE that it is under constant review as attempts are made to establish and justify the core purpose of the sector. This notion is supported by the review of further education colleges conducted in 2005 by Andrew Foster: 'Realising The Potential', which found that vocational colleges had no "core purpose". It comments on the failure of schools for the preparation of learners for college education, and a 'mismatch' between the: "aspirations of colleges" against tangible achievability and the "confusion about roles". Blackmore (2000) agrees and summarises the confusions due to the changes in educational purpose as being: "shifted from input and process to outcomes, from liberal to the vocational, from education's intrinsic value to its instrumental success" (Blackmore, 2000: 134).

It would seem that William Blake was ahead of his time in his critique of the controlling forces and was prophetic in his assumptions of the consequences of capitalism would mean for humanistic creativity and individuality. Like Blake, writers of modern times are still arguing and many of those who write and comment critically on today's 21st-century systems feel that it is through the medium of education that governments secure the chains of compliance in a wealth-measured system most effectively. Take Blackmore: "Education has, in most instances, been reshaped to become the arm of national economic policy" (Blackmore, 2000: 134). Further education has become no more than a tool employed by the systems of 'Reason' as a means to control society in order to promote national prosperity and the Power of those elected to be its leaders, with Reason's greatest triumph to date being the 'Frankensteinesque' creation of 'homo economicus' to the detrimental cost of the erosion of the true purpose of teaching and learning, which Stronach (2010) identifies:

> This is the first of the passage points – education must pass the test of the economic. Economic Man is now an unabashed goal. Educational effectiveness leads to economic productivity in the 'knowledge economy'. Repeat after me. . . .
>
> (Stronach, 2010: 29)

By the time Lord Lingfield reported on *Professionalism in Further Education* in 2012 these initiatives and "the turbulence of government policy" had become "challenges to a settled and consistent sense of professional identity among FE teaching staff" (Lingfield, 2012: 1). In fact Lingfield went further in his acceptance of John Hayes's accusation that "the sector has been 'infantilised and encumbered' by too much and too detailed intervention by government and its agencies." Lingfield also shared with this chapter that the only viable foundation for a better 'built' sector is greater autonomy and "a clearer set of aims, a better approach to the key policy and funding relationships with government, and a heightened understanding of its status" (Lingfield, 2012: 2).

The current Conservative, previously Coalition Government continues to make global competition its key aim for FE. In a speech given by David Cameron (2011) the Prime Minister stated:

> We've got to be ambitious if we want to compete in the world.
> When China is going through an educational renaissance, when India is churning out science graduates . . .
> . . . any complacency now would be fatal for our prosperity.

At present we have reached a stage in FE where the essence of education is removed, all that matters is the nation's place in the global marketplace. As Roy Fisher and Ron Thompson (2009) comment:

> learning has come to be regarded as a product to be sold and purchased like any other, with students positioned as consumers. The curriculum has been co-opted as a vehicle of 'economic progress', with largely unchallenged assumptions about its purposes as a means by which industry can be provided with efficient and pliable workers.

"McDonaldisation" (Ritzer, 1993) has now replaced 'Imagination' and 'Education' in FE – the term likening college education to the fast food empire McDonalds defined by Coles (2004) as:

> In students becoming consumers of a product based on the product being *predictable* (based on a set of outcomes), *calculable* (target driven), *efficient* (e-learning materials used for mass education, for example) and *controlled* in the sense that the curriculum and delivery are centrally determined.
>
> (Coles, 2004: 20)

It is apparent that the culture of managerialism which now controls FE leaves no room for education in its humanistic sense. Instead it is being defined as an economic process and measured in its success of producing a disciplined labour force, fully 'trained'. The managers who govern the system are separate from the 'training' process, being in place only to implement policy and measure levels of efficiency and productivity in order to ensure the success and growth of the business. Rowland (2003) comments on how this method is removed from true educational purpose:

> Understandably, if we want to ensure value for money, we need to be able to predict and measure. The fact that learning – or at least the more imaginative or critical aspects of learning – does not so readily submit to prediction and measurement is unfortunate.
>
> (Rowland, 2003: 20)

Moreover, no longer are only students, colleges, towns, regions and counties pitted against each other in matters of performance in education. Now it is the national overall achievement that is marked alongside the rest of the world much like an "Olympic games of cultural performance" (Stronach, 2010: 24). The success of FE is no longer a' family affair' but one of national importance.

To 'use' human beings as a product for securing capital and business success may be unethical; however, the 'factory farming' of human capital is justified by calling the business 'further education'. A bitter pill. . . . It is a far cry from the supposed 'enlightenment' of the imagination that surrounds the argument for the true purpose of education, but it does evidence Blake's prophesies in *The Marriage of Heaven and Hell*. It must be said that Blake was a revolutionary against the systematic advancement of reason and much of his poetry was a shout at the controlling systems of the time. His poem 'London': "is a condemnation of the effect of the market on people's lives. It is a poem about the reduction of human life to something that can be bought and sold and how this degrades and demoralises people" (Cox, 1994). It would seem that though separated by 300 years the same revolutionary words are still being shouted by modern voices.

> In every cry of every Man,
> In every Infants cry of fear,
> In every voice: in every ban,
> The mind-forg'd manacles I hear.
> (Blake, 'London')

Gagging the voices: teachers

The systematic devaluing of professionalism of FE teaching staff that FE market structures have legitimised, has not only ensured the economically driven motives of the controlling powers are implemented, but also that potential critical opposition to its objectives is minimalised and that the trust that had once been placed in the professional is undermined and removed. This is seen in a speech by Estelle Morris (2001), the Secretary of State for Education under New Labour, who said: "Gone are the days when doctors and teachers could say, with a straight face, 'trust me, I'm a professional'" (2001: 19) and invited "others, including parents and business people" to debate "what will provide the basis for a fruitful and new era of trust between Government and the teaching profession". Morris goes on to add:

> It is important to trust our professionals to get on with the job. That does not mean leaving professionals to go their own way, without scrutiny – we will always need the constant focus on effective teaching and learning, and the accountability measures described above.
>
> (Morris, 2001: 26)

In layman's terms this speech translates as:

'You can no longer trust these people. What was once defined as a professional is no longer so, and it is up to society to say what they expect from these people. Professionals have failed to do the job properly when left to their own devices and the public deserve better. We (the government) will remove their autonomy and implement systems that will measure their effectiveness to do the job we expect of them.'

And this has indeed been the case. FE teachers are now measured for their worth in pounds and pence against target and performance data, each pound of their flesh offsetting the balance of the books between output of performance and funding input. It would seem that 'education' in its purest sense does not balance the books of business of the corporations. This was highlighted in a recent discussion with a teaching colleague about why they were planning to return to work in a secondary school, the teacher said:

> I don't feel like I'm making any difference and I certainly don't feel I am doing the job I wanted to do. I am just working in a factory, babysitting young people that have nothing else to do. Students can speak to me as they wish, shout in my face and spit at me, and there will be nothing said. Teaching in FE is not a two-way thing. I may as well work in a shop as work in FE the rules are just the same . . . the customer is always right.

Discussions with colleagues have led to various suggestions as to why teaching practitioners in FE ignore the loss of their autonomy. Some argue that 'care' for their students and their futures means they must tolerate the strict control that now governs their profession. It is also likely that to some teaching in FE is seen as just a job no different to any other. A further consideration is that in many FE colleges the majority of teaching staff come from vocational rather than academic backgrounds. They are individuals that have worked in industry first and 'fallen' into teaching seemingly by accident or fortune. Although having prior knowledge of industry is essential for a vocational FE teacher, it could be argued that previous employments mean they are unconsciously programmed to respond to corporate structures with business systems being the accepted norms. This idea is based on comments from Gleeson discussing the changes in FE, from contractual permanent teaching staff to "part-time trainers who are more amenable to control" (Gleeson, 1989). This results in the employment of 'ad hoc' employees who respond to the needs of the business rather than to the needs of education, employed by the hour or by the day. Whatever the explicit intention this does result in minimal formation of relationships with students and colleagues, or concerns with regards to any unethical systematic manipulation of educational purpose, thus, removing the possibility of potential criticism to implementation and utilisation of any new structures and policies.

This common sense curriculum creates the notion that modern human beings are unable to perform everyday simple tasks and need to receive instruction in how to present themselves in everyday life; they also do little in achievement of the acquisition of valuable work and knowledge skills that will be needed for an individual's chosen area of vocation. This is evident in feedback obtained through discussion with one employer who wanted to know 'what we actually taught them in colleges these days'. The employer was keen to offer employment in a hairdressing salon to a newly qualified hairdresser; however, five such 'trainees' had been and gone, all had left of their own accord after deciding that the real-life experience was much harder and not what they expected. The employer also commented that although most could perform simple hairdressing tasks well, very few had 'everyday skills' such as being able to talk to customers and other staff, or using initiative to perform simple tasks such as putting towels in the washing machine if they were dirty.

James Avis (2009) describes the real learning process as "one of identity formation and transformation" (Avis, 2009: 123) but argues that 'vocational' PCE is ignorant of this being primarily concerned with the delivery: "of learners who can contribute to and enhance the economy by developing forms of human and intellectual capital that align with the needs of industry". In order to demonstrate this Avis identifies the difference that exists in curriculum content between academic curricula which he states are largely associated with the privileged and middle classes and that of vocational curricula which are in place in vocational colleges for everyone else. This highlights how the employment of the curriculum in different institutions systematically ensures the existing structures which determines social order are maintained.

This chapter suggests that, due to the advancement of industrial and marketised systems being employed within vocational colleges, contemporary further education has lost its core educational purpose. The result of almost four decades of marketisation of the sector has been chaos and confusion regarding the core function of these institutions in terms of how they 'fit in' to the educational 'industry', in itself a contentious allocation. For some FE is a government 'wolf in sheep's clothing' within the education industry as a whole, and once accepted as a 'common sense' model for the business will be free to impose and justify destructive market systems across all areas.

Throughout this chapter, I have drawn on William Blake's poem "The Marriage of Heaven and Hell' to demonstrate the detrimental effect of the advancement of systems of Reason and the effect this has had on the autonomy and 'Energy' of human beings, who have eventually become enslaved by the structures of control. The words of Blake have also offered a prophetic insight in making comparisons between the woeful foresight of the poet and the state of FE today. The poem is also utilised to support the argument that suggests how possible resistance to structures are systematically quietened, by highlighting the issues that existed for Blake in 1789 and which have also been compared to the shouts of other 'revolutionaries' throughout the subsequent centuries, but which have gone unheeded, and by most unheard.

Many who have evaluated and written on the problems within FE highlight the problems that exist within post compulsory education; however, few can offer a solution, other than to return some essence of 'real education purpose' back into the sector, to recapture that which Blake has identified as being lost from the lives of human beings. Frank Coffield (2008), is one who suggests a return to teaching and learning should be the first priority for FE, while justifying the need for this by highlighting the failures of the marketised structures in basing FE motives around the national economy. Coffield offers four new priorities for the sector in an effort to return to the core purpose of education:

- "to inspire and enable individuals to develop their capacities to the highest potential levels throughout life, so that they grow intellectually, are well equipped for work, can contribute effectively to society and achieve personal fulfillment
- to serve the needs of an adaptable, sustainable knowledge-based economy [and society] at local, regional and national levels
- to play a major role in shaping a democratic, civilised, inclusive society
- to increase knowledge and understanding for their own sake and to foster their application to the benefit of the economy and society."

(Coffield, 2008: 60)

However, unlike Coffield, this research can make no attempt to offer a solution, for I feel that we are too far along the path towards self-destruction in both society and FE for it to be easily possible for a mass reawakening of the creative, autonomous 'Energy' of 'Everyman'. This is what Blake desired, imagining that his illuminated broadsides into the underbelly of Reason from inside the caves of the 'Enlightened' would stop this unimaginable future in its tracks. The contemporary parallels would have confused as well as alarmed him. Sadly though, however loudly Rintrah roars and shakes, history will be condemned to repeat itself until we start to listen.

Note

1 Reference to systems of mass thought control described in the novel *1984* by George Orwell.

References

Atkinson, E. and Satterthwaite, J. (2003) *Discourse, Power, Resistance: Challenging the Rhetoric of Contemporary Education*. Stoke on Trent: Trentham Books Limited.
Avis, J. (Ed) (1996) *Knowledge and nationhood: education, politics, and work*. Cassell.
James Avis (1997) Globalisation, the learner and post-compulsory education: policy fictions. *Research in Post-Compulsory Education*, 2: 3, 241–248
Avis, J. (2009) *Education, Policy and Social Justice, Learning and Skills*, 2nd Edition. London: Continuum International Publishing Group.

Barnes, P. (1985) *Red Noses*. London: Faber & Faber.

Blackmore, J. (2000) Globalization: A Useful Concept for Feminists Rethinking Theory and Strategies in Education, in Torres, C. A. and Burbles, N. (eds.), *Globalization and Education: Critical Perspectives*. New York: Routledge.

Blake, W. (1975) *The Marriage of Heaven and Hell*. Oxford: Oxford University Press.

Blake, W. (2012) *The Complete Works of William Blake*, Version 1. Delphi Classics: www.delphiclassics.com.

Cameron, D. (2011) Education speech. Accessed on 19/12/2017 at www.politics.co.uk/comment-analysis/2011/09/09/david-cameron-s-education-speech-in-full

Coffield, F. (2008) *Just suppose teaching and learning became the first priority . . . Learning and Skills*. Network: London

Coles, A. (2004) *Teaching in Post-Compulsory Education Policy, Practice and Values*. London: David Foulton Publishers Ltd.

Cox, J. (1994) Blake's revolution, A review of E P Thompson, Witness Against the Beast, William Blake and the Moral Law. *International Socialism Journal*, 62.

Fisher, R. and Thompson, R. (2009) Introduction, in Avis, J. *Education, Policy and Social Justice, Learning and Skills*, 2nd Edition. London: Continuum International Publishing Group.

Gleeson, D. (1989) *The Paradox of Training: Making Progress Out of Crisis*. Milton Keynes: Open University Press.

Hayward, G & Williams, R. (2011) Joining the big society: am I bothered? *London Review of Education*, 9: 2, 175–189.

Lingfield, R. (2012) *Lingfield Report 'Professionalism in Further Education'* accessed on 15/9/2017 at www.bera.ac.uk/timeline/lingfield-report-professionalism-in-further-education

Little, K. (1993) Masochism, spectacle, and the 'broken mirror' clown entrée: A note on the anthropology of performance in postmodern culture. *Cultural Anthropology*, 8:1, 117–129.

Morris, E. (2001) *Professionalism and Trust: The Future of Teachers and Teaching: A Speech by the Rt. Hon Estelle Morris MP, Secretary of State for Education and Skills, to the Social Market Foundation*, 12th November, 2001. London: Department for Education and Skills.

Nelson, J. and O'Donnell, L. (2012) *Approaches to Supporting Young People Not in Education, Employment or Training: A Review* (NFER Research Programme: From Education to Employment). Slough: NFER.

Ritzer, G. (1993) *The McDonaldization of Society*. London: Sage.

Rowland, S. (2003) Learning to Comply; Learning to Contest, in Atkinson, E. and Satterthwaite, J. *Discourse, Power, Resistance: Challenging the Rhetoric of Contemporary Education*. Stoke on Trent: Trentham Books Limited.

Stronach, I. (2010) *Globalizing Education, Educating the Local, How Method Made Us Mad*. Oxon: Routledge.

Chapter 18

Conclusion
Identity and the collective purpose of further education

Pete Bennett and Rob Smith

Over the last quarter century, further education in England has been found particularly vulnerable to colonisation by the market-orientated values associated with neoliberalisation. The incorporation of colleges that took place in 1993 was supposed to allow them to forge new, stronger identities as embedded engines of economic and skills development for local industry. But what the preceding chapters illustrate is that, instead, something has been lost.

This book began with a quotation from *King Lear*. The play explores what happens to Lear after he steps down from the throne and divides his kingdom between his three daughters. The basis of the division seems arbitrary to the audience: whichever daughter expresses her love of him in the most grandiloquent terms will get the biggest share of the kingdom. The youngest daughter, Cordelia, refuses to play along with the performance. Speaking truthfully, in answer to the question: *How much do you love me?* – she answers:

> *according my bond, no more no less*

and by refusing to take part in the performatives event Lear has set up, she is disinherited.

The tragic action that follows unfolds through the playing out of Lear's realisation that the two daughters who expressed their love so volubly are in fact hard-hearted and cruel. By the end of the play, the kingdom has been ravaged by civil war, Lear has descended into madness and all three of his daughters are dead. The final words are left to another disinherited child, Edgar who, having been reconciled with his father and having rescued the kingdom from an ambitious and scheming brother, is left to rule.

Predicating our exploration of Teacher Identity in this 'age of anxiety' on Shakespeare's darkest and most existential tragedy always ran the risk of concluding on a note of pessimism. As an experienced practitioner, Kirstie Harrington's inability to do much more than shudder at "what is to come" must be taken seriously.

> *Is this the promised end?*

– asks one of the Lear's advisors, Kent, surveying the ultimate consequences of Lear's appalling misjudgement, having spent half the play disguised, in "strategic compliance", unable to reveal his true identity. This echoes the feeling of loss that provides the starting point for many of the foregoing chapters. This is the same feeling of loss that now permeates many state schools in England and other parts of what used to be known as 'the public sector'. Practitioners in further education have battled with the notion of neglect, have rejected the label of the 'Cinderella Sector' (see Daley et al., 2015) whilst also wrestling with re-formulations of de- and re-professionalisation to explain, give voice to and attempt in some way to empower teachers in further education during this period. But the loss of status, autonomy and agency is not simply a phenomenological or ego-logical phenomenon. Instead it finds its origins in the sense of a wider collapse, of dissolution and the overthrow of a collective understanding about the purpose and meaning of further education itself.

This collection is an attempt to find the space to breathe and think and re-imagine: to understand that, however bleak the perspective, the voicing of critique in the present is the prerequisite to imagining a different and better future. Thus though what is collected here often toes a line in which policy and pain too often 'rhyme', this collection of essays, sharp critiques, written experiences and celebrations of progress still constitute Williams-style 'resources of hope'. The emphasis on creativity is particularly timely with the developing crisis in creative subjects in schools and colleges as they are squeezed out of the curriculum by an obsession with 'the basics'. Here once again is that instrumentalism, nihilistic and ethically hollow, stripping back the curriculum to that which can easily be measured to smooth the way to 'accountability'. Lyotard's prescience about the "tenor of the times", that "everywhere we are being urged to give up experimentation, in the arts and elsewhere" (Lyotard, 1993: 1) has never seemed more stark.

The challenge for practitioners who are living through this and for researchers and others, is to gain a vantage point and achieve a historical perspective on what for many continues to be lived experience. Whether or not such perspectives are heeded by policymakers, these feelings and perspectives must be communicated. The communication of experience is important because it keeps alive the values that inform practice even in the most hostile and undermining environments. This is what the writers of these chapters have attempted.

If the picture presented by the contributors seems sometimes grim, there are today more grounds for optimism than at any period since Callaghan's Great Debate speech of 1976 which signalled the beginning of instrumentalist government interventions in educational policy. And as we write, there is at least some sense that the worst excesses of surveillance-style regulation may be finally properly exposed to the light, with Matt O'Leary's work on classroom observation and 'grading' having been especially effective in this respect. In Frank Coffield's latest book: *Will the Leopard Change Its Spots? A New Model of Inspection for Ofsted*, there is a confidence that change is coming. Coffield begins by reminding us that empirical studies on the impact of inspection on student attainment is modest and indirect and that descriptive studies of the experiences of educators record a climate of fear and 'gaming' (Coffield, 2017: xii). Coffield proposes a new inspection model underpinned by five moral principles:

- Education should inspire the desire for continued and productive growth – are we creating cultures of and for lifelong learning?
- Cultures of fear should be replaced by cultures of trust – how much trust do teachers have in Ofsted?
- Challenge should be matched by support
- Dialogue is crucial
- Adopting an Appreciative Enquiry approach would reject a deficit-based approach.

Coffield's hope, like ours here in word and deed, is to promote a formative approach in which we might learn new methods and approaches collaboratively. He is also keen, in keeping with the core British value of democracy, to work more democratically. He longs for the creativity of students and staff to be released rather than schools positioned as exam factories and further education colleges as skills factories. All this is contextualised by the kinds of practical reflexive activities that are demonstrated in this volume: that ongoing ethical negotiation of identity might with time and patience build a better world.

The collection can be seen then as a response to Franco Berardi who suggests we have lost any kind of feasible idea of the future. According to Berardi: "In the last three decades of the century the utopian imagination was slowly overturned, and has been replaced by the dystopian imagination" (Berardi, 2011: 12). He identifies the damage that only radical action can retrieve or redeem: "Corporate capitalism and neoliberal ideology have produced lasting damage in the material structures of the world and in the social, cultural, and nervous systems of mankind" (Berardi, 2011: 8). These accounts are an attempt to recover the loss noted in Berardi's critique: the "absence of an active culture, lack of a public sphere, void of collective imagination, palsy of the process of subjectivation" (Berardi, 2011: 9).

The tide of marketisation that has rolled out in the last two-and-a-half decades may have permeated all areas of the public sphere, the claim being that the competition this fostered has resulted in a raising of standards (Willetts, 2011); but the more recent global economic turmoil and the collapse of the models of leadership that underpinned the great adventure of neoliberalism in the 1990s and 2000s have brought into question all the gains claimed by market experimentation. The economic model underpinning neoliberalism currently faces a crisis in authority which raises significant doubts about its validity as a description of reality.

Ormerod (1994) charts the development of economics as a subject and how it has come to be dominated by a branch of the discipline that gravitated towards mathematics, seeing this as providing the veneer of the 'scientific' that could position economics alongside the physical sciences. Through the inception of a quasi-market, the organisation and management of further education appears to have travelled down the same path. So what are the consequences of a more or less exclusive focus on numbers as pre-eminent indicators of so-called 'performance'? It shouldn't surprise us if a blinkered fetishisation of metrics leads to a failure to spot the development of cultures that are not congruent with educational environments and may even damage the social processes that they are supposed to engage in. We might expect it to be the role of Ofsted to focus on this aspect of colleges and schools, but unfortunately, as Frank Coffield has noted and several of the contributors attest, Ofsted has instead assumed a position in the vanguard of the metrics brigade; indeed inspections revolve around the enforcement of the use of number as an orthodoxy, as though its prime function was to ensure the legitimacy of this fixation.

Performativity and its consequences

For teachers in further education, the collapse of the neoliberal order can be evidenced in the bifurcation of consciousness it has brought about. One thread that unites the narratives informing these chapters is the growing awareness of external economic and financial forces that need to be appeased, whose demands on teachers' time supersede any parochial focus on pedagogy or the lives and learning of the students in their classes. This economisation of consciousness results in a kind of monetised reflexivity that shifts teachers' attention away from their primary values connected to their pedagogical role and moral concern.

In some circumstances, it also undermines the potential of teachers to act as catalysers of hope that foster transformative learning experiences (Duckworth and Smith, 2018). This is because of the dispiriting and alienating impact of the (primarily data-driven) tasks and activities that have evolved as a consequence of marketisation and in response to the spread of managerialist cultures.

The connection between the loss of a bigger collective purpose for further education and the systems of accountability and performance data production that characterise college governance is not lost on the contributors to this volume. 'Feeding the monster' – to use a particularly evocative term from the collection – captures the sense teachers have of sustaining the systems of 'governmentality' (Foucault, 1978: 87) that depend on (specious) performance data, while remaining cognisant of the monstrous self-reproduction of the system of simulation that is thereby sustained.

The erosion of the established purpose and locally rooted identity of many colleges of further education is conditioned by performativity. The production of data by individual institutions within a competitive market reinterprets accountability as a market-orientated set of practices that clearly connect to neoliberal models of governmentality. Performativity is defined by Stephen Ball in the following way:

> Performativity is a technology, a culture and a mode of regulation that employs judgements, comparisons and displays as means of incentive, control, attrition and change based on rewards and sanctions (both material and symbolic). The performances (of individual subjects or organisations) serve as measures of productivity or output, or displays of 'quality', or 'moments' of promotion or inspection. As such they stand for, encapsulate or represent the worth, quality or value of an individual or organisation within a field of judgement.
>
> (Ball, 2003: 216)

A structural pressure that makes marketised further education more susceptible to performative pressures is that the majority of qualifications taken in colleges are assessed and completed over one or two years. This has the effect of making every cohort the equivalent of a Year 11 cohort in a school. Apart from shaping cultures within further education colleges, performance data also function within the marketised and political landscape as a central aspect of the choice mechanisms which the operation of the FE market supposedly relies on. The proper functioning of the market mechanism depends on customers' use of accurate data as 'market information'. In this mechanism (and neoliberal economics is founded on a view that social organisations function like massive machines) consumer choice raises standards on the part of a producer as good performance is rewarded by additional customer take-up. The centrality of the use of performance by government shows no signs of decelerating. Indeed, the use of such data is seen as a key strategy in the operation of education markets. *FE Choices* – part of the 'FE public information framework' (SFA, 2014) – provides a good example; it facilitates a comparison of the performance of 'similar' colleges through the use of number.

However, there have been continuous (as yet unheeded) warnings about the accuracy and validity of the performance data produced by further education providers. Alison Wolf (2011), among others, has noted how widespread 'gaming' practices are (see also Fletcher, 2011). Rob writes:

> Even at a distance of twenty years, I can remember the moment I first realised how embedded performative practices were with regards to data in further education. Early in my teaching career, in the foreword of a promotional brochure, the principal where I was teaching trumpeted the college's academic achievements. He boasted of a 100% pass rate in A level Modern Foreign Languages. As the German teacher was a friend of mine, I congratulated him when I next saw him. But he pulled a face. "Yes. It was a 100% pass rate but I had only one A level student last year."

Beneath the surface humour of such an anecdote lurks the disturbing cultural practice of the institutionalised misrepresentation of data that is a consequence of market competition.

That there are issues associated with the neoliberal use of performance data in driving improvement in public sector organisations is not new. Ranson, for example (2003), explores this 'regulation' in relation to its impact on trust. Haney (2000) provides a vivid example of this phenomenon in his critique of the so-called Texas miracle effect. Also, Goldstein (2013) illustrates how high stakes market environments lead to 'optimisation behaviour' on the part of teachers and schools. But it seems that only now we are getting a full picture of the epistemological crisis that neoliberalisation has spawned: not only does the numerical data not fulfil its function in terms of offering an accurate picture of activity or quality, but the cultures and models of professional identity that evolve as a consequence of 'deliverology' (Ball et al., 2012) are not anchored in firm moral ground.

There are further signs of the way the neoliberal 'project' is chafing against what it is to be human. Recent history suggests that current notions of professionalism may be irrevocably tainted by neoliberalisation. The narratives that provide evidence for this usually remain at the local level or, are unvoiced as a result of private 'settlements' and confidentiality clauses. But those that are beginning to surface present a picture in which compliance with management and loyalty to the employing organisation often for the purposes of securing competitive advantage, come at the cost of personal integrity and through the sacrifice of institutional honesty. Those who speak out in cultures like these are often victimised and lose their jobs. An unfolding legacy of performativity appears to be an institutional life that conceals a subterranean reality. It seems likely that there are more morally questionable practices lurking under the performative surface that require dragging out into the sunlight.

Accepting that marketising further education is the best way of organising it, under the current funding arrangements, hinges on a single question: *is it acceptable to view our young people's education and, contingently their futures, as commodities that can be designed, calculated for and traded?* We are writing this conclusion in the week that Scotland decided to make the smacking of children by parents illegal. During my own educational experience at school the slapping, caning and pumping of children by teachers was viewed as totally acceptable. It was a visible, even *integral* feature of the experience of education. By the time I began my own teacher education course, such overt violence was frowned upon. Looking back from our vantage point today, the slapping or beating of the children that we as teachers are here to educate, seems indefensible. But less visible forms of violence, the kind of symbolic violence written about by Bourdieu and Passeron (2013) seem to be prevalent, and further education appears to provide its share of evidence in relation to that.

While the imposition of specific educational trajectories on some young people isn't (yet) recognised as violence as such, it seems entirely possible that decades from now, the instrumentalist ethic that governs much of the policy driving further education, despite its claims to 'paternal libertarianism' (Thaler and Sunnstein, 2008) will be rejected. This rejection will not just be on the basis that marketisation was a clumsy and irrational way of managing colleges, but because it created the conditions in colleges for the objectification of students and the channelling, limiting, or worse, the crushing of their aspirations in the service of a (largely illusory) narrative of national economy.

There are consequences that come from depending on performative language and events. This dependence jeopardises the sense that our practice as educators is anchored in reality; in turn, that our educational work is acknowledged and represented accurately in the public sphere – which is surely a part of the connective tissue that contributes to our belonging and contribution to society as a whole. Our reliance on performative relations and data must be tempered if education is to offer the real possibility of opportunity and progress. The final lines of *King Lear* are worth returning to in this regard. The new king, Edgar, having witnessed Lear's decline and the destruction of the kingdom and, for a while at least, having had to disguise his own identity in order to survive, looks to the future foregrounding a new collective intention:

> *The weight of this sad time we must obey*
> *Speak what we mean, not what we ought to say.*

References

Ball, S. (2003) The teacher's soul and the terrors of performativity. *Journal of Education Policy* 18 (2): 215–228.

Ball, S., Maguire, M., Braun, A., Perryman, J. and Hoskins, K. (2012) Assessment technologies in schools: 'Deliverology' and the 'play of dominations'. *Research Papers in Education* 27 (5): 513–533.

Berardi, F. (2011) *After the Future*. Chico, CA: AK Press.

Bourdieu, P. and Passeron, J.-C. (2013) *Reproduction in Education, Society and Culture*. London: Sage.

Coffield, F. (2017) *Will the Leopard Change Its Spots? A New Model of Inspection for Ofsted*. London: UCL IOE Press.

Daley, M., Orr, K. and Petrie, J. (eds.). (2015) *Further Education and the Twelve Dancing Princesses*. London: IoE Press.

Duckworth, V. and Smith, R. (2018) *Further Education in England – Transforming Lives and Communities: Final Report*. London: UCU.

Fletcher, M. (2011) *Adult Further Education – the Unfinished Revolution, a 157 Group Policy Paper* [online]. Accessed October 26, 2015. www.157group.co.uk/sites/default/files/documents/adult_further_education_the_unfinished_revolution_2_policy_paper.pdf.

Foucault, M. (1978) 'On Governmentality' in Burchell, G. Gordon, C. and Miller, P. (eds.) (1998), *The Foucault Effect*. Hemel Hempstead: Harvester Wheatsheaf.

Goldstein, H. (2013) Evaluating educational changes: A statistical perspective. *Ensaio Avaliação e Políticas Públicas em Educação* 21 (78): 101–114.

Haney, W. (2000) *The Myth of the Texas Miracle in Education*. Accessed October 27, 2015. file:///C:/Users/ID121712/Documents/My%20Documents/Research%20Folder/2014~15/Oxford%20Symposium/Performative%20data/Haney%20Texas%20miracle.PDF.

Lyotard, J. (1993) *The Postmodern Explained: Correspondence, 1982–1985*. (D. Barry, Trans.). Minneapolis/London: University of Minnesota Press.

Ormerod, P. (1994) *The Death of Economics*. London: Faber and Faber.
Ranson, S. (2003) Public accountability in the age of neo-liberal governance. *Journal of Education Policy* 18 (9): 459–480.
Skills Funding Agency (SFA). (2014) *SFA: The Agency Story*. Accessed October 17, 2017. www.gov.uk/government/uploads/system/uploads/attachment_data/file/337715/The_Agency_Story.pdf. 17.10.17
Thaler, R. and Sunnstein, C. (2008) *Nudge: Improving Decisions about Health, Wealth and Happiness*. London: Penguin.
Willetts, A. (2011) *Speech to Universities UK Spring Conference*. Accessed October 7, 2017. www.gov.uk/government/speeches/universities-uk-spring-conference-2011.
Wolf, A. (2011) *Review of Vocational Education – the Wolf Report*. Accessed November 17, 2015. www.gov.uk/government/uploads/system/uploads/attachment_data/file/180504/DFE-00031-2011.pdf.

Contributors

Jennifer Addo is an experienced Health and Social Care Lecturer at South and City College Birmingham, and a Teaching and Learning Coach in the college's Quality department. After achieving an Honours Degree in Health Studies, Jennifer completed a PGCE (PCE) at the University of Wolverhampton. She went on to teach at the City of Wolverhampton College and also worked at Walsall College. Her current role has given her much insight into the many challenges that the Further Education (FE) sector and its teachers face, which fuels her research aims. Her research interests in the field of Vocational Education have focused on Assessment and Learning, the Politicisation of FE, Reflection and Positionality and Tutor Identity. Jennifer works as part of a team that organise and create effective staff development programmes, design and implement classroom observations; and reflection and progression sessions for teachers.

Anisa Ali is a Business Studies Lecturer at a local West Midlands College. Research interests are based around personal teaching experiences and teaching practice as well as the ideologies of different theorists.

Sandi Bates is Senior Lecturer in Post Compulsory Education at University of Wolverhampton. She taught for 20 years in FE, initially in Early Years and later as a Teaching and Learning Coach and Teacher Educator. She worked for the Institute for Learning, later the Educational Training Foundation in the role of Professional Formation Reviewer. Her special interest is improving the experience of students through supporting and educating teachers to engage with students using creative and innovative activities.

Pete Bennett is Senior Lecturer in Post Compulsory Education at the University of Wolverhampton, UK. He is co-author of *After the Media: Culture and Identity in the 21st Century* (2011) and of a range of communications, media and film textbooks for Routledge. He is also co-editor of *Barthes' Mythologies Today: Readings of Contemporary Culture* (Routledge 2013), *Doing Text: Media after the Subject* (Auteur 2016) and *Popular Culture and the Austerity Myth: Hard Times Today* (Routledge 2016). He recently contributed by invitation to Anti-Austerity and Media Activism, an online collaboration between Goldsmiths and openDemocracyUK. He is co-author and Chief Examiner of Communication and Culture, A level, and a regular provider of INSET to teachers.

Steve Coleby is a Training Manager with BAE Systems, previously serving as an Avionics Technician in the Royal Air Force. Having obtained Qualified Teacher Status in 2011, he maintains his interest and involvement in the education sector as a member of the Practitioner's Advisory Group for the Society of Education and Training as well as a Chair of Governors for a local school.

Chris Davies was Director of Curriculum and Quality at South Staffordshire College until Easter 2016. Chris has held a number of senior management roles in the further education sector, including Director of Teaching and Learning and Director of Teacher Innovation and Higher Education. His research interests include: the development and maintenance of teacher identities, and the impact of marketisation on the FE sector. Chris has presented at a wide variety of national conferences and events on teacher identity and the use of developmental approaches to lesson observations. Chris has also published in the *International Journal of Cloud Computing* on the use of cloud technologies to aid collaborative learning. Chris has regularly contributed to publications such as *Inside Evidence*, and *In-Tuition* on teacher identity and professionalism with the FE sector and the use of research to aid teacher development.

Alan Davis has been teaching construction (brickwork) for the past ten years, in secondary and further education settings. Prior to coming into teaching he worked on construction sites from the age of 16, gaining a vast amount of experience. Coming from a working-class background and leaving secondary school with very few qualifications, he went on to gain the Certificate in Education and an honours Degree in Further Education from the University of Wolverhampton. Recently he has been teaching the Award in Education and Training and the Certificate in Education and training, which he finds hugely satisfying. He says, "If I had to look back reflectively, I would say that I learned more at college when I left school than I ever did in secondary education."

Donna Drew is Course Team Leader of Media Studies at Bournville College of Further Education – now part of the South and City College in Birmingham. She has taught vocational BTEC Level 2 and Level 3 Media Studies for 8 years and A-Level Film, Media Studies and Communication and Cultural Studies alongside Film and Television Production Technology at level 4 and 5. Donna manages and assesses the Creative and Digital Media apprenticeships and engages with employers to place learners in work-experience and internship placements. Her interests are based around developing pastoral support to ensure success and developing online learning resources for Creative and Digital Media apprentices.

Catherine Gallagher has been a Lecturer in Teacher Education and Training for over ten years in several further education colleges in Birmingham and has taught every major teaching qualification during that time ranging from introductory courses in teaching to PGCE. Her subject area is Psychology and she is interested in how the OFSTED inspection framework, college inspections and classroom observations impacts on the individual lecturer. In her view, the requirements of OFSTED in order for a college to gain a "good grade" pervade every aspect of college life and it permeates every teaching and learning decision made by lecturers and managers.

Anne Groll is Senior Lecturer in Post Compulsory Education at the University of Wolverhampton. She spent 19 years in FE, including work for the Institute for Learning and also has experience working in educational research. Her current PhD research is based around communities of practice across the post compulsory sector. She is also especially interested in developing innovative approaches to teacher education.

Kirstie Harrington is a Lecturer at Birmingham Metropolitan College working within the Foundation Learning Department of the organisation. She also lecturers within the Lifelong learning/Adult Education Provision for the local authority, and is currently a postgraduate student at the University of Wolverhampton undertaking a Master's degree in Education. Her research interests are concerned with the marketisation of vocational FE, the redefinition of educational purpose and the effects this has on human beings.

Joe Harrison is a Lecturer in Outdoor Adventure and Uniformed Public Services at a Gloucestershire College. His research interests are based around experiential education, alternative methods of delivery, learner-facilitator rapport and learning environment.

Theresa Loughlin is Senior Lecturer in Post Compulsory Education (PCE) at the University of Wolverhampton. Her career spans 20 plus years in Further Education teaching business-related subjects and managing a department which included being a franchised partner for the Certificate in Education PCE with the university. Within the last four years, she has set up a small private training provider company alongside maintaining her association with the university which has recently become more permanent. Her research interests are firmly based at practitioner level and the tensions between policy and practice.

Emma Love is a Lecturer in Building Surveying at Birmingham City University. Her research interests are the cultural history of graffiti and the built environment with a particular interest in the City of Birmingham. Also an established photographer, she has recently held her first solo photography exhibition, Mr Birmingham, which was a collection of portraits of key ambassadors from Birmingham. She is currently working towards a PhD via the publication route: Perceptions, Deceptions, Contradictions and Innovations of European Graffiti.

Lou Mycroft is a Teacher Educator, writer and researcher, based at The Northern College in Barnsley and with the University of Huddersfield. She is co-author of *Further Education and the Twelve Dancing Princesses* and co-founder of democratic campaigning organisation Tutor Voices. Lou's work is about getting educators to think critically and reflexively for themselves, and to challenge the norms of education and their own practice as confident, informed 'Anti-Heroes'. She uses Thinking Environment techniques to work with potential, trainee and established teachers, through formal and rhizomatic CPD programmes. Her work is particularly focused outside traditional contexts for education, in communities, charities, trade unions, social enterprises and public services, operating across a virtual 'Community of Praxis', which assembles critical thinkers who equally believe in the power of education for social change.

Matt O'Leary is Reader in Education at Birmingham City University. Prior to this he was the co-founder of the Centre for Research and Development in Lifelong Education (CRADLE) and a principal lecturer in post compulsory education at the University of Wolverhampton. Matt has worked as a teacher, teacher educator, head of department and educational researcher for over 20 years in colleges, schools and universities in England, Mexico and Spain. Much of his work and research is rooted in the field of teacher education, particularly exploring the relationship between education policy and the continuous professional development of teachers. He is well known for his work on classroom observation and is regarded as one of the first educational researchers in the UK to investigate and critique the practice of graded lesson observations. He is also the author of the book *Classroom Observation: A Guide to the Effective Observation of Teaching and Learning* (Routledge 2014).

Matthew Parsons is a Civil Servant employed at a West Midlands college. As a Technical Instructor, he trains engineering tradesman in both initial and further Trade Training. His research interests centre around macro-issues such as the influence of economics, business and technology on educational uptake, delivery, direction and, particularly, their effect on the employment prospects of graduates of both Compulsory and Post Compulsory Education.

Joel Petrie has taught in the post compulsory sector in the northwest for over 20 years, initially with disabled students and then as a teacher educator. He has held elected college, regional and national NATFHE and UCU positions for much of his career, most recently on the national UCU Disabled Members Standing Committee. He is on the Board of *The Journal for Further and Higher Education, Research in Post-Compulsory Education*, and *Prism*. He is currently a middle manager in the City of Liverpool College, and is studying for an Educational Doctorate at Huddersfield University.

Claire Saunders is a Senior Lecturer in Learning and Teaching at Southampton Solent University. She also works as an Associate Lecturer for The Open University, lecturing in Childhood Psychology and Childhood Studies. She has over 20 years' experience in education, working in both the primary and higher education sectors and is working towards an EdD with The Open University.

Kay Sidebottom is an experienced Teacher Educator, currently based at two colleges in the north of England where she teaches on CertEd/PGCE and degree programmes. She specialises in creative and innovative approaches to teaching, focusing on new approaches to equality and diversity, use of technology and reflective practice. Her work is grounded in social purpose principles, which hold at their heart a belief in the power of education to transform lives and achieve social justice

Rob Smith is a Reader in Education at Birmingham City University and Director of the Centre for the Study of Practice and Culture in Education (CSPACE). He has extensive experience of writing and publishing collaboratively. His body of work explores the impact of funding and marketisation on FE provision. He has researched and written extensively in collaboration with FE and HE practitioners. His recent research with Vicky Duckworth focuses on further education as a space for transformative learning.

Stuart Smith is now a client manager and senior lecturer at Staffordshire University within the faculty of Computing, Engineering and Sciences. He is award leader for FDSc, BSc and MSc awards for the Ministry of Defence. He has coaching and mentoring qualifications and is an NLP practitioner using these skills within the university and performance coaching for an U15 girls football team. Since leaving the Royal Air Force he has started a higher degree qualification through the University development team.

Elizabeth A. Stephenson has over 20 years' experience as a Senior Lecturer in health care, specialist community nursing (district nursing) practice and professional education. She works predominantly with postgraduate health, social care and allied professionals who are undertaking professional teacher development. Liz also works with student teachers from the post compulsory sector. Her research interests are in relation to adult learning, specifically enquiry-based learning in higher education. Liz is currently undertaking doctoral studies at the University of Birmingham.

Sir Alan Tuckett is Professor of Education at the University of Wolverhampton, past president of the International Council of Adult Education and a visiting professor at the University of Leicester and the International Institute for Adult Education in Delhi. He is an internationally recognised expert in adult education and advises UNESCO on adult and lifelong learning. From 1988–2011 he was Chief Executive of the National Institute of Adult Continuing

Education, where he led a research and development programme totalling some £45 million, advised ministers on adult learning policy, and created the annual Adult Learners' Week. He writes widely – his most recent book is *Seriously Useless Learning* co-authored with Ian Nash. He received a knighthood for services to education, particularly in support of adult learning in January 2018.

Julie A. Wilde is Senior Lecturer in Post Compulsory Education at University of Wolverhampton. Her research interests are based around personhood – the self, teaching practice and action using philosophical, political and ethical practices.

David Wise originally trained as a secondary Business Studies teacher. He had substantial experience working in secondary and further education in a number of roles before becoming involved in teacher education. He taught as part of the ITE team at Walsall College and from there joined the University of Wolverhampton, teaching and taking on a Personal Tutor role on the PGCE. David's research interests have focused on the process of continuing professional development within teacher education. This interest stems from his previous experience both in secondary education and as an Advanced Practitioner in the further education (lifelong learning) sector. He completed his own PhD that focused on Reflective Practice in 2015. After a long battle with illness, David died in April 2017. This book is dedicated to his memory.

Victoria Wright is an experienced Teacher Educator and has recently completed a doctorate. She is a Senior Lecturer in Post Compulsory Education at University of Wolverhampton. Her research interests are lesson observation feedback and observation processes, autoethnography as a way of writing educational research, and reflexive practices with particular reference to 'care of self' (as interpreted by Foucault).

Index

abstract space, further education as 29, 33
action, reflection on 41–42
affirmative politics, rhizomatic working and 171–2
"Aims of Education, The" (Whitehead) 25
Alho-Malmelin, M. 118–19, 121
apostasy, defined 123
apprenticeships 105–6
Arendt, H. 61–68
Atkinson, D. 65–66
Atkinson, E. 180
austerity 3, 9–10
Australia: teacher certification in 28; vocational education courses in 105
authorities associated with EBL 57
autonomy and reason in further education 179–87; education within FE, purpose of 180–4; *Marriage of Heaven and Hell* comparison 179–80; teaching staff professionalism, devaluing of 184–7
Avis, J. 181, 186

Bacon, F. 21
Ball, S. 192–3
Ball, S. J. 151, 155
Bargh, M. 7, 8
Barry, J. 121
Barthes, R. 67, 102
Basis voor Actuele Kunst (BAK) Utrecht 171
Baudrillard, J. 3–4, 107
Beck, J. 81
Berardi, F. 191
best practice 132
Biesta, G. 61, 62, 120
Blackmore, J. 182
Blake, W. 179–80, 182, 184, 186–7
Bloch, E. 35–36

Bolton, G. 45, 46–49
Boocock, A. 122
Boud, D. 39
Bourdieu, P. 23–24, 31–32, 130–1, 194
Bradley, D. 100
Braidotti, R. 170, 172
Briggs, A. R. J. 89
Brookfield, S. 40–41, 56, 57, 58, 156
Brooks, R. 77
Brown, E. 76, 77
Burke, G. 105

Cameron, D. 183
capitalist realism 2
cartography, rhizomatic working practices and 172
change: flexion from 47; reflection on 44
change agent, further education teachers as 21–25
Cheers test, learning environment and 97
Cladingbowl, M. 157
Coffield, F. 82, 117, 123, 140, 187, 190–1
Coles, A. 183
'Come to the Edge' (Logue) 51
Commission on Adult Vocational Teaching and Learning (CAVTL) report 106, 111
communicative action theory 39
community as curriculum rhizome 171
Community of Praxis 174–6
constellations of rhizomatic working practices 172–4
context: flexion from 48; reflection on 45
Cope, P. 154
Cormier, D. 171
Cote, J. 82
Craig, D. 77
critically reflective teachers, developing 156–7

critical race theory 7
critical reflection 40–41
Critical Theory 40
Crowther, N. 82, 92–93

Daley, M. 120
Dearing Report, The 58
Debord, G. 97–98
De Certeau, M. 102, 104
Defence School of Aeronautical Engineering 161
Deignan, T. 53, 55
Deleuze, G. 172, 176
Dennis, C. 123–4
Dewey, J. 25, 55; on reflective thinking 38–39
differential space, further education as 29–30
dromology 5–6
Duckworth, V. 51

EBL *see* enquiry-based learning (EBL)
Ecclestone, K. 41
economics *vs.* education 71–79; democratic disconnects 78–79; money, nature of 72–74; overview of 71; production triad 74–75; productive credit economic models 77–78; scarcity and 71–72; Student Loan Scheme 75–77
education: within FE, purpose of 180–4; Freire on purpose of 24; scarcity and funding 71–72
Education and Training Foundation (ETF) 117, 144, 148
Education as Mythology (Peim) 6, 9
Education Professional Standards 62
education *vs.* economics 71–79; democratic disconnects 78–79; money, nature of 72–74; overview of 71; production triad 74–75; productive credit economic models 77–78; scarcity and 71–72; Student Loan Scheme 75–77
Edward, S. 140
Elliot, G. 123
Engeström, Y. 147
England: apprenticeships in 105–6; drop-out rate of teachers in 35; teacher certification in 28–29; vocational education courses in 105–6
English, F. 119
English Bank Act of 1844 74
enquiry-based learning (EBL) 51–59; authorities associated with 57; described 51; ideational functions of 54–55; identity functions of 55–56; introduction to 51–53; origins of 52; problematising 53–54; relational functions of 55; stages to 52; strategies 58–59; subjectivities within 57–58; technologies of 56–57
Entry to Employment 105
Erlandson, P. 64
ethical praxis 61
evidence: flexion from 47–48; reflection on 45
Exley, S. 139
experiential learning 39–40; stages of 39

Fairclough, N. 54
Fazaeli, T. 8
FE *see* further education (FE)
fear, in teaching practice 135–6, 137
Fendler, L. 56
Fenwick, T. 82
Fisher, M. 2
Fisher, R. 183
fitness to practise 153–4
flexion model 46–49; change, flexion from 47; context, flexion from 48; defined 46; evidence, flexion from 47–48; values, flexion from 48
forgotten-middle child, further education as 22
Foster, A. 22, 182
Foucault, M. 11, 51–52, 53, 55, 56–58, 99, 152
14–19 Diploma 105, 112
Freire, P. 24, 30
Fry, R. 39
further education (FE): as abstract space 29, 33; austerity and 3, 9–10; autonomy and reason in (*see* autonomy and reason in further education); change agent, teachers as 21–25; contexts 3–4; defined 1; as differential space 29–30; as forgotten-middle child 22; Foster review of 182; history 1–3; identity and 10–12; identity construction for student teachers in 61–68; *King Lear* comparison 189–90; Lefebvre and 29–30; marketisation of 81–93; Newbuild™ 96–104; performativity and 25–26; post-incorporation sector 81–82; professionalism within, sector 82–83 (*see also* professionalism in further education); propositions 3–4; purpose of 180–1; resistance/creativity 9–10; social inequalities and 23–25; timescales 4–7;

Tuck on neoliberalisation 7–9; vocational teaching and (see vocational teaching, further education policy and)
Further Education National Training Organisation (FENTO) standards 141

General National Vocational Qualifications 105
Ghaye, A. 42–43
Ghaye, K. 42–43
Gibbs, G. 39
Gipps, C. 154
Gleeson, D. 83, 86, 120, 139, 185
Goldstein, H. 194
Gordon, N. 65
Gottlieb, E. 119
Gove, M. 130
graded lesson observations 33; Ball critique of 151–2; Foucault on 152
grading, symbolic violence in 133–4
Greaves, D. 41
Guattari, F. 172, 176
Gupta, S. 41
Gutting, G. 57

Habermas, J. 39
habitus concept 136
Hafez, R. 173
Halpin, D. 121
Hancock, M. 112, 113
Haney, W. 194
Hansen, D. 120
Hard Times (Dickens) 163
Harrington, K. 189
Harrison, J. K. 65
Harvey, D. 104
Hayes, J. 117–18, 182
Hayward, G. 181
Heidegger, M. 96
Higgins, C. 62, 63
Honey, P. 39
Hughes, J. 45
Human Condition, The (Arendt) 62, 63
hyperrealities theory 107
Hölderlin 96

ideational functions of EBL 54–55
Identities project 174, 177
identity: EBL and, functions of 55–56; further education and 10–12
identity construction for student teachers 61–68; actions and 64; freedom and 64–65, 67; professionalism and 65–66; reflection and 63–64; subjectness/action and 61–62
Illich, I. 119
Initial Teacher Education (ITE) 28, 61, 140; lesson plan use and 32; teacher educators and 28–36; teacher's identity on 35; values and 30–32
in-service teachers, divisions of 28
Institute for Learning (IfL) 116–17, 141
ITE *see* Initial Teacher Education (ITE)

Jackson, N. 147
James, D. 86
Jauhiainen, A. 118–19, 121
Jephcote, J. 83
Johnson, S. 98
Jones, A. 53, 54, 55, 56
Journal of Thought, The (Placha) 24

Kennedy, H. 120
Kerfoot, D. 121–2
Kes (Loach and Bradley) 100
Kinsella, E. 63
Knights, D. 83
knowing-in-action 41
knowledge-in-action 41
Kolb, D. A. 39

La Belle, T. 119
labelling 31
Lareau, A. 24
Lave, J. 147, 172
leadership 172
learning styles inventory 39–40
Learning Works: Widening Participation in Further Education (Kennedy) 120
Lefebvre, H. 29–30, 35, 102–4, 106–7
Leicester unconference 173
Leitch, S. R. 55
lesson observations, validity and reliability of 151–8; contextual background to 152–3; critically reflective teachers, developing 156–7; introduction to 151–2; post-inspection Ofsted policy shift 157–8; teacher development, prioritising 155–6; teacher performance, evaluating 153–5
Levine, C. 82
Lingfield, R. 117–18, 182
Lingfield Report 3, 28, 130
Lipovetsky, G. 4
Loach, K. 100
Locke, J. 24

Logue, C. 51
'London' (Blake) 184
Lucas, N. 82, 92–93
Lumby, J. 119
Lyotard, J. 190

Malcolm, J. 101
Malcolm, M. 58
managerialist positivism 135
marketisation of FE sector, teacher identity and 81–93; importance of 82–83; introduction to 81; post-incorporation context 81–82; research question study/findings of 84–92
Marriage of Heaven and Hell, The (Blake) 179–80, 184
Massive Open Online Course (MOOC) 171
McCormick, R. 58
Mezirow, J. 39
Middleton, R. 76
Mills, C. W. 1
money 72–74; commercial credit as 73; functions of 72; production and value of 72–74
Moon, J. 38
Morris, E. 184
Morrissey, S. P. 100
Motion, J. 55
Mumford, A. 39

natality 61, 62
National Association of Teachers in Further and Higher Education (Natfhe) 116
national deficit 73
Nelson, J. 181
neoliberal/neoliberalism: defined 1; further education in England and 29; nihilism and 7–8; *weltbild* 7, 9, 36, 130
Newbuild™ 96–104
nihilism 7–8
No Child Left Behind (NCLB) 5, 6
nomadic working 171

observations, teacher education 139–49; author's experiences of being observed 145–6; example of 143; graded/ungraded models of 139–40; Loughlin autobiography 140–2; outstanding teacher, identifying 146–7; overview of 139; pre-service students, working with 147–8; quality and 144; Wright autobiography 142

observation schemes 33–34
O'Donnell, L. 181
Office for Standards in Education (Ofsted) 62, 82, 129–37; authoritative judgement of 134; Bourdieu and Passeron theory of 130–1; Coffield's new inspection model for 190–1; fear in teaching practice from 135–6; 4-point scale 153–4, 158; Gleeson on influence of 139; habitus concept and 136; high stakes regulatory power 134–5; introduction to 129–30; measuring progress 131–3; model of PCE teacher requirements 146; national context of 130; partnership inspection 131; pedagogic authority and 133–4; policy shift of 157–8; symbolic violence in grading and 133–4; technical rationality in colleges and 136
Ofsted *see* Office for Standards in Education (Ofsted)
O'Leary, M. 139, 149, 190
Operation Mindcrime of Reason 180
Organisation for Economic Co-operation and Development (OECD) 2
Ormerod, P. 191–2
outstanding teacher, identifying 146–7

Page, D. 90–92, 122
partnership inspection 131
Passeron, J.-C. 31–32, 130–1, 194
Pattison, S. 119
PCE *see* post-compulsory education (PCE)
Peck, J. 1
pedagogic action 31; twofold arbitrariness of 31–32
pedagogic authority 31, 133–4
peer support, critical reflection and 40–41
Peim, N. 6, 9–10, 56, 57, 58, 99, 101
performativity 25–26; accuracy and validity of performance data 193–4; consequences of 192–5; defined 193; marketised further education and 193
PGCE *see* Postgraduate Certificate in Education (PGCE)
Placha, T. C. 24
post-compulsory education (PCE): PGCE in 61–62; purpose of 180
Postgraduate Certificate in Education (PGCE) 38; in PCE 61–62
posthumanism 170
potentia principles 172, 173, 174, 176
potestas principles 172, 175
practice, reflection on 42–45

Practice of Everyday Life, The (De Certeau) 104
pre-service students, working with 147–8
Price, B. 52
problem-based learning (PBL) 52
problem-solving model 38–39
Production of Space, The (Lefebvre) 102–3
production triad 74–75
professionalism in further education 116–25; English context of 116–18; faith, apotasy and 123–4; introduction to 116; religious metaphors in 118–22
Professionalism in Further Education (Lingfield) 182
professional knowledge, reflection as 45–46
Programme for International Student Assessment (PISA) 2
prolepsis 144

qualification, for education 62
quality *vs.* teacher education observations 144, 149

race for humanization concept 24
Ranson, S. 194
'Realising The Potential' (Foster) 182
Reddy, S. 175
reflection as professional knowledge 45–46
reflection-on-action 41–42
reflection-on-change 44
reflection-on-context 45
reflection-on-evidence 45
reflection-on-practice 42–45; core foci of 44–45; example 42–44
reflection-on-values 45
reflective practice 38–49; critical reflection 40–41; experiential learning 39–40; flexion adapted model of 46–49; literature on 38–44; reflection as professional knowledge 45–46; reflection-on-action 41–42; reflection-on-practice 42–45; reflective thinking and learning 38–39
reflective thinking and learning 38–39
relational functions of EBL 55
rhizomatic working practices 170–7; cartography and 172; community as curriculum 171; Community of Praxis 174–6; constellations of 172–4; Identities project 174, 177; Leicester unconference 173; politics and 171–2; posthumanism 170, 176; snow day pop-up course 174; Tutor Voices 174; #ukfechat 173
Richardson, G. 118

Robinson, K. 76
Robson, J. 83
Rogers, T. 77
Romain, P. 139
Rose, N. 51, 52, 54, 57
Rouxel, D. 123
Rowland, S. 183
Royal Air Force (RAF) 161–9

Sachs, J. 83
Salisbury, M. 83
scarcity, education and 71–72
Schön, D. 41–42, 63–64
Shain, F. 83
Shaw, G. B. 124
Silver Book 82
Simmons, R. 121
Simons, S. 173
simulations 3–4
16–19 Study Programmes 107–8, 112
Smith, R. 82
snow day rhizomatic pop-up course 174
social inequalities, further education and 23–25
socialisation, for education 62
social space 102–3
Society for Education and Training (SET) 118, 124
Sociological Imagination, The (Mills) 1
strategic action field of incorporation 92–93
Stronach, I. 182
Student Loan Scheme 75–77
subjectification, for education 62
subjectivities within EBL 57–58
Sullivan, A. 23–24
symbolic violence 31–32; in grading 133–4

Tabula Rasa concept 24
Taubman, D. 124
Taylor, C. 3, 61, 65, 171
Taylor, L. 139–40
teacher agency, defined 82
teacher development, prioritising 155–6
teacher education *vs.* quality observations 144, 149
teacher educators: observation schemes and partnership 33–34; Ofsted and 32–35; values and 30–32
teacher educators, ITE programs and 28–36; context of 28–30; future of 35–36; Ofsted and 32–35; symbolic violence and 31–32; values and 30–32

teacher identity: defined 82–83; importance of, and professionalism 82–83; marketisation of FE sector and (*see* marketisation of FE sector, teacher identity and); military context of 161–9; reflection and 38–49 (*see also* reflective practice)
teacher performance, evaluating 153–5
teaching, as revolutionary 24–25
Teaching, Learning and Assessment in Further Education and Skills-What Works and Why (Ofsted) 33
teaching staff professionalism, devaluing of 184–7
technical colleges 105
technologies of EBL 56–57
Thinking Environment 175
Thompson, R. 183
Thompson, T. 121
timescales 4–7
Tomkins, S. 124
tracking progress 132
Train to Gain 105
Tuck, E. 7–9
Türkkahraman, M. 25
Tutor Voices 174
Twitter 173

#ukfechat 173
United States: teacher certification in 28; vocational education courses in 105

Vähäsantanen, K. 82
values: flexion from 48; reflection on 45; teacher educators and 30–32

Van Manen, M. 66
Virilio, P. 5–6
vocational teaching, further education policy and 105–14; counter-productive policy intervention findings 112–14; funding cuts findings 110–11; introduction to 105–6; performance data findings 109–10; policy context 107–8; present and presence 106–7; recruitment findings 111–12; research project 108–14

Walshaw, M. 58
Warford, M. K. 144, 147
Waugh, C. 116–17
Weininger, E. 24
weltbild 7, 9, 36, 130
Wenger, E. 147, 172
We Think That's the Future: Curriculum Reform Initiatives in HigherEducation (Higher Education Academy) 58
Whitehead, A. N. 25
Whitehead, S. 121–2
Willcocks, L. P. 56
Williams, R. 104, 181
Will the Leopard Change Its Spots? A New Model of Inspection for Ofsted (Coffield) 190–1
Wilson, F. 121
Wilson, H. 124
Wolf, A. 78, 81, 93, 106, 112, 193
Wright, V. 147

Žižek, S. 7
zoë 175, 176
Zukas, M. 101